Discovering Dylan Thomas

Discovering Dylan Thomas

A Companion to the *Collected Poems*
and Notebook Poems

John Goodby

University of Wales Press
2017

www.uwp.co.uk

British Library CIP Data
A catalogue record for this book is available from the British Library

ISBN   978-1-78316-963-4
eISBN   978-1-78316-964-1

The right of John Goodby to be identified as author of this work has been asserted in accordance with sections 77 and 79 of the Copyright, Designs and Patents Act 1988.

MIX
Paper from
responsible sources
FSC   FSC® C013604
www.fsc.org

Typeset by Eira Fenn Gaunt, Cardiff
Printed by CPI Antony Rowe, Melksham

i.m. Kenneth Goodby
(1932–2016)

The rivers of the dead

Veined his poor hand I held, and I saw
Through his unseeing eyes to the roots of the sea.
'Elegy', Dylan Thomas

Contents

Acknowledgements

As usual, my main thanks and gratitude go to my family: Nicola, Kate and George.

Thanks are also due to Swansea University for their purchase of Dylan Thomas's fifth notebook in December 2014, and granting me a research sabbatical at the end of 2014. For their support of Dylan Thomas-related activities in 2014 I would particularly like to thank Kirsti Bohata of CREW (Centre for Research into the English Literature and Language of Wales), and the staff of Swansea University's Research Institute for the Arts and Humanities (RIAH).

As with the *Collected Poems*, I acknowledge, too, a debt of gratitude to Siân Bowyer and staff at the Manuscripts Collection at the National Library of Wales, Aberystwyth, Mike Basinski and the staff at the Special Collection Library of the State University of New York at Buffalo, Rick Watson and staff at the Research Library at the Harry Ransom Center at the University of Texas at Austin, the Department of Manuscripts at the British Library in London, and staff at Swansea University Library.

One of the benefits of working on Dylan Thomas is that it is unusually productive of new friendships, and the refurbishing of old ones. I would like to take this chance to thank the many friends and encouragers who supported my work in various ways during the Dylan Thomas centenary, when this book was conceived, planned and part-written – Hannah Ellis, Dylan Thomas's grand-daughter, and her father, Trefor Ellis; Hilly Janes; Andrew Dally, editor of the Dylan Thomas blog; Matt Hughes of the Dylan Thomas Birthplace; Branwen and Julie Kavanagh of Twin Headed Wolf; James Keery; Toni Griffiths and Fred Jarvis; Ned Allen, Leo Mellor, and members of the Cambridge

University English Faculty; Jeff Towns; Dai Smith; Charles Mundye and Chris Wigginton of Sheffield Hallam University; Gabriel Heaton and Toby Skegg of Sotheby's; Lyndon Davies and Penny Hallam; Allan and Helen Wilcox; Wu Fu-sheng and Graham Hartill; Dan Llywelyn Hall; Martin Smith-Wales and Nick Andrews of BBC Wales; Peter Stead; Nerys Williams of University College Dublin.

Finally, special thanks are due to my postgraduate students and colleagues, several of whom who gave advice and support during the sometimes difficult birth of this volume: Rhian Bubear, Ade Osbourne, Rob Penhallurick, and Steve Vine.

For permission to quote from Dylan Thomas's poetry thanks are due to the Dylan Thomas Estate, David Higham and Co. and New Directions Press.

Abbreviations of titles of books by Dylan Thomas

N1, *N2*, *N3*, *N4* and *N5* = the poetry notebooks kept by Dylan Thomas between April 1930 and August 1935 (*N1–N4* are collected in Maud, 1989; see below).

18P	*18 Poems.*
25P	*Twenty-five Poems.*
DE	*Deaths and Entrances.*
ICS	*In Country Sleep.*
CP52	*Collected Poems 1934-1952* (London: Dent, 1952).
QEOM	*Quite Early One Morning*, ed. Aneurin Talfan Davies (London: Dent, 1954).
LVW	*Letters to Vernon Watkins*, intro. Vernon Watkins (London: Dent/Faber, 1957).
TML	*The Map of Love.*
TP71	*The Poems*, ed. and intro. Daniel Jones (London: Dent, 1971).
EPW	*Early Prose Writings*, ed. Walford Davies (London: Dent, 1971).
CP88	*Collected Poems 1934–1953*, eds Walford Davies and Ralph Maud (London: Dent, 1988).
NP	*The Notebook Poems*, ed. Ralph Maud (London: Dent, 1989).
CS	*Collected Stories*, ed. Walford Davies, intro. Leslie Norris (London: Dent, 1993).
UMW	*Under Milk Wood*, ed. Ralph Maud and Walford Davies, intro. Walford Davies (London: Dent, 1995).
CL	*The Collected Letters*, ed. Paul Ferris, 2nd edn (London: Dent, 2000).
CP14	*Collected Poems: The New Centenary Edition*, ed. John Goodby (London: Weidenfeld & Nicolson, 2014; pbk repr. 2016).

Introduction: After 'DT–100'

Discovering Dylan Thomas fulfils the promise I made in my 2014 centenary annotated edition of the *Collected Poems* of Dylan Thomas. Given Thomas's continued popularity with the general reading public, and the commercial imperatives this entailed for his estate, his agents and his publishers, the *Collected Poems* was always going to take the form of a trade edition for a mass market, whatever my preferences, as an academic, might be. Thus, while Weidenfeld & Nicolson generously allowed me almost two hundred pages for annotations, the need for readerly accessibility nevertheless played a rather larger role in determining the extent of the critical apparatus than would have been the case for the collected poems of a less marketable poet.[1] As a result, as I explained in the Introduction to the *Collected Poems*, I gave priority in the edition to maximising the number of poems it contained, and this meant that I had to exclude from it 'variant passages and poems'. These I said I would publish in 'a future *Guide*', and *Discovering Dylan Thomas* is that guide.

However, as the word 'guide' suggests, this book is more than just a gathering of material which could not be fitted into the *Collected Poems*.[2] It includes such material, of course – poems, additional annotations, and the 'variant passages' I mentioned – and also a list of the glitches which crept into the text of the poems in 2014, since corrected in the 2016 paperback edition (these are listed in Appendix 3).[3] But *Discovering Dylan Thomas* has a very different rationale to the *Collected Poems* and is not merely a supplement to it, for all that it gathers together my director's cuts and will benefit substantially from being read alongside *CP14*. That rationale is primarily a critical and scholarly one, unshaped by commercial criteria, even though I hope this book will appeal to some non-academic lovers of Thomas's poetry too. A coherent work in its own right, it offers, for example, critical histories for most of the poems, at a level of detail which would never have been tolerated in the edition, as well as material which has come to light in the two years since the edition was published. This material includes the rediscovered poem 'A dream of winter', reprinted just once (in the USA) since its appearance in the journal *Lilliput* in January 1942.[4] Most crucially of all, it includes the results of my study of a fifth Thomas notebook (*N5*), hitherto unknown, a successor to the four covering the period April 1930 – April 1934. The fourth notebook ends with 'If I were tickled by the rub of love', dated 30 April 1934; poems 'One', 'Two' and 'Three' in the fifth notebook are undated, the first with a date being 'Four' ('Especially when the October wind'), which is dated 1 October 1934. This suggests strongly that it is a direct continuation of the fourth notebook, with the first three poems having been entered in it between May and September 1934. In all, the fifth notebook contains a total of sixteen poems (six of which were destined for *18 Poems*, ten for *Twenty-five Poems*), including several of Thomas's finest and most original.

As with so much relating to Dylan Thomas, the story of the discovery of the notebook is both entertaining and intriguing. As homeless newly-weds, Dylan and Caitlin Thomas stayed at the home of Yvonne Macnamara, Caitlin's mother, in Blashford, Hampshire, often for extended periods, in the late 1930s. We know that during these stays Thomas wrote poetry; we know, moreover, that he often took his poetry notebooks with him on his travels in order to do so, and was prone to mislay them. This was evidently what happened in the case of *N5*; a note discovered with the notebook, in the hand of Louie King, one of Mrs Macnamara's domestic servants of the time, tells us that she was given it with other scrap paper from the house with an instruction to burn it in the kitchen boiler. She saved it from destruction, however, and from then until her death in 1984 the notebook lay hidden in a drawer. It was presumably inherited by Louie King's family, but its existence remained secret until late 2014. It had no impact, therefore, on the 1971, 1988 or 2014 editions of the poems, or on Ralph Maud's editions of the collected notebook poems of 1967–8 and 1989. It is undeniably, and by some way, the most significant addition to the corpus of Thomas's work to have appeared since 1941 – and, since Swansea University decided, with admirable determination, to acquire it when it came up at Sotheby's in December 2014, I was lucky enough to be the first Thomas scholar to examine it, in January 2015. The results of these initial labours are incorporated in what follows

Without pre-empting research which is still ongoing, it can be said that the new notebook changes our understanding of Thomas's work in at least three basic respects. First, it gives a clear idea of the order in which the poems of 1934–5 were written, one which is at odds with the order agreed hitherto (details of the corrected order, as well as further information about the notebook, can be found in Appendix 2). Secondly, recording as it does Thomas's development immediately before and after his departure from Swansea for London in December 1934, N5 gives the lie to claims that he did little work when he hit the capital for the first time. On the contrary, he continued to write purposefully, tackling ever more complex forms and subjects during the first half of 1935. Thirdly, while it does not contain any previously unseen poems, N5 includes several for which there had previously been no autograph manuscripts or drafts, including two of the most complex and innovative, 'Altarwise by owl-light' and 'I, in my intricate image'. As a result, we can see how the poems were conceived, and, in several cases, follow the final stages of their composition. The tripartite 'I, in my intricate image', for example, is entered in the notebook as three separately numbered poems (one of which is separated from the other two by another poem), raising the possibility that Thomas did not initially consider it to be a single work. In addition, as with many of the other poems in N5, Thomas altered 'I, in my intricate image' after he had entered it. In many cases the alterations are fairly minor, and the poems are very close to their published versions. But in several, and 'I, in my intricate image' is one of these, the alterations are so extensive in places that they amount to fairly sustained efforts of poetic composition and recalibration. (Quite a few poems, for example, were revised in some way when Thomas was in Donegal in summer 1935, as his records of the date and place of his labours show.) Crucially, the interpolated material (and almost all the deleted material) is decipherable. All of this means that N5 deepens the insight we have into Thomas's astonishingly rapid development as a poet from spring 1933 onwards, in many ways completing the picture revealed by the third and fourth notebooks.

There was a fortuitousness about the timing of the appearance of *N5* in November 2014 and the rediscovery of 'A dream of winter' in autumn 2015. Thomas is both a popular writer *and* a demanding and difficult one, a hybrid blender of traditions and cultures. As a result, critical ambivalence has surrounded his work from the start. The response to the problem of how to present his work in 2014 was, in many quarters, to dumb him down. By unexpectedly appearing at the tail end of the centenary, notebook and poem served as timely reminders, first, that the body of texts we refer to as 'Dylan Thomas' is not fixed or static and, second, that his significance can only be fully understood through sustained engagement with his poetry. This is not, of course, to belittle the many genuinely imaginative populist responses of the year; Thomas's own genius and taste for mass media cultural forms should warn anyone against snobbery.[5] (Indeed, 'DT–100', as it was branded, was arguably the first genuinely inclusive, all-Wales cultural phenomenon (rugby tournaments aside) since the establishment of the Welsh Assembly in 1997.) But some corrective to the excesses was undoubtedly necessary by late 2014, and the new material helped to reinforce the claims for Thomas's seriousness and the range of his achievement as a poet. It provided, that is, additional fuel for the critical project of reinterpreting Thomas which has been in train for over a decade now, one which in turn has implications for the way mid-twentieth-century poetry is understood more generally. I briefly touch on this contextual aspect at the end of the Introduction. For now, however, I discuss the main aim of *Discovering Dylan Thomas*, namely, as a guide to the texts and intertexts of individual poems.

'Clap its great blood down': some thoughts on annotating Dylan Thomas

Discovering Dylan Thomas is organised in three sections. Part one, 'Supplementary Poems', includes poems I had wished to include in the *Collected Poems*, but could not for reasons of space, plus 'A dream of winter', which came to my attention only after the hardback appeared and was included in the 2016 paperback edition.[6] Part two, the meat of the book, begins with a discussion of Thomas's juvenilia and youthful plagiarism and the light they shed on the role of mimicry in his work.

It continues by glossing allusions and references on a poem-by-poem basis, explicating textual cruxes, and giving details of publication, critical histories, variant poems and passages for each poem in *CP14* and the supplementary section of this book. These details include the material drawn from my research on *N5*.[7] It should be noted that the publishers of the *Collected Poems* have not allowed me to alter the order of the poems in its latest edition in line with the discoveries about the chronology of their composition made in *N5*. However, I have followed this new order in *Discovering Dylan Thomas*: this means that there is mismatch between the order of entries in this book and that of the poems of the period 1934–5 in *CP14*. Appendix 2 gives the correct order of composition in a handy form. Part three of *Discovering Dylan Thomas* consists of three appendices, giving publication details for the main poetry collections Thomas published in his lifetime, a description of *N5*, and an errata list for the hardback edition of *CP14*.

The material included in 'Supplementary Poems' reflects the principles of inclusion I operated in compiling the *Collected Poems*, and it is worth saying a few words about these. As Seamus Perry noted in his *LRB* review, I could have made these principles rather more explicit; suffice it to say that my aim was simply to include all the published poetry, with the exception of juvenilia and two notebook poems which had been published but not collected, plus others that were good and/or interesting enough, with priority given to those which did not substantially repeat others. Thus, 'Jack of Christ', published in 1960, a good, but rather long poem that resembled other early poems, did not make the cut. 'The Woman Speaks', which was published in Thomas's lifetime, but also remained uncollected, had to be left out. Both are included here. Also included are two more examples of notebook versions of poems rewritten by Thomas in the late 1930s, the originals of 'The spire cranes' and (in extract) 'After the funeral'. Ditto the first versions of three poems in *N4*, rewritten by Thomas within *N4* at a later date, 'That the sum sanity', 'Grief, thief of time' and 'I fellowed sleep'. I was less interested in the juvenilia, and poems from the first notebook, the weakest of the five. Too much fuss has been made of Thomas's juvenilia, it seems to me, because they are easy targets for the attention of those unable or unwilling to get to grips with the infinitely better mature poetry, as if precocity is sufficient warrant for sustained attention. I should add here that the items of juvenilia I included in *CP14* – the three poems from the story 'The Fight' – were interesting to me precisely because they were juvenilia in a problematic, debatable sense; 'The Fight' was written in 1938, and the poems may be Thomas's pastiching of his teenage affectations. By including them I was flagging up the degree to which Thomas's juvenilia and very early poems often blur the boundaries between self-revision and imitation, invention and appropriation. However, I have relented and add other, more genuine, items of juvenilia here, namely 'Forest picture', 'Idyll of unforgetfulness' and 'In borrowed plumes'. The first two show a certain individuality of phrasing, while the last is a reminder of how Thomas's paradoxical form of originality was related to his uncanny ability to inhabit the styles of others. 'A dream of winter', as I've already noted, is also included, as is the weakest of the wartime verse letters, 'The postman knocks'. Finally, there is a Yeats pastiche written a quarter of a century after 'In borrowed plumes', 'An old man or a young man'.

Part two, the annotations and variants section, includes variant passages from poems and entire alternative versions for four 1940s poems, 'On a Wedding Anniversary', 'Lie still, sleep becalmed', 'Last night I dived my beggar arm' and 'Holy Spring'. Most exciting of all, I include here – published for the first time – an early draft version of one of Thomas's greatest 1940s poems, 'A Refusal to Mourn'. I continue to exclude, without regret, several scraps of doggerel from the early letters, the unfinished satire 'Oxford', a parody of Frederic Prokosch's 'The Dolls' and the duller pastiches from *The Death of the King's Canary*.

The bulk of Part two consists of textual annotations and critical histories. These are acts of anamnesis, a step towards restoring the basic critical literacy that has been lost by many where Thomas is concerned, and thereby towards a properly informed critical conversation about his poetry. The critical histories present the main lines of critical interpretation; the aim is to give readers the means by which to assess the poems for themselves. The entry for 'A Winter's Tale', for example, offers a précis of critical responses by Linden Huddlestone, James Keery, W. S. Merwin, William York Tindall, Jacob Korg, William T. Moynihan, Seamus Heaney and myself, placing in context the briefer notes given in *CP14*, plus additional details of the poem's narrative structure, its pastoral tropes and historical and literary contexts.

Allusions in the poem not noted in *CP14* – to 'Little Gidding' and 'East Coker', the book of Revelations, Robert Southwell, Keats' 'Bright Star' sonnet and 'La Belle Dame sans Merci', and Kierkegaard – are recorded. All of this gives the reader a richer and more nuanced sense of how far Thomas's own opinion – that the poem was a 'failure' – can be upheld in the face of critical opinions that range from 'one of the finest poems of this century' to mere 'Disney fantasia'.[8]

Ruminations on the need for, and efficacy of, annotations to Thomas's poetry were voiced by William Empson as long ago as 1954, and his comments (as for most of what he said about Thomas) are still pertinent:

> Kathleen Raine has at last told me that Mnetha is a suitable character in one of Blake's Prophetic Books; but this acts only as a reassurance that the line meant the kind of thing you wanted it to, not really as an explanation of it. 'That'll do very well', as Alice said when she was told the meaning of a word in 'Jabberwocky', because she knew already what it ought to fit in with. I think an annotated edition of Dylan Thomas ought to be prepared as soon as possible and that a detail like that ought to go in briefly, though it would be hard to decide what else ought to go in.

Empson was right, it seems to me, to believe that it is 'hard to decide' what 'ought to go in', beside the very obvious. His need for a gloss of 'Mnetha', however, indicates one area requiring treatment, namely the recurring themes and symbolic clusters which determine the atmosphere of Thomas's poems, whether those pertain (like Mnetha) to Blake or others – Ancient Egypt, film, the body as a suit of clothing, and so on. In more specifically linguistic terms, I have also glossed most of Thomas's characteristic devices, in particular his reconditioned idioms – 'up to his ears', 'coin in your socket', 'a grief ago' – and the more complex instances of his wordplay. I have frequently singled out pun, his favourite device, settling for sample cases of those which are ubiquitous, such as sun / S/son, 'die' as death and orgasm, etc. The knottiest prosodic schemas are set out in full, in order to illustrate Thomas's craftsmanship but also as a reminder that traditional form was the catalyst that allowed him to forge his process style. The cruxes created by complex sentences (usually strings of appositive clauses), or the disguising of main verbs, are also glossed. I would note that despite his reputation for obscurity, Thomas's vocabulary is not difficult in the usual sense – words like 'parhelion' are very rare, one-offs. They have been glossed, naturally, but the point is that Thomas is a poet of etymologies not inkhornisms, of the *OED* rather than the thesaurus. His real lexical challenge is in the short, apparently simple terms, which he repeatedly uses: 'cock', 'grain', 'seed', 'bone', 'wax', 'marrow', 'weather', 'worm', 'film', 'ghost' and 'fork', for example, in the first two collections, 'bolt', 'chain', 'reel', 'stone', 'key', 'tear', 'ride' and 'maze' in *DE*. They are difficult because they describe and enact process, and therefore have multiple meanings, varying in sense within and between poems. Again, glosses can only be illustrative given the ubiquity of the poetic shorthand.

The best way of understanding how Thomas wrote is, of course, to examine drafts and variants where these exist. They range from the replacement of single words to whole stanzas and complete and near-complete variants, such as the astonishing 'A Refusal For An Elegy' of November 1944, a draft of 'A Refusal to Mourn', already mentioned – this resembling the final poem in many ways, but with some telling small differences, and a very different second stanza. (Poignantly, since it pre-dates the liberation of the Nazi death camps by the Allies in January 1945, it also lacks the final version's allusion to the Holocaust in 'Zion' and 'synagogue'.)

If Empson is right to say that we cannot always expect 'explanations' for Thomas's poems, he perhaps concedes too much to the detractors when he claims that any annotations will simply confirm what we 'know already' about the poems. The poems are certainly always about 'process' – the profound inter-involvement of the forces of growth and decay, of everything from molecules to galaxies, and their existence in a state of perpetual flux and change. But 'know already' is slightly too deterministic; it needs to be distinguished more carefully from the *canard* that Thomas wrote the same poem over and over again. However similar their themes, the poems' value is as unique linguistic events – to use Thomas's oft-cited phrase, they work 'from' rather than 'towards' words,[9] each doing so in a unique, never-to-be-repeated way. Annotation should help to highlight this uniqueness by clarifying the textual and social contexts of each poem, as well as simply telling us where names like 'Mnetha' come from. This is particularly important in Thomas's case since, in the early poems in particular, he disguises and buries these contexts and sources, often alluding to them in only the most glancing way.

Reading and influences: 'Anything in the world so long as it is printed'

Despite this, the place where any annotator has to start is with Thomas's 'influences'. Of course, no poet can be reduced to their reading, reading is not synonymous with the sources of a poem, and sources, in any case, do not necessarily tell us very much about a poem's meaning. Nor do poets learn of things solely through their reading, certainly not in the garrulous artistic *milieux* and multi-media society Thomas inhabited. Thomas is unusual, however, in the way he so often hides his allusions, or distances them: does the 'dolphined sea' of 'Where once the waters of your face' come from Yeats, or *Anthony and Cleopatra*, or anywhere at all (but there is always a somewhere)? As a result they are often discounted or missed, with the result that he can seem not very well read – or, worse, to write in some naïve, 'inspired' way. Because of this, and because the reader is often in need of some kind of purchase on the more difficult poems, it is important to unearth as much empirical evidence as possible, albeit this should be offered in a way that does not nail the poem to a single interpretation.

More interestingly – if less immediately useful to the struggling reader – there is the question of just why Thomas alludes to and echoes other writers so obliquely. Most poets want you to get their allusions, after all, or why use them in the first place? It seems to me that the secrecy and covering-up has to do with the *way* Thomas's poems mean rather than *what* they mean, what we might call their general strategy of obscurity. Dylan Thomas was a trickster-poet, one who resisted the display of metropolitan insider knowledge which allusion, quotation and echo often signify. Defining himself against Eliot and Auden, with their well-bred canonical assurances, he opted instead for a subversive, cryptic mode of allusion. This has fostered the impression that he was not very well read, or even that he was a philistine who read nothing but thrillers, detective fiction and Dickens as an adult. This in turn accords with the legend, and may have been part of an effect

Thomas was trying to create, but it does not fit the facts. When I began working on the *Collected Poems*, I drew up a list of possible sources I ought to read, initially based on accounts of Thomas's own accounts of his reading. Its range surprised me, even allowing for the fact that he surely exaggerated occasionally. The poetry that most obviously shaped his own is well known – it includes the Bible, the Metaphysical poets, Renaissance and Jacobean poetry and drama, Milton (his favourite poem was reportedly 'Ode on the Morning of Christ's Nativity') and Blake ('I am in the path of Blake, but so far behind him that only the wings on his heels are in sight' (*CL*, p. 34)).[10] Other favourites included Beddoes, Whitman, T. S. Eliot, the Sitwells, Richard Aldington, Wilfred Owen, W. B. Yeats and W. H. Auden. Then there is the fiction he enjoyed – and we should recall that Thomas in the mid-1930s presented himself to editors as a poet and short story writer equally, and that the early fictions and poetry explore the same sexualised, Gothic modernist moods and landscapes, and share numerous verbal parallels. Fiction was evidently crucial to his poetry, and it is clearly shaped by prose writers as different as Caradoc Evans, Arthur Machen, the Powys brothers, Aldous Huxley, D. H. Lawrence (he described reading *The Plumed Serpent* for 'the hundredth time' (*CL*, p. 87)). Joyce, indeed, with his 'revolution of the word', was as important as any poetic predecessor; we know that in 1933 Thomas bought himself two Faber-published extracts from *Work in Progress* as a Christmas gift.[11] And, given his taste for experimental prose, it should come as no surprise to learn that the chief model for the stylistic shift in his poetry in 1938–41 was Djuna Barnes's *Nightwood*.

My task, of exploring Thomas's reading, was aided by his early keenness to dispel any notion that he was a benighted provincial. His description of father's library for Pamela Hansford Johnson, for example, was an exhaustive one:

Dad has a room full of all the accepted stuff, from Chaucer to Henry James; all the encyclopaedias and books of reference, all Saintsbury, and innumerable books on the theory of literature. His library contains nearly everything that a respectable highbrow library should contain. My books, on the other hand, are nearly all poetry, and mostly modern at that. I have the collected poems of Manley Hopkins, Stephen Crane, Yeats, de la Mare, Osbert Sitwell,

Wilfred Owen, W. H. Auden, & T. S. Eliot; volumes of poetry
by Aldous Huxley, Sacheverell & Edith Sitwell, Edna St. Vincent
Millay, D. H. Lawrence, Humbert Wolfe, Sassoon, and Harold
Munro; most of the ghastly Best Poems of the Year; two of the
Georgian Anthologies, one of the Imagiste Anthologies, 'Whips
& Scorpions' (modern satiric verse), the London Mercury Anthology,
the Nineties Anthology (what Dowsonery!); a volume of Cambridge
Poetry & Oxford Undergraduate Poetry; most of Lawrence, most
of Joyce, with the exception of Ulysses, all of Gilbert Murray's
Greek translations, some Shaw, a little Virginia Woolf, & some
E. M. Forster. (*CL*, p. 93)

Thomas went on to give evidence of his omnivorous tastes throughout
the 1930s, often referring to books he was reading or reviewing. Later,
as a reader and writer for the BBC, he broadcast on poets ranging
from Philip Sidney to Alun Lewis, Dryden to W. H. Davies, as well
as acting in productions of works that included *In Parenthesis* and
Paradise Lost. Despite denials, he was *au fait* with French symbolist
and surrealist verse (probably via the Paris-based journal *transition*),
and was supplied with translations of Kierkegaard, Rilke, Novalis,
Rimbaud, Lorca and other European writers by friends such as Norman
Cameron and Vernon Watkins. Well before their critical recognition
in British critical and academic circles, Thomas was alert to the new
voices in American poetry, including those of Randall Jarrell, Allen
Tate, John Crowe Ransom, Edgar Lee Masters, John Berryman and
Richard Wilbur: Robert Lowell and Theodore Roethke feature in a
broadcast he recorded in July 1952. He was capable of drawing an
informed contrast between Dreiser and Thomas Wolfe, and had a
particular penchant for underrated and eccentric writers such as Ruth
Pitter, Sir Thomas Browne and Walter de la Mare.

Many readers will concede this much, of course, but still argue that
Thomas's reading was nevertheless not really 'rounded'; what do they
know of literature that only literature know? Again, it seems to me
that this underrates Thomas's knowledge and curiosity. No one would
claim, I think, that he was a scholar, or that he read widely in non-
literary areas such as philosophy, theology, history, botany, science,
or politics. But it is all too easy – especially given some of the exaggerated claims made for his expertise in astronomy and suchlike in the

1950s – to dismiss him as a narrowly focused *idiot savant*; encyclo-paedic, granted, when it came to poetry, but lacking contextual know-ledge.[12] The over-inflated claims were rightly ridiculed by Daniel Jones, who claimed his friend had had no interest in any studies 'with names ending in -ology, -onomy, -ography, -osophy, -ic, -ics, or, even, to a large extent, just -y (history, botany) . . . Dylan did not know by heart The Koran, the Zend Avesta, the Upanishads, the Lun Yu, and had no access to the Kabbalah' (Jones, 1977). But Jones overdid the demystification. Of the texts he listed, we know, for instance, that Thomas received the *Koran* as a gift for Christmas 1933 from none other than Jones himself.[13] We also know that Thomas read popular science books, newspapers, studies of politics and current affairs, science fiction, jazz and film journals, and much other printed matter. Like many other poets, he was a magpie reader with an above-average taste for glitter and for the arcane.

When I was seeking out what Thomas had read, then, I cast my net as widely as possible. Trawling the Victorian poets, I read Francis Thompson and George Meredith (finding echoes of both) as well as Gerard Manley Hopkins. I bore in mind that Thomas expressed a 'theoretical dislike' only of the Romantics, and found echoes of Words-worth, Keats and Byron to prove it. I knew that the Georgians, too, so frequently mocked in his letters, had made an impression, as the echoes of Brooke's 'The Great Lover' in 'There was a saviour' show. In reading so widely I was also able to eliminate from the reckoning some of Thomas's favourite works, such as Henry Miller's *Tropic of Cancer*.[14] Even so, 'influence' is often more a case of mood and milieu than simple allusion or echo, and much lies beyond the scope of annotation, which is a clumsy tool at best.

It is possible to say, nevertheless, that when Thomas began writing poetry again in 1944, after a gap of over two years, his use of allusion had changed. Perhaps because he was now, as a father and husband, embracing rather than resisting his own place in the cycle of process, he began to deploy allusion in a more traditional way. The use of Wordsworth's Immortality Ode as a template for 'Fern Hill' (1945) is the most obvious example, but similar examples can be found for all of the later, longer pastoral poems. Moreover, the poets evoked there are often of a smoother, more Virgilian kind than previously: Arnold, Keats, Chaucer and Traherne have supplanted Beddoes,

Milton and Donne. It is as though Thomas's sense of how directly he should draw on the central English poetic canon became more expansive as his own work edged towards permanent inclusion within It. 'Fern Hill' and 'Poem in October' read like poems that already have anthology inclusion in mind, examples in a new mode of his talent for subversive mimicry and adaptation.

As I've noted, however, Thomas's allusive strategies were more often about hiding, not revealing, his sources. One reflection of this is his occasional feigning of ignorance of work he knew perfectly well; of Hopkins, Welsh poetry and surrealism, for example.[15] This can be partly attributed to an outsider's defensive cockiness; having left school at sixteen, Thomas knew there were gaps, or what the university-educated might perceive as gaps, in his reading. He also knew that the difficulty his readers had in getting a handle on his poetry usefully burnished its aura of mystery and novelty. As a result, he turned disadvantage to account, even to the point of occasionally feigning ignorance to enhance the impression of autonomous self-invention. On the make in the metropolis, he availed himself of its desire for a pure, untutored, elemental genius, as his taste for role-playing and the omnivorous quality of his reading suggests. As Kenneth Rexroth put it in 1948, '[Thomas] . . . made the same violent assault upon official culture [as Hart Crane]. The thin erudition of the previous generation, the result of judicious schooling and back numbers of *The Criterion*, seemed dull and idle stuff beside his wolfing of books.'[16]

In this sense, the image of the purposeful autodidact requires a caveat or two. A few months after itemising the contents of his father's 'library', when he knew Johnson better, Thomas gave a very different account of his reading habits to the systematic one his earlier lists had implied; he was, he told her, someone who spends his mornings browsing 'translations out of the Greek or the Film Pictorial, a new novel from Smith's, a new book of criticism, or an old favourite like Grimm or George Herbert, anything in the world so long as it is printed' (*CL*, p. 101). This eclecticism is confirmed by other self-descriptions and accounts by friends, and anticipates the account of how, as a teenager, he would write imitations of 'whatever I was reading at the time . . . Sir Thomas Browne, de Quincey, Henry Newbolt, the Ballads, Blake, Baroness Orczy, Marlowe, Chums, the Imagists, the Bible, Poe, Keats, Lawrence, Anon., and Shakespeare'.[17] The poems, in their often oblique ways, testify to this 'wolfing' appetite; unpick their apparently seamless tone a bit, and you find a bewildering variety of discourses and tones, with allusions and echoes ranging from Schopenhauer to shock and horror thrillers. The less guarded lists, then, undermine, even mock, the more straightforward ones, stressing a promiscuous mingling of texts, many outwith the canon, subverting whatever smacks of prescriptiveness. There is a comic point to them, but they are not merely haphazard; rather, they seem purposefully unpurposive, calculated to bring about novel lexical juxtapositions, cut-ups of genre and register. This is a major reason why, however much one tries to truffle out the 'sources' of Thomas's forging of the process poetic in 1933–4, it is nearly impossible to trace many of the stages by which he created it; the fact that he made wordplay and textual heterogeneity the fundamental principles of his poetry at this time arose from a mode of reading and dealing with texts which is so complex and fugitive as to be impossible to fully trace.

Although born from a recognisably Modernist citational abyss, then, *18 Poems* is very different to *The Waste Land* or *The Cantos* in smothering its allusions deep within its traditional forms, rather than flaunting them on a broken, variable verse surface. Ironically, given the charges of obscurity, Thomas's early poems would be *less* difficult to understand if he had used the more technically 'advanced' collage techniques of *The Waste Land*; criticism has long since caught up with collage, but still has problems with such varied material so slyly wrapped in regular forms and (just about) regular syntax. It is for this reason, I think, that John Bayley described reading poems such as 'When, like a running grave', as being like an 'obstacle course' in which 'even the most careful and devoted reader' can be tripped up and '[i]t is as if the attitudes to language of Donne, Blake, and Swinburne were all to be encountered in the same poem'.[18]

'Half-realised borrowings': Thomas as intertextualist

Thomas's Modernist metaphysical poetry had many of the qualities mid-century critics like Bayley admired, but it also often flouted the limits they set. As a result, by about 1960, it had come to mark one of the points beyond which such criticism could not go. In Winifred

Nowottny's brilliant study, *The Language Poets Use* (1962), a *tour de force* reading of 'There was a saviour' leads to the conclusion that several of its allusions are so recondite that Thomas could not have reasonably expected most readers to identify them.[19] And while Nowottny did not believe that a full accounting for allusions was necessary for the poem to succeed, she was worried by whether the fainter echoes of other texts were unintended or deliberate; 'Compost or Cue?', as she put it. It all depends, of course, on what we mean by 'reasonable'. Thomas seems to have believed that, since we are never wholly in control of our language, and hence a poem's sources, it is right to register this within the poem itself; non-'reasonable' in this context does not mean irrational, but truer reasonableness.[20] No poet is able to wholly account for everything in a poem, of course; but Thomas makes it a conscious principle to allow for a residue of unexplained, unresolved material in his. This gives them a textual unconscious which works to thwart the separation of 'Compost' (genetics) and 'Cue' (meaning) which Nowottny felt was so necessary; they anticipate, that is, some of the new ways of thinking about literature which would emerge just a few years after Nowottny's book, in particular the concept of intertextuality associated with Mikhail Bakhtin and Julia Kristeva.[21]

In intertextual terms, trying to account for a poem simply by tracking it to its sources is not only impossible but, to some extent, beside the point.[22] Or, as Thomas once put it himself, justifying his avoidance of allusion to 'conscious influence[s]', the mere 'heredity' or 'descendency' of a poem 'isn't worth a farthing'.[23] In 1922 *The Waste Land* had made a creative principle of the fact that all poems are 'fragments' of others. But Thomas avoids such an ironic parade by his subversion of the allusive protocols, violating the convention by which other poets are permitted to retain their identities within the host text.[24] Alert to allusion-hunting, he will even sometimes lure the unwary into over-explication with what Barbara Hardy calls 'deceptive allusions'.[25] In a similar way, aware of his own compromised relationship towards the textual mulch from which his poems grew, Thomas's poems often incorporate an understanding that language use itself is shaped by echo, false parallelism, phrasal slippage, palimpsestic overlay. They recognise that the creative process is not fully knowable or susceptible of authorial control, and in so doing allow the linguistic unconscious an enhanced degree of autonomy.[26] Mastery *over* language is renounced as an illusion, even as virtuosic creativity *within* language is flaunted. Sound, un- or half-conscious intertextual echo, will invariably shape sense in poetry, we might say; rather than deploring it, or pretending it can be eliminated, better to be conscious of its inevitability and make that part of your conscious poetic practice.

Thomas's procedures anticipate analyses of poetic language by contemporary poet-theorists such as Denise Riley, who has noted that 'Sound runs on well ahead of the writer's tactics. The aural laws of rhyme precede and dictate its incarnation—and this is only one element of an enforced passivity in the very genre where that irritating thing "creativity" is supposed to most forcefully hold court.'[27] 'Enforced passivity' in Thomas is the backdrop to a drama of self-making on the part of the hybrid, Anglo-Welsh subject; thus, interlinked allusions to Freud, *Hamlet* and Eliot's 'The Problem of Hamlet' in *18 Poems*, constellate his relationship with a poetically usurped father and adolescent sexual angst in poems such as 'My world is pyramid', while also mimicking the Joycean 'chaosmos', the universe of process, to which everything belongs. More fugitive intertexts include the 'process' of 'A process in the weather of the heart', a reference to the 'philosophy of process' of Alfred North Whitehead, whose *Science and the Modern World* (1926) Thomas is known to have read. Like other popular science writers of the day, Whitehead tried to reconcile modern physics with a spiritual principle, and this effort is mediated in Thomas by the intertextual code of his family's Unitarianism.[28] Typically, the allusions are blatant *and* cryptic, subversive and an attempt to channel the linguistic unconscious. It is the threat to this from a more (auto) biographical poetry which, it seems to me, haunts the turning-point poem, 'Once it was the colour of saying' of 1938.[29]

The stylistic turning-points of his career – in 1933 (the Nazi seizure of power) and 1938 (the Munich Agreement) – hint at the fact that Thomas's intertextuality taps an 'out of joint', overdetermined historical unconscious too. Far from being escapist, for many of his contemporaries, as R. George Thomas noted, his poems 'accurately mirrored' 'the febrile grotesqueness' of the 1930s, with a poem such as 'The force that through the green fuse' understood by many 'as a fairly clear realization of unknown sources of physical suffering that must lie ahead of us, most probably in gas warfare or Guernica-like devastation' – this because, not despite, their 'macabre' quality. Paradoxically, it was the poems' lack of reportage that ensured that 'the nightmare quality in the drift towards Hitler's war . . . was echoed more closely in Thomas's non-political verse than in any of the Home Guard poems of C. Day Lewis or . . . Spender.'[30]

Thomas and 'the English tradition': future research

To align Thomas with history in this way is to raise questions about his own place in the history of English (and British, and Welsh) poetry, questions which have a material bearing on why we should pay attention to his work today, and on how we might be rewarded by it. The most distinctive aspect of his reputation has always been its anomalous relationship to the standard narratives of twentieth-century poetry, whether 'mainstream' or 'alternative'. Even at the height of his critical acceptability, in the 1950s and 1960s, he did not fit easily within them; and, since the late 1970s, uneasy tolerance has been replaced largely by dismissal or patronage – that he is, at worst, a kind of fake poet, and at best merely an interesting one, in a dead end, fascinating-but-inconsequential way.

My case in *CP14* and *Under the Spelling Wall* is that Thomas's response to Modernism, informed by Joycean attitudes to language, New Country's revival of form, Lawrence's expressionist Modernism and Blake's iconoclasm, gathered under the sign of his own hybrid Anglo-Welsh identity, was an event of major significance in the development of the English lyric. I argue there that if it is taken as seriously as it should be, a radical rethinking of standard narratives of mid-century poetry is required. However, as I also note, this would inevitably threaten long-cherished beliefs, particularly anglocentric ones – in particular the myth of the 1930s as 'the Auden decade' and the 1940s as poetically dire – as well as acquiescence in the primacy of 'the English tradition' of plain-style discursive-empirical poetry, from Hardy to the present.[31] Partly as a result, despite the positive reception of *CP14* as an edition, almost no reviewer referred to the literary-historical case it advanced – namely that Thomas, author of the experimental 'Altarwise' and anthology classics like 'Fern Hill', problematises the division of British poetry into 'mainstream' and 'alternative' strands, and straddles the fault-line opened up in English poetry by *The Waste Land*.[32] Thomas's poetry, dealing with major existential issues (birth, being, sex, faith, death, with an emphasis on the question of (im)mortality), fused the traditional forms revived by Auden and his followers with Modernist content. Following Gabriel Pearson's 1971 review of Daniel Jones's edition of Thomas's poems, I rejected the idea that Thomas and Auden were simply polar opposites, finding their much-touted opposition best understood in terms of what they initially *shared* – that, as poets of post-1929 crisis, they belonged to the same 'spiritually-orphaned generation', responding apprehensively to a looming world war with different forms of 'nervy apocalyptic jokiness' – and that they should therefore be regarded as complementary, 'the sundered halves of the great modernist poet that English [*sic*] poetry, after Eliot, failed to throw up'.[33]

In formal terms, both Thomas and Auden also belonged to a conservative, distinctively British attempt to domesticate avant-garde disruptiveness, which was under way as they were starting their careers. As the poet-critic Drew Milne notes, this established that the only kind of Modernist-derived British poetry sanctioned by the mainstream was, for many decades, that which presented itself as the inheritor of pre-modernist English poetry, and especially as 'retrospective conceptions of the modernism of seventeenth-century poetry'.[34] The best expression of this process was Empson's *Seven Types of Ambiguity* (1930), which built on Eliot's criticism, but valorised polysemy and structural complexity in 'a major development of modernist poetics within criticism'. It offered a blueprint for the rewriting of earlier poetry according to Eliotic tenets and for 'writing modernist poetry by other [i.e. critical] means'.

Both Auden and Thomas reflected this trend towards containment; however, while Auden rejected Modernism after *The Orators* (1932), Thomas maintained an intense dialogue with it until at least 1938; indeed, his ratchetting up of polysemy and fugitive allusiveness, above even Empsonian levels, was a challenge to its domestication. Then, in 1938–9, Thomas's version of 'nervy apocalyptic jokiness', now tempered by his experience of marriage and parenthood, supplanted its previously dominant Audenesque twin on the poetry scene, in the form of the New Apocalypse group of poets. Throughout the war, and for some years afterwards, Thomas set the tone for British poetry, and not just that of his own generation. During this period there existed both a new visionary-apocalyptic Modernism and a renewed 1920s Modernism: the outcomes included not only W. S. Graham's *The Nightfishing* and Lynette Roberts's *Gods With Stainless Ears*, but Eliot's *Four Quartets*, David Jones's *The Anathemata*, and H. D.'s *The Towers Fall*. Far from being a wasted decade, as Movement ideologues later claimed, the 1940s was one of the richest of the century.

The consequences of how the Thomas–Auden split has been construed have shaped British poetry to the present day. Broadly speaking, poets following Auden's example tried to curb what they saw as Modernism's excess of linguistic and metrical defamiliarisation in an effort to make formal control of tension and ambiguity the cornerstone of a continuing humanist enterprise. Those inclining towards Thomas and/or experiment, fewer in number (but including W. S. Graham, Ted Hughes and Sylvia Plath), rejected liberal humanism and its reliance on pre-modern concepts of language and the self. Yet despite this divide, there have always been poetic practices which blurred and overrode it. Since the early 2000s, this divide has become – in the era of the internet and print-on-demand technology – increasingly difficult to police. As a result, Thomas's subaltern, tricksterish credentials and his pioneering role as a flouter of distinctions (not to mention his rôle as a proto post-colonial 'mimic man', biomorphic body-writer and pacifist prophet of ecological crisis) make him an increasingly appropriate representative figure of mid-twentieth-century poetry for our own times.

An overhaul of standard accounts of 1930s and 1940s poetry and its relationship to the present-day scene is long overdue. Critics such as Andrew Duncan and James Keery have for some time been preparing the way by teasing out the 1940s inheritance shared by such unlikely bedfellows as Hughes, Plath, Roy Fisher, Geoffrey Hill, Philip Larkin and J. H. Prynne, as well as tracing the influence of W. S. Graham on poets, such as Denise Riley, associated with the 'Cambridge School'. Further exploration of the relationship of Thomas's poetry to their work and that of others will follow, as well as of his as-yet-unexplored intertexts and contexts, from crossword puzzles to Paul Celan and John Cowper Powys. These will help to flesh out a richer, more genuinely nuanced and paradoxical history than we currently have. It is with this future prospect in mind that *Discovering Dylan Thomas*, in its oblique and supplementary way, is offered as a contribution towards establishing Thomas's dissident place near the heart of that history.[35]

Notes

1   The recent Faber *The Poems of Basil Bunting* (2016), splendidly edited by Don Share, is a case in point: while the two poets arguably require a similar level of editorial attention, the 570 pages of the Bunting include 330 pages of annotations and textual variants, while the 440 pages of my edition of Thomas contain 190 pages of annotations, with no variants. The Bunting retails at £30.00 and is aimed at a specialist poetry audience; the Thomas was initially priced at £20.00, with discounts, falling to £16.99 for the paperback edition of 2016.

2   This is the place to admit to the fact that I was required to perform a rather hasty reduction (of around 60,000 words) to my annotations for the *Collected Poems*, in March–May 2014; on some occasions I felt as if I were playing a blue-pencil version of Jenga: one slip, and the entry would collapse into a heap of verbal debris.

3   These glitches were noted only by Seamus Perry in his review for the *London Review of Books*. Perry was kind enough to describe them – damnable in an editor, in truth – as 'slips'. As a leading Oxford academic, Perry's largely positive piece was significant, and signals a growing *rapprochement* between the academic-critical establishment and Thomas. This was matched by Cambridge University, home of Thomas's *bête noir* F. R. Leavis, which organised a centenary symposium in October 2014. Only the *Times Literary Supplement* reviewer Michael Caines (true to past *TLS* form) proved unable to forgo the old Thomas-as-drunkard stereotypes (his article was titled 'Buying a pint for Dylan Thomas') (Caines 2014).

4   The reprint was collected in *The Doctor and the Devils and Other Stories*, published by New Directions Press in 1966.

5   The centenary witnessed numerous inventive attempts to find twenty-first century equivalents for his own multi-media and mass media involvements, ranging from an *Under Milk Wood* opera by John Metcalf and exhibitions of Peter Blake prints, to a 48-hour Dylanathon and a slew of radio and television programmes and films featuring the likes of Tom Hollander, Elijah Wood, Charlotte Church and Michael Sheen. BBC Wales, in particular, excelled itself, ditching the sepia-tinted approach it had adopted in 2003 (the fiftieth anniversary of Thomas's death) in favour of an imaginative and varied response. Its main event was a

Thomas-and-radio themed weekend at Laugharne in April, which included items ranging from quiz programmes, to an episode of *The Verb*, a series of Radio 4's *The Essay*, input from Radio 6, and a Radio 3 choral programme; but there were many other highlights. As well as one-off broadcasts, such as an Aardman animation of 'The hunchback in the park', and a commissioned biopic, the BBC established a Dylan Thomas website, making available large amounts of archive material in one place for the first time.

In academic terms, the year saw some Welsh universities involved in a rather undignified competition with each other to grab a slice of the Thomas action, and a few dark mutterings about 'outsiders' (such as myself) muscling in on his work. However, these negative responses were offset by successful conferences at Swansea and Cambridge Universities, and the emergence of a new generation of young, Thomas-interested and theory-savvy critics. As is so often the case, academia (which includes the author, of course) was less important in the grand scheme of things than it liked to think; the biggest failures of 2014 by far stemmed from the uncritical embrace by the leadership of Literature Wales of a market-defined 'accessibility', 'choice' and 'impact' agenda, which led to a focus on Thomas's life at the expense of his writing. This, in turn, ensured the lack of a lasting legacy of appreciation of his work by the wider public in Wales. At an institutional level, the chief outcome of 'DT-100' level was a new alliance of previously distinct 'stakeholders' in the Thomas 'brand' – Literature Wales, the Dylan Thomas industry, a newly corporat-ised university sector, local businesses – most of them devoted to ignoring the unruly energies and subversive lessons of the poet while harnessing his aura to their PR operations. Paradoxically, the relative failure within Wales at an institutional level (another example of a longstanding cultural cringe, it could be argued) was in marked contrast to the response elsewhere, where organisers and audiences proved to have outgrown the old taste for Thomas stereotypes and clichés. For more details see my article: *http://poetrywales.co.uk/wp/1905/and-i-am-dumbed-down-to-tell/*

6 I also republished 'A dream of winter', with an introductory note, in *P.N. Review*, 42/2 (November/December 2015, issue 226), 3.

7 In *CP88* Davies and Maud annotated inconsistently and at times rather unhelpfully. Much of the annotation was biographical, and there was no mention of critical viewpoints differing from their own, for example. For 'Altarwise by owl-light' – the acid test, as Thomas's densest poem – they gave fifteen brief glosses for 140 lines of poetry (fourteen for the first five sonnets, but just one for the second five). It seemed as if the editors had been hamstrung by having to jointly agree on everything.

As if to show how it could be done, the *Selected Poems* (2000), edited solely by Walford Davies, gives twenty-nine notes for the five parts of 'Altarwise' it includes. Ralph Maud's annotations to the notebook poems are also, of course, exemplary.

8   The first assessment is by Linden Huddleston, the second by Seamus Heaney (Heaney, 1992, 1995).

9   Thomas's point, repeated throughout his life, was that much poetry, like realist prose, began with a pre-existing idea for which the poet then sought to find words (working 'towards' them). As opposed to this, he felt that they should 'work from words, from the substance of words and the rhythm of substantial words'; that is, from verbal material which pre-existed the labour of writing the poem (*CL*, pp. 147–8, 208).

10 It's fair to assume that Thomas also knew some Blake criticism; his father's library contained the first critical study, S. Foster Damon's *William Blake, His Philosophy and Symbols*, of 1924.

11 Three extracts were published in pamphlet form by Faber: *Anna Livia Plurabelle* (1930), *Haveth Childers Everywhere* (1931) and *Two Tales of Shem and Shaun* (1932). Thomas bought two (he does not say which two) as a present to himself for Christmas 1933, (*CL*, 91).

12 The classic case of extreme over-interpretation is Elder Olson's reading of 'Altarwise by owl-light' through the Hercules legend and the movement of the constellations during the course of the year (Olson, 1954).

13 See the letter to Pamela Hansford Johnson of 25 December 1933: 'My gifts are arrayed in front of me: . . . a new edition of the Koran from a friend who writes music' (*CL*, p. 91).

14 Thus, Thomas enjoyed (and reviewed) Samuel Beckett's *Murphy* and Flann O'Brien's *At Swim-Two-Birds*, for example, but they appear to have left no trace in his poetry. The only overt trace of Miller is the name-checking of *Tropic of Cancer* and *Tropic of Capricorn* in 'Altarwise by owl-light', and the dedication to him of 'Lament'.

15 Thomas denied knowledge of Hopkins's poetry in his correspondence with Henry Treece. For his knowledge of *cynghanedd*, see the note to 'I dreamed my genesis', below, and Mererid Hopwood (2004). Thomas's declaration of his complete ignorance of surrealism to Richard Church in 1936 was a particularly blatant fib, coming as it did in the year in which he appeared at the International Surrealist Exhibition and gave a poetry reading with Paul Éluard. On the other hand, his denials of knowledge of some poets – Hart Crane, for example – ring true. Usually, the safest course is to assume that if it seems as if Thomas could have read or learnt something, he probably had.

16 Kenneth Rexroth, 'Introduction', *The New British Poets*, New York: New Directions, 1949, p. xx.

17 Thomas's correspondence, especially in the 1930s, mentions scores of other writers In passing, among them Archibald MacLeish, Christina Rossetti, Rémy de Gourmont, Stella Gibbons, e. e. cummings, Laura Riding, Robert Graves, S. J. Perelman, James Thurber, Beachcomber and P. G. Wodehouse. Thomas was a fan of mystery, detective, fantasy, horror and sci-fi genres and children's literature (he praised *The Hobbit* on its appearance, in 1952). Perhaps the best example of the independence of his taste – 'eclectic' is too euphemistic, 'indiscriminate' too censorious is his exuberant, prescient advocacy of Amos Tutuola's *The Palm-Wine Drinkard* in a 1952 *Observer* review.

18 John Bayley, *The Romantic Survival*, 1957, pp. 194, 207.

19 Thus, '[a]nyone who brings literary allusion into a commentary on a poem must be hag-ridden by uncertainties. How is allusiveness to be established? Even if it is established what does it mean? . . . Even if it can be shown that an allusion is deliberate as well as verifiable, what limits are to be set to the limits of the allusion (and its context) to the concerns of the poem in which it is included? . . . if the works drawn upon by a poet have only the status of compost . . . it would be absurd to talk about the meaning of the "compost"; to study [it] is to study the genetics of the poem, not [its] meaning , , , But if the echoes are deliberate . . . [this] is an aspect of the meaning of the poem.' Winifred Nowottny, *The Language Poets Use*, 1962, pp. 204–5.

20 The oscillation between conscious and unconscious elements is nicely registered in Thomas's 1938 letter to Henry Treece about his composition methods: 'I make one image, – though "make" is not the word, I let, perhaps, an image be "made" emotionally in me then apply to it what intellectual & critical forces I possess.' *CL*, pp. 328–9.

21 Kristeva coined the term in 1966. 'Intertextuality' resists the notion that meaning resides in the text, and that the writer communicates directly with the reader in an intersubjective way. Rather, it takes meaning to be mediated through, or filtered by, 'codes' supplied by other texts, or 'intertexts', and as being produced by the reader in relation not only to the text itself but also by the network of texts around it, accidental as well as optional or obligatory. Revealingly, given the extent to which Thomas's poems unsettle the border between originality and derivation, intertextuality is often mistaken for plagiarism.

22 The empirical fallacy on which this kind of procedure is based had already reached its apotheosis in Thomas's own time, with John Livingston Lowes's exhaustive, brilliantly limited analysis of Coleridge's 'Kubla Khan', *The Road to Xanadu* (1927).

23   In May 1934, consoling Pamela Hansford Johnson over a rejection slip
she had received, Thomas reminded her that most editors 'look at the
influences first and the individuality afterwards. If a poem, in the John
Donne descendency, is fairly good, they print it; if very good, in the
Tennyson descendency, they refuse to. What they never realise', he adds,
'is that the convention, the heredity, of the poem, doesn't matter a
farthing. It's the individuality of the poet . . . that really matters.' If she
were to 'tack on' the 'conscious influence of Donne, Tourneur, Traherne
or . . . Hopkins', she would be published 'all over the place & be the
moment's wow in every public salon' (*CL*, p. 158).

24   Thus, for Don McKay, Thomas wrenches his mythic and literary materials
from their contexts in a way such that 'the aggression—the *kidnapping*
[would be a better description]—is itself a telling feature of the symbol
in its new Thomas-controlled situation. Accordingly, the act of allusion
itself forms part of the symbol's signification'. It is forcefully dislodged
from its original context as a way of striking a blow at authoritative
systems: 'his style of allusion serves notice that he will be no slave to
another man's, even when he has stolen pieces of it.' Don McKay, 1985/6,
p. 382.

25   See Hardy's gloss of the phrase 'stones of odyssey' in the note to 'Altarwise
by owl-light', IX, below.

26   As Northrop Frye noted: 'what we think of as typically the poetic creation
. . . [is] an associative rhetorical process, most of it below the threshold
of consciousness, a chaos of paronomasia, sound-links, ambiguous sense-
links, and memory-links very like that of a dream', this being responsible
for lyric's 'oracular' and 'unconscious' priorities. Northrop Frye, *Anatomy
of Criticism*, London: Penguin, 1957, pp. 271–2.

27   Denise Riley, 'Is There Linguistic Guilt?', *Critical Quarterly*, 39/1 (Spring
1997), 83.

28   Whitehead was one of the first British physicists to understand Einstein's
theories and their implications, and in his role as populariser of the new
physics was the Stephen Hawking of the 1920s. His sense of nature as
perpetual process, the interconnectedness of atomic and cosmic events,
of their simultaneity and perpetual potentiality (the idea that whatever
is going to happen is already happening), of the impossibility of full
communication in language ('there is always a background of presuppos-
ition which defies analysis by reason of its infinitude') and scepticism
towards ratiocinative logic ('Logic, conceived as an adequate analysis of
the advance of thought, is a fake') are all found in Thomas.

29   This poem is one of Thomas's most complexly allusive pieces, adapting
as it does Rimbaud's synaesthetic sonnet 'Voyelles' and invoking his

truncated poetic career at the moment when Thomas himself was seeking to get beyond his own prodigious but costive early style. Thomas's later mocking description of himself as 'the Rimbaud of Cwmdonkin Drive' is, in this sense, his gloss on the poem, which signifies its own wry take on the French original by falling one line short of the fourteen it nominally requires.

30 R. George Thomas, 'Dylan Thomas and some early readers', *Poetry Wales*, 9/2 (Autumn 1973), 12.

31 Goodby, 2013, pp. 19–20.

32 Goodby, 2013, pp. 452–4.

33 Gabriel Pearson, 'Gabriel Pearson on Dylan Thomas', *The Spectator Review of Books*, 20 November 1971, p. 731.

34 Drew Milne, 'Modernist Poetry in the British Isles', in Alex Davis and Lee Jenkins (eds), *The Cambridge Companion to Modernist Poetry*, Cambridge: Cambridge University Press, 2007, p. 153.

35 For the link with Celan see James Keery's discussion of their common root in German expressionism and French surrealism. James Keery, 'The Burning Baby and the Bathwater', *P.N. Review*, 31/6 (July–August 2005), 59, cited in Goodby, 2013, p. 451.

PART I

Supplementary poems

Forest picture

Calm and strange is this evening hour in the forest,
Carven domes of green are the trees by the pathway,
Infinite shadowy isles lie silent before me,
Summer is heavy with age, and leans upon Autumn.

All the land is ripe. There is no motion   5
Down the long bays of blue that those cloudy headlands
Sleep above in the glow of a fading sunset;
All things rest in the will of purpose triumphant.

Outlines melting into a vague immensity
Fade, the green gloom grows darker, and deeper the dusk: 10
Hark! a voice and laughter – the living and loving
Down these fantastic avenues pass like shadows.

Idyll of unforgetfulness

To have seen countries which were glorious,
Immutable, and ardourously consecrated;
To have known them in their blue-hued valiance,
Felt their serenity of ripple-woven loveliness;
To have heard their vague, rhapsodic singings,   5
Their silences in silver quietness of sleep,
And listened when a slow, starred slumber wrapt the moon,
To the voices of the wind caught in the cradle-petals of the night:
These were my desires, eternal as mountains,
These were the whisperings that sighed on my lips at dusk,   10
These the imaginings, tender and blossomed with futility,
That played in voiceless frolic at the threshold of my heart.
These countries I have not visioned,
Which bathe themselves in a ravishment of snow;
Their grasses, each a tiny ecstasy,   15
Have not adored my body as it softly smoothed their skin.
But I have known the still ardour of equability;
I have known the mystery of the sea to be mantled about me;
I have felt the silk wind brush my lips;
I have made my throat an arbour for forgotten songs.   20
The sea has been breeze-serene sapphire,
And blue-tipped birds have rippled it,
And the sun has smoothed it with quiet fire,
And I have reflected its colours in the peace of my eyes;
It has been vague, and made of shadow,   25
With little, odd mists waved in the path of its echo,
When everything slept and the smell of the waves was strange;
The foam has lingered into white, little flowers,
And changed with the wind into indistinct patterns of frolic,
And my fingers have touched the glass of the waters,   30
And hours made little I have dipped my arms in their rapture;
Little white-lipped faces have peered up at me,
And eyes have been grove-green catching mine from the
          depth of the silence;
Voices have called, and the answers lemural whispers from the sea;
And covering all has been a quietude, and a singing from
          flake-bare throats   35
Now the sea has a flowering of foam;

Hidden in delicate mists are they that beckon,
They of the pale, sea-wan beauty, they of the home
Of the pale-green, delicate fishes, silver as sighs,
Their voices are dim; they have passed, 40
In the carpeting of the dusk, obscurely and elusively,
Enveloping themselves in the laden eve;
The darkness is illimitable, green shadow,
And the whisper caught in its pageant of tawny pearl,
Green-shadowed panoply enveloping all its strangeness
      and softness of stealth. 45

In Borrowed Plumes
II. W. B. Yeats

There was a pearl-pale moon that slid
Down oceans of ambrosial sky,
Under the drooping of the day's dusk-lid
Where darkness and her wine-waves lie,
And at that full nocturnal hour   5
She twined her splendid, curving hair,
And bent her body like a flower,
And glided through the evening air
Light as a cloud and petal-fair.
She gained the garlanded and leaf-green mound   10
That tapered like a dove-gray hill,
To sink upon the deep grass without sound,
To press her face upon the lilting ground,
And twine her yellow hair like daffodil.
She raised fine, luscious fruit up to her lips,   15
Tasted the round grape in full-throated sips,
Smoothed upon her mouth the lovely pear,
When through the darkness coiled about the place,
The terror-scented darkness passion-dim,
A silver spider crawls, and weaves his web about her hair,   20
And weaves his silken rapture everywhere,
And looks into her wave-wild face,
And wonders why she weeps at him.

The woman speaks

No food suffices but the food of death;
Sweet is the waxen blood, honey the falling flesh;
There is no fountain springing from the earth
Cool as the waxred fountains of the veins;
No cradle's warmer than this perished breast,   5
And hid behind the fortress of the ribs
The heart lies ready for the raven's mouth,
And lustreless within the ruined face
The eyes remark the antics of the hawk.

A sniper laid him low and strewed his brains;   10
One would not think the greenness of this valley
Could in a day be sick with so much blood;
What were young limbs are faggots on the land,
And young guts dry beneath the sickened sun.
Let me not think, O God, of carnage,   15
Of ravens at the hero's meat and nerves
Pecking and nestling all the time of night.

The grass he covers is a pretty green;
He has the still moon and the hundred stars;
He learns the carrion pickers of the sky,   20
And on his shoulders fall their world of wings,
And on his ears hosannas of the grave.

His narrow house is walled with blades of grass,
Roofed with the sky and patterned with blond bones;
The birds make him his cerements of plumes,   25
Cerecloth of weed, and build an ordured bed.

Since the first flesh of man was riven
By scalpel lightning from the rifted sky,
Man's marrow barbed, and breast ripped with a steel,
All that was loved and loved made the fowls' food,   30
Grief, like an open wound, has cried to heaven.

No food suffices but the food of death;
Death's appetite is sharpened by the bullet's thumb;
Yet he is dead, and still by woman's womb
Hungers for quickening, and my lonely lips   35
Hunger for him who dungs the valley fields.

There shall be no mute mourning over his acre,
Sorrow shall have no words, no willow wearing;
Rain shall defile and cover, wind bear away
The saddest dust in all this hollow world.   40

Old men whose blood is hindered in their veins,
Whom cancer crops, whose drinking rusts, these die;
These die who shovel the last home of man;
The sniper dies; the fingers from the sky
Strangle the little children in their beds;   45
One day my woman's body will be cold.

So I have come to know, but knowledge aches;
I know that age is snow upon the hair,
Wind carven lines around the drooping mouth;
And raven youth will feast but where he will.   50

Since the first womb spat forth a baby's corpse,
The mother's cry has fumed about the winds;
O tidal winds, cast up her cry for me;
That I may drown, let loose her flood of tears.

It was a haggard night the first flesh died,   55
And shafted hawks came snarling down the sky;
A mouse, it was, played with an ivory tooth,
And ravens fed confection to their young.

Palm of the earth, O sprinkle on my head
The dust you hold, O strew that little left;   60
Let what remains of that first miracle
Be sour in my hair. That I may learn
The mortal miracle, let that first dust
Tell me of him who feeds the raging birds.

Grief, thief of time, crawls off

Grief, thief of time, crawls off
With wasted years and half
The loaded span of days.
Marauding pain steals off
With half the load of faith   5
That weighed thee to thy knees.

The old forget their cries,
Lean times on evil seas,
And times the wind blew rough,
Remember the sea-boys   10
Riding sea-bear and horse
Over the salty path.

The old forget the grief,
And the hack of the cough,
And the friends fed to crows,   15
Remember the sea-youth,
And plucking wild radish,
And seed that was promise.

Grief is the price of peace,
And age forgets the cries,   20
The thief of time steals death.
Remember the prince's price,
Remember all thy days
Thy thieven load of faith.

Jack of Christ

I

For loss of blood I fell where stony hills
Had milk and honey flowing from their cracks,
And where the footed dew was on the pools
I knelt to drink the water dry as sticks.
Where was no water ran the honeyed milks,   5
And where was water was the drybacked sand.

I met the ghost of water on the paths,
And knelt before the ghostly man of milk;
Where was no honey were the humming wraiths
Descending on the flowers' cup and stalk.   10
Where was no water there the image rides,
And where was water was the stony hand.

For lack of faith I fell upon the desert
Where eagles tenanted the single palm;
Where was no god I heard his windy visit,   15
And saw the spider weave him on her loom.
And where god was his holy house was sculptured,
A monster lie upon the maddened sand.

For lack of love I fell where love was not,
The plains by the still sea, and there love sat,   20
My child did knock within her happy heart.
And where love was sat fever on her throne,
My child did burn and scream within her womb
And where love lay was laid her hot-veined brat.

At last I came to a remembered cave,   25
There made my lodge, and sucked the fallen figs,
Where no thief walked leapt through my neighbour's grove,
My skin not waxen old upon my dugs.
Where no thief was there came the padded knave
To set his famined hands upon my fat.   30

The thief of light did sew upon my lids
His chequered shades, and at my open ear
The thief of sound poured down his fluids,
The thief of speech was busy at the jaw.
When all was peace there came these palming lads   35
To nick my senses but to leave the breath.

II

Jack my father, let the knaves
Fill with a swag of bubbles their sad sacks,
No fingers press their fingers on the wax
Red as the axe, blue as a hanging man.   40

Jack my father, let the thieves
Share their fool spoil with their sad brood of sneaks,
No silver whistles chase them down the weeks'
Daybouldered peaks into the iron van.

Let them escape, the living graves   45
Be bared of loveliness and shorn of sex,
Let sense be plundered and the dryboned wrecks
Of words perplex the sad tides of the brain.

Let them run off with laden sleeves,
These stolen bubbles have the bites of snakes,   50
These sacked wines raise a thirst no liquor slakes,
No victual breaks this hunger son of pain.

Lust and love both be your loves,
Wean the well-loved on one symmetric breast,
Please the one-minded hand, and suck to rest   55
The body pressed upon one flesh and bone.

One dies all die, all live one lives,
And slopes and vales are blessed as they are cursed;
Both sweet and bitter were the last and first
Truths to be nursed with their same mother's groans.   60

Where is no god there man believes,
And where god is his homage turns to dust;
God who is all tells in his desert gust
That one man must be all and all be one.

When the knave of death arrives, 65
Yield the lost flesh to him and give your ghost;
All shall remain, and on the cloudy coast
Walk the blithe host
Of god and ghost with you, their newborn son.

III

The girl, unlacing, trusts her breast, 70
Doubts not its tint nor how it leans;
Faith in her flesh maintains its shape
From toe to head
Their maiden cloths the stars unslip,
And from her shift the worn moon turns 75
One bosom to her lover's bed
Red in the east.

Should the girl doubt, a sallow ring
Would rim her eyes and sphere her breast;
And should the stars blush as they strip, 80
Ashamed of light,
Their manypointed light would drop;
If the moon doubts, her dew is dust;
If day lacks faith, it turns to night,
And light is done. 85

It shall happen that time's venom
Darts to your cheek and leaves its scars;
Burning like age upon your mouth,
The old-veined wind
Shall bear away the kiss of youth; 90
And it shall happen that the stars,
Lorn of their naked welcome,
Shoot as they fade.

Trust, in the first, the desert hills,
And milk will move along their udders;   95
Let the hilly milk sit sweet
Upon the tongue,
And honey quiet every gut;
Trust the lips the honey colours:
Lips are smiling, always young,   100
Though the flesh falls.

The girl, unlacing, trusts her breast:
Forever shall the breast give milk;
The naked star stands unashamed:
It shall forever.   105
You who believe the stony hand,
And, groaning, trust the needles' stroke,
Shall be star-fathered on the air
And Jack of Christ.

I fellowed sleep who kissed between the brains

I fellowed sleep who kissed between the brains;
Her spinning kiss through my lean sheets
Stopped in the bones.
I fathered dreams as races from the loins
And sleep, pit-wombed, who kissed the pits.   5

Sleep shifts along the latches of the night;
The shifting night inched in as she
Drew back the bolt;
My fellow sleep who kissed me in the heart
With her salt hairs unlocked the sky.   10

I fellowed sleep who drained me with a kiss;
Where went but one grave-gabbing shade
Now go the stars;
Now stirs a ruined moon about my bed;
And worlds hang on trees.   15

A Dream of Winter

Very often on winter nights the halfshaped moonlight sees
Men through a window of leaves and lashes marking gliding
Into the grave an owl-tongued childhood of birds and cold trees,

Or drowned beyond water in the sleepers' fish-trodden churches
Watching the cry of the seas as snow flies sparkling, riding,   5
The ice lies down shining, the sandgrains skate on the beeches.

Often she watches through men's midnight windows, their winter
     eyes,
The conjured night of the North rain in a firework flood,
The Great Bear raising the snows of his voice to burn the skies.

And men may sleep a milkwhite path through the chill, struck
     still waves   10
Or walk on thunder and air in the frozen, birdless wood
On the eyelid of the North where only the silence moves,

Asleep may stalk among lightning and hear the statues speak,
The hidden tongue in the melting garden sing like a thrush
And the soft snow drawing a bellnote from the marble cheek,   15

Drowned fast asleep beyond water and sound may mark the street
Ghost-deep in lakes where the rose-cheeked nightmare glides
     like a fish,
The Ark drifts on the cobbles, the darkness sails in a fleet,

Or, lying down still, may clamber the snow-exploded hill
Where the caverns hide the snowbull's ivory splinter,   20
Fossil spine of the sea-boned seal, iceprint of pterodactyl.

Oh birds, trees, fish and bears, singing statues, Arkfloods and seals
Steal from their sleeper awake as he waits in the winter
Morning, alone in his world, staring at the London wheels.

The postman knocks. By Cain, he knocks once more!

The postman knocks. By Cain, he knocks once more!
I spring from bed. Then, rising from the floor
Where I have fainted, rush to the door and fall
Again. Youth, what a joy is youth! The hall
Is dark with dogs. They bite me as I pass.   5
My dear dumb friends! I'll put some powdered glass
Today in their Bob Martin's. That'll teach
Them manners. And now at long last I reach
The dog-and-child-chewed mat and find? – yes, yes!–
A bunch of letters from the far U.S.   10
Ah, what epistolary pearls unseen
Blush in these envelopes! what hippocrene!–
'Be my pen-pal' from Truman. Or 'Dear Friend,
Shall we arrange a *personal* Lease-Lend?'
From Betty Hutton. Or 'Will you play for me   15
An Air on my G. String?' signed Gypsy Lee.
Or 'We salute you Script-King!' from MacArthur,
Hecht, and Wilder. Or a plea to bath her
From Miss Colbert. But, alas, vain hopes!
There's nothing in those Sam-stamped envelopes   20
But a request to write on 'Wither Art?'
For 'Cyclorama', 'Seed', 'Rubato', 'Fart',
'Prognosis', 'Ethic', 'Crucible', and 'Clef'–
And other small reviews that pay sweet F.

An old man or a young man

An old man or a young man,
And I am none of these,
Goes down upon the praying mat
And kneels on his knuckled knees
Whenever a fine lady   5
Does his poor body good.
And if she gives him beauty
Or a cure for his hot blood,
He weeps like one of the willow trees
That stands in a grave wood.   10

A wise man or a mad man,
And I am both of these,
Whenever a woman pleases him
With what she does not need—
Her beauty or her virtue,   15
Her sin or her honeyed pride,
Or the ice cold price she puts upon
Her white hot maidenhood—
Weeps like one of the willow trees
That stands in a grave wood.   20

Old or mad or young or wise,
And she is all of these,
Whenever a poor man needs her
She does her best to please:
For, oh, she knows in the loveless nights   25
And in the nights of love
That bitter gratitude is all
A loving woman can have—
And she weeps like one of the willow trees
That stands in a grave wood.   30

PART II

Annotations, versions and drafts

* Indicates a poem in the supplementary poems section

Juvenilia: a note on plagiarism, parody, and finding a style

In a draft of his radio talk 'How to be a Poet', held at the Harry Ransom Center in Austin, Dylan Thomas whimsically refers to 'the career upon which I embarked at the age of seven and a half (writing, as I fail to recall, a quarrelsome poem with the title of They Are All Wrong).' That first effort has not survived, but many pre-notebook poems have. The earliest are either comic verse or on conventional subjects: romantic and nature lyrics, elegies for the First World War dead. Evidence of a talent for versifying and mimicry, they say very little about the direction Thomas's poetry was to take. At some stage – perhaps when he was thirteen or fourteen – he appears to have sent a batch of such poems to Robert Graves, who recalled, much later: 'I wrote back that they were irreproachable, but that he would eventually learn to dislike them . . . Even experts would have been deceived by the virtuosity of Dylan Thomas's conventional, and wholly artificial, early poems' (Graves, 1955).

The young Dylan's main outlet at this point was the *Swansea Grammar School Magazine*, which had published his 'The Song of the Mischievous Dog' in December 1925, at the end of his first school term. I have included in the Supplementary poems section two of the best poems he published there, 'Forest picture' and 'Idyll of unforgetfulness'. Like many of his early poems, the second of these was set to music by his best friend of his school years, Daniel Jones, the 'Dan' of the short story, 'The Fight'. A year older than him, and equally precocious, Jones was a crucial influence on Thomas's poetry, broadening his grasp of modernist art and music as well as literature, and encouraging him to experiment. The two collaborated in musical-literary schemes, including radio 'broadcasts' at 'Warmley', the Jones family home, and wrote plays, songs, stories and poems together (Jones *TP71*). Three notebooks of these lyrics and an illustrated playlet 'Bismuth', known collectively as the 'Walter Bram' notebooks after a joke character invented by the pair ('Bram' is the Welsh for 'fart'), are also held at Austin, along with numerous other items on individual sheets and scraps of paper.

The poems in the notebooks, in Jones's handwriting, are in sub-imagistic, consciously precious styles, and might be considered the flipside to Thomas's 'public' poems of the time, a reaction against conventional style producing another, more hermetic one. However, it is impossible to determine the extent of Thomas's authorship, as opposed to Jones's, in any of this material, and consequently I do not include any examples here. Among the loose items in the Austin archive there are also a number of very short pieces made up of disjunctive lines alternately supplied by the pair, suggestive of the surrealist *cadavre exquis* technique.

From around the time he met Daniel Jones, at the age of eleven, Thomas seems to have tried to develop a modern poetic style of his own – that is, before starting the first of the Buffalo notebooks in April 1930, which can be said to mark a formal commencement of this quest. For several years an imagist-modernist vein of work co-existed with the already-established one of conventional verse aimed at family and friends other than Jones. Thomas probably became increasingly exasperated by the latter, sometimes having to write it to order, even as he was unwilling to quite say farewell to it (his final contribution to the *Swansea Grammar School Magazine*, for example, came as late as 1931, after he had left school).

This behaviour, it seems to me, has some bearing on the plagiarism of which he was guilty in early adolescence. As we now know, several of the poems he wrote out, and at least two he either had published, or tried to publish, were not his own. 'His Requiem' appeared under Thomas's name in the 'Wales Day by Day' column of the *Western Mail* on 14 January 1927, and is mentioned in 'The Fight'. However, it was identified as being the work of Lillian Gard (who had published it in *The Boys' Own Paper* in November 1923) when it was republished in *The Poems* in 1971, nearly fifty years later. The theft is an 'act of stealth' to which Thomas virtually confesses in the story itself (that 'stolen quill'):

> On my bedroom walls were pictures of Shakespeare, Walter de la Mare torn from my father's Christmas *Bookman*, Robert Browning, Stacy Aumonier, Rupert Brooke, a bearded man who I had discovered was Whittier, Watt's 'Hope', and a Sunday school certificate I was ashamed to want to pull down. A poem I had printed in the 'Wales Day by Day' column of the *Western Mail* was pasted on the mirror to make me blush, but the shame of the poem had died. Across the poem I had written, with a stolen quill and in flourishes: 'Homer Nods' (*CS*, 160–1).

Since then, it has also come to light that 'Sometimes', a poem Thomas tried to pass off on the school magazine, was rejected because its editor recognised it as being the work of a minor versifier, Thomas S. Jones. In the light of these revelations, it seems to me that two other poems published under his name in 1927, 'The Second Best', which appeared in *The Boy's Own Paper* in February, and 'If the Gods had but given', published in the *Western Mail* in July 1927, with their stale language and trite sentiments, should also be considered suspect.

Other, unpublished, autograph poems in the Thomas archive at Austin have been shown to be by other poets, among them, as Jeff Towns notes, 'It can be done' and 'The Secret Whisky Cure' (Ellis, 2014). As in other cases, Thomas made small alterations to the poems to make detection more difficult. Another poem in the same Austin group, 'La Danseuse', transcribed in Florence Thomas's handwriting, and with margin corrections by D. J. Thomas (suggesting that Thomas had at least convinced his parents it was his own work), was recently identified by Charles Mundye as the work of the minor Edwardian versifier James Allan Mackereth (Mundye, 2015).

What does this tell us? Only the very few who are pathologically determined to depict Thomas as a charlatan would claim that these youthful thefts cast a shadow over his poetic achievement. And yet, of course, like the reversion to notebook poems in the late 1930s, they *do* say something about him. The most obvious thing, of course, is the sheer urgency of his desire to write and be recognised. But more interestingly, the urgency can be said to point to Thomas's liminal, outsider situation – Anglo-Welsh, between languages, rural and urban worlds, working- and lower-middle-classes, piety and atheism, and lacking a university education – and the tactics he adopted not so much to overcome these qualities (in the usual margins-to-centre way) but to make them advantages rather than disadvantages. In particular, we need to consider the role of subversion and provocation in his forging (both senses) of a writing self and style, and in shaping his dealings with literary authority. It is revealing that one of the most striking aspects of his 'plagiarism' is the sheer badness of the poems Thomas used – his own better poems of the time (such as 'Forest picture' and 'Idyll of forgetfulness') being more striking and original than those he purloined. Was he, then, playing a game of amusing himself by exposing the bad taste of authority, on the sly, and for his own purely personal satisfaction? Perhaps, though it is worth remembering that the conventional poems Thomas wrote in this period (1925–31) often read as pastiches or parodies – and, like the more sophisticated efforts in *The Death of the King's Canary*, dating from around 1941, and 'An old man or a young man', written in the early nineteen fifties – it is difficult to tell whether they are homage or critique.

The fine line between original and copy is illustrated, however, by two poems of April 1930. In that month Thomas published the Yeats pastiche 'In Borrowed Plumes' in the *Swansea Grammar School Magazine* and entered a serious poem in his early Yeatsian manner, 'Osiris, Come to Isis', in the first of the Buffalo notebooks. In other words, it is not just that the equivocal response to a source reflects uncertainty towards the discourses of poetry and authorship; it is also that copying, imitating and creating go together. Each seems to have acted as a spur to the others – as if the mockery, pastiches and even thefts were a way Thomas had of stirring his own poetic activity while simultaneously negotiating with power, a youthful trickster's registering of resistance, even as he strove for approbation, putting on a display to impress at the same time as he covertly cocked a snook at authority: parents, teachers, editors, writers, critics, publishers. The tongue-in-cheek denial of a knowledge of surrealism to Richard Church in 1936, for example, like the red herrings served up to naïve enquirers after the meanings of his poems throughout his life, seems like an adult continuation of this behaviour. More to the point, it is at least arguable that the tension between real and fake, and different notions of 'sincerity', is enacted in the teasingly indeterminate intertextuality of the process style by which he discovered his individual poetic 'voice' in 1933–4.

* Forest picture

Early 1928; published in the *Swansea Grammar School Magazine*, March 1928, p. 19, collected *TP71*. Occasional dated Romantic vocabulary ('carven', 'Hark!') and general *mise-en-scène* apart, this piece is impressive in the clarity of its description and argument, qualities enhanced by avoidance of end-rhyme, telling enjambement at l. 9 and the mature phrasing of l. 6.

Idyll of unforgetfulness

Written, according to Daniel Jones, in February 1929; published *Swansea Grammar School Magazine*, March 1929, pp. 15–16. Collected in *TP71*, p. 221, with Jones's note: 'Musical setting for soloists, chorus and orchestra.' 'Idyll' may have been written specifically for such a setting; it shows the influence of the Imagistes and Edwardian exoticists like Flecker, and owes something of its languorous mood and textures to Tennyson's 'The Lotos-Eaters'. The verbal music is rich, and the handling of complex syntax and irregular line-length impressive for a fourteen year-old.

In Borrowed Plumes; II. W. B. Yeats

Published in *Swansea Grammar School Magazine*, April 1930. Collected in Maud (1989), but not *TP71*. Maud notes: 'This imitation of W. B. Yeats' early style was the second of two parodies on the theme of "Little Miss Muffet". The first told of the intrusion of the spider as Ella Wheeler Wilcox might have handled it' (Maud, 1989, 233).

Poems from 'The Fight'

First published in the short story 'The Fight', in *Portrait of the Artist as a Young Dog* (1940), these three lyrics are collected by Maud (1989) in the 'Early Rhymed Verse' section of his edition of the first four notebooks, where they are dated 'c. 1930'. The story is Thomas's comic account of his first meeting with Daniel Jones, and details their early adolescent precocity. Like the other stories in the collection, however, it also has the serious purpose of critiquing the affectations of his younger self; as Maud rightly notes, 'There is a slight tone of self-mockery in the way [the poems] are brought into the story, and we cannot be absolutely certain that the titles and the poems themselves were not made up later, expressly for the story.' All three of the poems serve critique and 'self-mockery' in some way ('Warp', for example, describes 'parhelions' with portentous elaboration, picking on a thesaurus-word which we know to have been one of Thomas's favourites as an adolescent).

In including these poems in *CP14* I was fully aware that it was quite possible that the twenty-four-year-old Thomas tampered with the originals, assuming these to have existed. Their inclusion and placement seemed inappropriate, as a result, to one reviewer of *CP14*, but he missed the point that while these lyrics – unlike 'Forest Picture' and 'Idyll of Forgetfulness' – may be doctored, even faked, they represent perfectly the importance of hybridity and game-playing to Thomas's work, then and subsequently, and thereby problematise the simplistic notions of originality, sincerity and self-expression by which discussions of it have been dogged.

To-day, this hour I breathe

As might be expected of the source for 'To-day, this insect' (1936), this is a poem about the act of writing and its paradoxes, the differences and similarities between space and time, the division between empirical sense-evidence and faith ('sight and trust'), and the idea that certainty is uncertain ('a fable') – all major subjects in Thomas's mature poetry. Paradox is symbolised by an aircraft that flies despite being made of 'iron' (Thomas may have been thinking of the famous 'Spirit of St. Louis', flown by Charles Lindbergh on the first solo transatlantic flight in 1927, one of the first all-metal frame aircraft).

if the lady from the casino

Maud (1967) feels Thomas wrote this poem when he was drunk. However, given the habitual care he exercised in the ritual transcribing of poems into the notebooks, this seems unlikely. Its 'irrational' features – inconsistent initial capitals, misspellings, doubled letters, disjunctive grammar, leaps of thought – may be better understood as a one-off attempt at Surrealist automatic writing.

Out of the sighs

No link is made in *N2* between the two poems amalgamated to make 'Out of the sighs', and both appear as separate poems in a BL typescript. Davies and Maud conjecture in *CP88* that they were joined at Christmas 1934, and that this composite was submitted, unsuccessfully, to *Poetry* (Chicago). The poem shows Thomas adapting Jacobean soliloquy to frame disappointment in love, objectify adolescent angst, and analyse the mechanisms of self-delusion by which the ego maintains its sovereignty.

Before the gas fades

The date of 6 February 1933 may link the gloomy tone to Hitler's seizure of power just days before, on 30 January; for many of the more politically aware young, a new world war in which they would be sacrificed suddenly appeared likely. Thomas's work had developed a socially aware strain in later 1932, in the poems of the notebook, now lost, covering summer 1932 to January 1933; a group of 'collateral poems', conjectured to be derived from it by Maud (1989), reflect the socio-political themes of the *New Lines* anthology of April 1932.

Was there a time

The first version of 'contained' was twenty-one lines long; Thomas shortened it in his revision, copied on the facing page in *N3* and dated 'December 1935'. The first stanza of the original version is more positive than in the final version, exhorting the reader to 'Hold on, whatever slips beyond the edge, / To hope, a firefly in the veins; to trust / Of loving'. In dropping it, Thomas ensured the poem's tone was set by what had been the second stanza of the original, which questions the efficacy of art. The bleak paradox that 'hope' can only be preserved by never being allowed expression and therefore may as well not exist is characteristic of other early poems which cut away the ground they stand on in a rather simplistic way, such as 'Out of the sighs'. Davies (1972) calls it an 'exercise in tonal quotations from an unwritten Jacobean tragedy, whose knowingness ("So the blind man sees best") is in effect bogus because in a vacuum'.

4 **maggot** = plural 'maggots' in the original; the change increased the power of the image, which anticipates the Cadaver figure of 'When, like a running grave'.

'We who were young are old'

Like Auden, Thomas explores a generational sense of impending apocalypse, but in passive terms. The only 'message for the earth' is 'Faith fixed beyond the spinning stars', religious or 'any other', and the poem's conclusion sees even this assertion as a whistling in the dark to keep collective spirits up. The paradoxes of being capable of asserting faith while not necessarily sharing it are fundamental to the process poetic. The abhorrence of vivisection of l. 43 is a feature of the writings of F. T. Powys and John Cowper Powys, both Thomas favourites.

Out of a war of wits

The evenings of discussion described in 'war of wits' occurred in the years 1932–4; Thomas, and his friends Bert Trick, the painter Fred Janes, Tom Warner, a composer, and a dozen or so other more or less regular attenders gathered once or twice a week: they were 'young men who were really passionately interested in literature, art, music, politics, and the perennial subjects of philosophy, religion, and ethics', as Trick put it. Those attending more informal day-time get-togethers are known as the 'Kardomah Gang', after the café where they met in Swansea town centre. For the best account of this milieu, see Hilly Janes (2014). Trick's memoir notes:

> It was at these meetings of the coterie that Dylan was at his most brilliant. Wit, invective, word magic, and mimicry amounting to sheer genius were given full rein. This was Dylan's natural habitat. These sessions beginning early in the evening invariably went on

till the early hours of the following morning. Many were the times I skipped out of 5 Cwmdonkin Drive, my arms full of books, my head full of stars and feet of feathers, I didn't walk down the hill to my home, I was levitated. There was no need for strong drink, we were intoxicated with words – ideas and words. The magic of language was ours: the play of words to produce paradox, to twist the tail of a platitude to make an epigram, to change the juxtaposition of words in mundane prose to produce an explosion. These were things which fascinated us and became our common currency. (Trick, 1966)

The phrase 'war of wits' was taken up in 'Holy Spring' in 1944 (see below), a poem about real war, and as such was the very last contribution made by the Buffalo notebooks to Thomas's later poetry.

In wasting one drop

A poem that expresses the fear that masturbation will exhaust the speaker's ability to match true love when he finds it. Masturbation (and nocturnal seminal emission) feature in several early poems (cf. 'My hero bares his nerves', 'Jack of Christ'), and invariably signifies deathliness and wastage. Thus, while Thomas championed sexual freedom and openness, as his letters to Pamela Hansford Johnson show, he inherited something of the Victorian taboo against masturbation which, at the time, was often viewed, even by those committed to sexual realism, as a sin against 'real' sex, that is, penetrative intercourse. Thomas may have been following D. H. Lawrence's lead in this, as in other areas. Lawrence's 1930 essay 'Pornography and Obscenity' is a good example of the puritanism threaded through his rejection of orthodox restrictions on sexuality (in part, the result of a Nonconformist upbringing similar to Thomas's); it presents masturbation as 'the solitary vice' of tradition, and links it to pornography and 'doing dirt on sex', invariably resulting in 'shame', 'anger', 'futility' and 'humiliation':

In masturbation there is nothing but loss. There is no reciprocity. There is merely the spending away of a certain force and no return.

The body remains, in a sense, a corpse, after the end of self-abuse. There is no change, only deadening. There is what we call dead loss. And this is not the case in any act of sexual intercourse between two people. Two people may destroy one another in sex. But they cannot just produce the null effect of masturbation. (D. H. Lawrence, 'Pornography and Obscenity', in James T. Boulton (ed.), *Late Essays and Articles* (Cambridge: Cambridge University Press, 2004), p. 245.)

I have longed to move away

The final, revised version of this poem, written on the facing page, in *N3*, is dated 13 January 1936; it had already been published in *New Verse* in December 1935, so Thomas was entering it for the sake of record. Revision had involved reducing forty-one lines to twenty, equalising stanza-lengths, and eliminating social specifics (e.g. 'some sulphurous reminder of November'). Korg claims the 'death's feather' image is synecdochic for the wings of the Angel of Death; another possible source is Wilfred Owen's 'The Show': 'I . . . shivered earthward like a feather. / And Death fell with me'.

See, on gravel paths under the harpstrung trees

4 **mock** = first of a series of terms ('moans', 'vain', 'leper', etc.) hinting at a rather maudlin and morbid 'self-dramatization'. 17 **unbosoming** = romantically self-conscious echo of Keats's 'To Autumn': 'Close bosom friend of the maturing sun'.

The ploughman's gone, the hansom driver

In asserting uncaring technological mastery over nature, humanity has become carrion, 'cold, with their horses, for raven and kite', even if 'nature' in the cosmic sense remains 'unaltered'. However, the simple antipathy towards the machine on display in this poem anticipates the more complex and interesting man-machine cybernetic fusions of later poems such as 'All all and all'.

13–15 *Waste Land*-style satire, deleted in *N3*. 27 **iron saddle** = the
Massey-Ferguson tractors, which replaced the horse as the main source
of power in British agriculture between the wars, had steel drivers'
seats.

And death shall have no dominion

The opening line, one of Thomas's best-known, is taken from St Paul's
Epistle to the Romans 6:8–9: 'Now if we be dead with Christ, we
believe that we shall also live with him: Knowing that Christ being
raised from the dead dieth no more; death hath no more dominion
over him.' However, its context was provided by lines from the poem's
predecessor in *N3*, 'Twenty Two', which Thomas immediately recycled:
'Man's wants remain unsatisfied till death. / Then, when his soul is
naked, is he one / With the man in the wind, and the west moon, /
With the harmonious thunder of the sun'. Maud (1968) sees it as 'a
poem on the topic of death, trying out the thesis that death shall have
no dominion . . . running counter to adjacent doubt poems such as
[Twenty Two and] Twenty Four', arguing that, as a result, 'And death'
should not be regarded as the first 'process poem'. Most critics disagree,
and view it as the breakthrough poem it surely is.

As James A. Davies (1996) notes, the flanking poems also refer to
WWI, and like many WWI-related poems, the N3 version asserts a
faith in individual survival after death. This is particularly apparent
in the unequivocal fourth stanza, which Thomas dropped in his 1936
revision:

And death shall have no dominion.
Under the sea or snow at last
Man shall discover all he thought lost,
And hold his little soul within his fist;
Knowing that now can he never be dust,
He waits in the sun till the sun goes out;
Now he knows what he had but guessed
Of living and dying and all the rest;
He knows his soul. There is no doubt.
And death shall have no dominion.

Revision also reduced the ten- and eleven-line stanzas to nine lines, and introduced a more distinctive lexis – e.g. 'swords of evil' became 'unicorn evil' – as well as wordplay, more typical of *N4*, in stanza 3.

The outcome of revision was a poem more equally caught between rhetorics of belief and non-belief in resurrection than the *N3* version. The result is vitalistic, rather than doctrinal, an assertion of the eternal nature of the life-force and a non-dogmatic spiritual principle in a post-Darwinian and -Einsteinian universe. However, its non-inclusion in *18P*, and Thomas's unwillingness (according to Vernon Watkins) to include it in *25P*, suggests that he felt the poem even as revised to be 'imitatively biblical and heavy-handed', in a 'prescriptive' rather than 'presentational' style', as it has, with some justice, been described (McNees, 1992). Haste to publish a second collection probably had much to do with its inclusion in *25P*. Nevertheless, it remains more than what G. S. Fraser called 'a set of large but empty rhetorical gestures . . . not facing death but cheering himself up' (Brinnin, 1961); it is the progenitor not only of Thomas's own visionary process poetry, but ultimately of the apocalyptic-modernist mode in British 1940s poetry (Goodby (2013), Keery (2003)).

2 **Dead men naked** = originally 'Man, with soul naked'. 25 **hammer through daisies** = cf. Thomas Lovell Beddoes, *Death's Jest Book*, 'Turning to daisies gently in the grave; Thomas Hardy, 'Voices from Things Growing in a Graveyard': 'now I wave / In daisy shapes above my grave'.

Within his head revolved a little world

Elements of realist observation and visionary insight intermingle in this poem as Thomas gradually began to realise the potential of the latter in what would become his process poetic.

26 **through every hole** = originally 'from nose to arse'. 29 **Pole-sitting girls** = the American, Richard 'Dixie' Blandy set a new and well-publicised world flagpole-sitting record of seventy-seven days in 1933. 33, 49, 63 **Where, what's my god . . .** = a common trope in religious poetry; cf. George Herbert's 'The Search': 'Where is my God?'

We lying by seasand

The issue of *Poetry* (Chicago) in which this poem was first published, in January 1937, was an 'English [*sic*] Number' edited by W. H. Auden and Michael Roberts.

The poem dramatises an antagonism between the colours yellow and red; *The Waste Land*, with its watery death and resurrection and 'red rock' lurk here, with Eliot probably one of the 'deriders' the poem mocks. 'Bound' to yellow, wishing the red rock's disappearance but unable to fend off its 'arrival', the speaker reflects Thomas's growing taste for Blakean contraries and microcosmic perspectives (ll.14–15 recall Blake's 'To see the world in a grain of sand', the opening line of 'Auguries of Innocence', asserting the ethical consequences of an interconnected creation). Edith Sitwell's *Sunday Times* review of 1936 called it an 'unsurpassable technical achievement'; if over-generous praise, this is a reminder of the poem's rich synaesthesia and music.

Largely written in iambic pentameter, it has much alliteration and internal and end rhyme patterning, using full rhyme, pararhyme and *rime riche*.

No man believes

Thomas's belief that faith could exist only if it was continually threatened, a version of negative theology, lasted throughout his life. By the same logic, denial of god (or process as god), even blasphemy, presupposed faith. Revealingly, for the publication of 'No man believes' in *Adelphi*, Thomas capitalised 'god' throughout. McNees (1992) takes it to be a poem of faith, discerning ten commandment-like 'basic assertions couched in negatives' leading to 'a final affirmative faith reached through the process of "breaking and making", analogous to the Eucharistic fraction and communion'. Less dogmatically, she notes that the speaker does not submit to death in order to be reborn, but 'actively kills the natural objects of his world and presumes to resurrect them himself'. Echoing Hillis Miller (1966), she claims that he does not die himself, or die on behalf of created things after their deaths, with this 'sacrificial dimension' only entering in the later work.

24 there was no final full-stop in *N3*; Thomas added one for *Adelphi* publication.

Why east wind chills

N3 'Thirty Seven' was reduced from fifty lines to twenty-six and entered on a facing page, dated 21 January 1936, while 'Thirty-Seven' was itself a reworking of *N1* 'XLI', of 12 September 1931.

The repeated 'Why' reveals Thomas's probing of the limits of ratiocinative thought; his conclusion is that the world will never be totally knowable until, as 'Thirty Seven' gothically puts it, 'the worms feed at my face', or 'the stars go out' – the apocalyptic end of time and of the universe. In this it anticipates one of the basic ideas behind 'A Refusal to Mourn'. James A. Davies (1998), in a comparison of the *N3* and final versions, suggests a subtext of social revolt, which became reduced in the published poem to an image of the communist salute at lines 11 and 26.

As with 'No man believes', Thomas resisted the temptation to use a regular stanza form throughout; in metrical terms, iambic tetrameter lines predominate but with significant pentametric variation.

1 **Why east wind chills** = cf. Sir Thomas Browne, *Pseudodoxia Epidemica* Book 6, Chapter 10: 'yet were it no easie problem to resolve, Why Grasse is green?' The ur-version of this poem, *N1* 'XLI', opens: 'Why is the blood red and the grass green / Shan't be answered till the voice is still'. 20 **till the stars go out** = cf. Blake's 'Auguries of innocence': 'If the sun and moon should doubt / They'd immediately go out.'

Greek Play in a Garden

The narrator of the radio feature 'Return Journey' (1946) claims that he 'used to have poems printed in *The Herald of Wales*; there was one about an open-air performance of *Electra* in Mrs Bertie Perkins's garden in Sketty.' The story 'The Mouse and the Woman' (1936) also alludes to the play: 'There had been seven women, in a mad play by a Greek, each with the same face, crowned with the same hoop of mad, black hair. One by one they trod the ruler of turf, then vanished. They turned the same face to him, intolerably weary with the same suffering.' The themes of murder, mourning, revenge and matricide which Thomas encountered in Sophocles's play may well have shaped his poetic development in late 1933, and, despite seeming rather conservative beside Thomas's other poems of the period, this is a remarkably assured exercise in traditional style.

Praise to the architects

Thomas's criticisms of the New Country poets are trenchant, if impressionistic, and reveal his deep differences with them. The most succinct expression of his mixture of respect for, and suspicion of, Auden's poetry appears in his contribution to Geoffrey Grigson's special Auden issue of *New Verse*, published in 1937 to mark Auden's thirtieth birthday. More personalised versions of this are to be found throughout his letters of the 1930s, such as the one to Trevor Hughes of January 1934, or more elaborately to James Laughlin, his US publisher, of 17 May 1938:

> [Auden is] . . . the heavy, jocular prefect, the boy bushranger, the school wag, the 6th form debater, the homosexual clique-joker. I think he sometimes writes with great power . . . He's exactly what the English literary public think a modern English poet should be. He's perfectly educated (& expensively) but still delightfully eccentric. He's a rebel (i.e. an official communist) but boys will be boys so he is awarded the King's Medal [for Poetry]; he's got a great sense of Humour; he's not one of those old-fashioned, escapist Bohemians (which means he doesn't get drunk in public, that he dresses like a public school-master not like a 'silly artist'). (*CL*, 346)

As Gabriel Pearson (1971) shrewdly notes, however, Thomas and Auden have more in common than is usually realised, or than either of them probably understood. And as Stan Smith (2001) observes, Thomas's early poetry is steeped in Auden, even as it twists him to new purposes.

8 followed in *N3* by the line 'Who steps on the gas'. 13 **Auden** = Thomas's objection here is to what he felt was Auden's glib, insufficiently corporeal or psychically probing radicalism.

'Find meat on bones'

Maud (2003) claims that this poem, rather than 'And death shall have no dominion', is the first process poem. In *25P* and *CP52* the speech marks enclosing the son's speech close at the end of stanza 4, leaving stanza 5 to be spoken by some third voice. In *N3*, however, the final quote marks occur at the end of stanza 5, and are restored in *CP88* on the grounds that the 'you' of l. 41 makes most sense if addressed by the son to the father; I follow suit.

Technically, this poem shows Thomas's increasing expertise in traditional lyric form; it uses eight-line stanzas in tetrameters, with shorter trimeter or dimeter fifth lines (and seventh line in the final stanza), with pararhyme *abbbaaab*, except in stanza 4.

8 **ram rose** = to a query by Desmond Hawkins in 1936, Thomas replied: 'It's funny about ram. Once I looked up an old dictionary and found it meant red, but now I can't find it in any dictionary at all. I wanted ram in the poem to mean red *and* male *and* horny *and* driving *and* all its usual meanings. Blast it, why doesn't it mean red? Do look up and see for me' (*CL*, 244). 22 **merry** = *N3* has 'lovely'. 26–9 **And the man . . . foul fiend to heel** = *N3* has 'And the bird no bullet sting / Rebel against the reason's wrong / That penetrates the drum and lung / And cataracts the soul'. This suggests that 'man' is individual mortal man on its first appearance and a general principle of humanity, or spirit, on the second.

* *The woman speaks*

N3 'Forty Eight', where it is subtitled '(From A Play)' and 'The Woman Speaks' in the margin above the opening line; dated 'July 1933'. An MS in the BL is entitled 'From A Play To Be Called, "Ravens"'; as Daniel Jones (1971) noted, this suggests a connection with 'Greek

Play in a Garden'. Published in *Adelphi* (March 1934) with the title 'The Woman Speaks'.

Thomas had sent the poem to Pamela Hansford Johnson in mid-September 1933, adding that 'though complete in itself', it is 'a woman's lament from an unfortunately unfinished play', and that it should not 'cast aspersions on the nature of my sex' (*CL*, 40). However, when an impressed Glyn Jones wrote him a fan letter after its *Adelphi* appearance, he replied: 'The woman speaks but the young man writes, and your doubt as to my sex was quite complimentary, proving (or was it merely my uncommon name?) that I do not employ too masculine a pen' (*CL*, 120). Thomas considered revising it when listing it, in a letter to Johnson of 2 May 1934, among the poems he would include in *18P*, however, It was not republished until *Poet in the Making* (1967). Several details – dead young soldier, green valley, sun – suggest sources in Sophocles, Rimbaud's 'Le dormeur du val', Wilfred Owen and the ninth century Welsh Heledd Cycle, in which Heledd, sister of the suggestively named Cynd*dylan*, laments the destruction of his hall and townships and, most bitterly of all, the eagles which will feed on his flesh.

Ears in the turrets hear

Tower imagery plays a significant role in Thomas's early work, symbolising the isolated artist. He could plead guilty to solipsism, although he defended himself against the charge to Vernon Watkins in 1936: 'living in your own private, four-walled world as exclusively as possible isn't escapism, I'm sure; it isn't the Ivory Tower, and, even if it were, you secluded in your Tower know and learn more of the world outside than the outside-man who is mixed up so personally and inextricably with the mud and the unlovely people' (*CL*, 248). Exploring the tension between the world and the isolated (but not necessarily 'escapist') artist, 'Ears in the turrets hear' uses an imagery of built structures, doors and windows to suggest the penetrability of body and self by the outside world, and the extent to which this is desired and resisted. The poem's delicate soundscape delineates the shifting border between inner and outer worlds, symbolised by eye and ear, the organs most responsible for their interaction.

Dactylic dimeter, occasionally shortened or lengthened (at ll. 8, 9, 12 and 25), gives the poem its peculiar rhythm, and the sense of anxiety and liminality finds expression in the oscillation between nine- and seven-line stanzas, concluded with a couplet, and in irregular end-rhyme and mix of full rhyme, pararhyme, and vowel and consonant combinations (e.g. 'bay' and 'ships' giving a portmanteau rhyme with 'grapes').

That sanity be kept

Victor Neuberg, the editor of the *Referee*'s 'Poets' Corner' feature, introduced this poem to his readers as 'perhaps the best modernist poem that as yet I've received.'

Goodby (2013) argues that W. H. Auden (the aerial observer of 'Consider this and in our time') and T. S. Eliot (cf. 'Morning at the Window') jostle together in it without having yet fused in Thomas's trademark style. The title recalls 'That the sum sanity', dating from 24 August 1933, suggesting a composition date of late summer 1933.

Shall gods be said

For its publication in *25P*, Thomas dropped the fourth and sixth stanzas of 'Fifty Two' in *N3*, producing one of the group of minor short lyrics (such as 'Was there a time') which helped him pad out the volume. Stanza 4 ran:

> Shall it be said that this moon's face
> Is but the face reflected of some god
> Admiring the acres of his brow?
> Does gods' blood die [*sic*] the sun?

The last stanza (6) read:

> The gods of stone our fathers worshipped
> Are brass and wood if gods weep rain.
> If gods thump thunder, then the clouds
> Are gods and water, and the bark is brass.
> All things are god if gods are thunder.   5

Its abstraction and lack of social context led Davies (1972) to criticise this poem for its 'pure inconsequence'.

The hand that signed the paper

Behind this poem lie the unravelling of the rackety post-Versailles peace and the influence of Thomas's socialist friend, Bert Trick, and (perhaps) an extended pun; as Davies (2000) argues, '"Arms" may . . . be a hidden metaphor: *finger joints, hand, sloping shoulder*'. Not long after writing it, Thomas wrote to Pamela Hansford Johnson indicting arms manufacturers:

> [Y]ou know that the Union Jack is only a national loin-cloth to hide the decaying organs of a diseased social system; you know that the Great War was purposely protracted in order for financiers to make more money; that had it not been for the shares in the armament firms the War would have ended in three weeks; that at one point in the war French and Germans were shelling each other with ammunition provided by the same firm, a firm in which English clergymen and politicians, French ambassadors and German business men, all had a great deal of money invested. (*CL* 105)

Revision consisted largely of deleting the fifth stanza of N4 'One':

These five blind kings have quills for sceptres;
Each has a parchment for his shield,
Debates with vizier words what time he shatters
The four walls of the world.

This eliminated repetition and the *Arabian Nights*-like 'vizier', maintaining emphasis on the impersonality of tyranny. Keith Selby (Bold, 1990) finds theme, form and prosody interweaving to an unsuspected degree, in 'tight, formal quatrains in the Augustan mode, regularly iambic', except that:

> first and third lines . . . actually contain an additional, eleventh syllable. This has the effect of jarring the rhythm by leaving an

amphibrach [metrical foot of unstressed, stressed, unstressed syllables] hanging at the end of the line. The effect is further increased by the sudden return to a regular iambic in the second and fourth lines of each quatrain. Again, and just as happens with the grammatical structure of the lines, we are left waiting for closure, but . . . metrical rather than grammatical . . . The fifth foot does arrive . . . but is then followed by another, unexpected, syllable. Again, the effect is uncanny, giving the sense that there is no rhyme or reason to things. Power, again, is absolute.

That the sum sanity

An MS of the *N4* 'Four' first version of this sonnet at Austin, dated 24 August 1933, is set out in couplets. Line 12 ('I would make genuflexion with the sheep') originally read 'I would reverse my collar to the sheep'. In spring 1934 Thomas revised the poem with an eye to collecting it in *18P*, and this substantially new version appeared in the *Swansea and West Wales Guardian* on 8 June 1934 titled 'Twelve'. However, Thomas eventually decided against including it in *18P*. It read:

That the sum sanity might add to nought
And words fall crippled from the slaving lips,
Girls take to broomsticks when the thief of night
Has stolen the starved babies from their laps,
I would enforce the black apparelled cries, 5
Speak like a hungry parson of the manna,
Add one more nail of praise on to the cross,
And talk of light to a mad miner.
I would be woven a religious shape;
As fleeced as they bow lowly with the sheep, 10
My house would fall like bread about my homage;
And I would choke the heavens with my hymn
That men might see the devil in the crumb
And the death in a starving image.

The only critical commentary is by James A. Davies (1997), who argues that both versions have 'a priest-like narrator who wishes to

offer inadequate counsel to what appear to be victims of 1930s depriv-
ation.' My notes follow for the second version:

2 **words fall crippled** = the change makes clearer the disfigured >
inhibited > religiously repressed sense of version one (but Thomas
may have felt that if his first version was rather over-elaborate, his
second was too direct). 3 **Girls take to broomsticks** = *a* become
domesticated; *b* become hag-like (witches) because of repression. 3–4
the thief of night . . . babies from their laps = the god of repression
(the real Devil) has denied the procreative, sexual urge. 4–7 **enforce
the black apparelled cries . . . mad miner** = examples of deliberately
hypocritical behaviour, intended to exacerbate the gap between official
religion and the spiritual hunger it purports to satisfy. 9–10 **I would
be woven a religious shape; / As fleeced as they bow lowly with
the sheep** = I would be as religious-seeming and as sheep-like (pun
on 'fleeced' as 'robbed') as 'they' [who] 'bow' [in prayer] with the
flock: i.e. priests, as deluded as those they lead in worship. 11 **My
house would fall like bread about my homage** = the established
church would collapse around me. Thomas may have in mind the
great Nonconformist hymn 'Guide Me, O Thou Great Jehovah', sung
to the tune of 'Cwm Rhondda', often known as 'Bread of Heaven'.
Cf. also 'the bread-sided field', Altarwise by owl-light' IV; 'bread and
milk mansion', 'I make this in a warring absence'. 12–14 **And I
would choke the earth . . . starving image** = as in version one, the
speaker sees himself as an anti-prophet, whose praise of 'the heavens'
will expose the lack of spiritual sustenance promised by religion, seen
as creating the opposite of the liberation it promises ('the devil in the
crumb . . . death in a starving image' – an image of Christ starving
for the lack of compassion with which it is wielded, and that starves
those who seek its succour).

* Grief, thief of time, crawls off

N4 'Five', dated 26 August 1933.
The first version of 'Grief thief of time' (*CP14*, 79). Comparison
with the later one, which dispenses with the commas in the opening
line, illustrates Thomas's habit of creating obstacles to spur the writing

process and test the ability of the lyric to accommodate innovation and 'difficulty'. In this case, the removal of punctuation entailed a reshaping of the ensuing narrative to accommodate the new meaning, producing a contorted sense and fluid syntax which more fully enacted process, albeit at the risk of obscurity. The narrative of the *N4* original seems clearer, although it is not wholly free of ambiguity. The grief and faith of youth are forgotten as you age, alleviating the burdens they represent; the old edit out the bad bits of the past to create an ideal form of it in which they once simply '[plucked] wild radish / And seed that was promise.' The price they pay for their peace is the loss of 'grief', and death itself – the existential edge of existence – and the poem ends with a call on the old to 'remember' Christ's sacrifice and the burden of faith 'all thy days'. The poem would therefore seem to ironically invert the generational predicates of Ecclesiastes 12:1: 'Remember now thy Creator in the days of thy youth, while the evil days come not, nor the years draw nigh, when thou shalt say, I have no pleasure in them.' Arguably, the poem's 'message' has to do with the socio-political situation of summer 1933; mass unemployment, political crisis at home and the rise of fascism abroad (with a new world war threatening as a result) mean the young are old before their time, while the old, by comparison, seem youthfully irresponsible. The price of peace, it might seem, is eternal grief. Thomas's dissatisfaction with the first version of the poem may stem from its unequivocally Christian co-ordinates, and the glibness with which 'price of peace' slides into 'prince of peace'; his second attempt certainly avoids any smoothness or orthodoxy.

22 **prince's price** = probably a reference to Christ and his sacrifice.

Before I knocked

Thomas sent 'Before I knocked' with 'The Woman Speaks' to Pamela Hansford Johnson in a letter of 15 September 1933, telling her that she might not like it as it was 'distinctly unfashionable'. The preceding poem in *N4*, 'Shiloh's seed shall not be sown', has a footnote referring to the prophet Johanna Southcott (1750–1814), a domestic servant who identified herself with the 'woman clothed with the sun' of

Revelations and promised to give birth to a son, the Shiloh of Genesis 49:10 (cf. 'The seed-at-zero'), and its unorthodox stance on the incarnation carries over into this one.

'Before I knocked' marks an important stage in the evolution of the process poetic, especially its biomorphic, incarnational and anti-ratiocinative aspects, as Thomas himself understood. To Johnson in November 1933 he claimed: 'There is more [of the visionary quality] in the poem "Before I knocked" [than 'I fellowed sleep'], more of what I consider to be of importance in my poetry.' Critics have agreed; Aneirin Talfan Davies (1964) describes the opening stanzas as a 'declaration of man's solidarity with nature' while Martin Dodsworth (1972) makes the poem part of his discussion of Thomas's relationship to Blake. Simply put, this argues that Thomas's obscurity is bound up with the attempt to 'short-cut the reason, by bringing the mind to bear upon a representation of reality which is resistant to a reduction to the mind's own reasonable terms'. The rational structures of his poems permit them to be read as riddles and unriddled, indicating that, like Blake, he does not prize irrationality or obscurity (the common charge), but wishes to redeem reason from its reductive tendency, and therefore 'seeks out the inexplicable elements in human experience' with which to confront it. The choice of antenatal subject-matter is intended precisely to 'establish imaginative truth as an element necessary to temper the arrogance of intellect'. This is why, for example, the speaker of 'Before I knocked' recalls existence even before it was formed, and why the succeeding metaphorical descriptions of the sexual act, conception and gestation work to imply the context of mystery within which these apparently straightforward events occur. Stanzas 3 and 4 hint at the Holy Land and crucifixion, and in stanza 7 the speaker identifies himself as a 'dying christ', the lower case 'c' suggesting Christ in his mortal, everyman aspect, or even slang for his father's detumescent penis (cf. 'A saint about to fall'). In the final stanza we get 'doublecrossed', 'the great word of the poem' for Tindall (1962); it encapsulates what Maud (2003) calls its 'tone of grievance', yet it has a dark wit and amplitude that transcends narrow complaint.

The poem is in iambic tetrameters, organised in eight-line stanzas and a quatrain, with twenty-three end-rhymes on *er*.

1 **knocked** = begged entrance; with slang sense 'was (knock)ed up' by sexual intercourse. cf. 'joy is no knocking nation', 'When, like a running grave'; the movement of the foetus: cf. 'The Enemies': 'And women with shapes in their wombs would feel a new knocking as they bent over the steamy tubs' (*CS*, 17). 5–6 **Mnetha's daughter . . . sister to the fathering worm** = as well as *Tiriel*, cf. Blake, *Book of Thel*; Thel, the unborn soul, inhabiting 'the vales of Har', fears entering the world of time and suffering. The lowly worm instructs her in the knowledge that all creatures are brethren, and that to be food for worms is an essential act in the cycle of birth, death and renewal. Mnetha also serves in Blake as an anagram of 'anthem' and 'the man'. 9 **Felt thud beneath my flesh's armour** = Dodsworth (1972) notes that 'thud' is not yet the embryo's heartbeat but 'the rhythm of orgasm . . . "beneath" . . . has a very specific reference to the creating father's penis at the doors of the womb, the "armour" within which, "in a molten form", the sperm has fertilized and will realize its flesh. But this specificity works to reinforce our sense of the mystery of creation itself which escapes all measure and for which we have no adequate words.' 25 *N4* has an additional stanza:

My milk was curdled by the thunder;
The lightning forked into the jaw,
The lilac gums, that kissed me murder;
Deep in my bowels jumped the fire,
The false lips cursed me like an adder
Who bares his sting to wound the air.

43 *N4* has an additional quatrain:

A virgin was my sad-faced dam,
My sire was of wind and water.
Get thee behind me my blood's tempter,
I cried out when the blood was dumb.

42, 44, 46 **christ . . . Him** = lower-case 'christ' is Jesus as everyman, although as Tindall (1962) notes, for Thomas 'Any father deceives any mother by engendering death'. McNees (1992) discusses the issue of upper- and lower-case usages throughout the poem, and the way in which Thomas's 'purpose[ful] confusion' of identity allows the final stanza to be read as 'a united rebellion by Christ and Thomas against God'; **doublecrossed** – Tindall's relish of 'doublecrossed' as 'qualifying the solemnity of man's fate with levity' was not shared by Johnson or Barbara Hardy, the latter claiming that 'the exhibitionist would-be shock associations with . . . American slang diminish the larger resonances, and close with an emphasis on the vehicle rather than the tenor [of the metaphor]'; she views it as a failure of control rather than as a radical disruption (Hardy, 2000). Cf. note to 'doublecrossed', l. 18, 'When once the twilight locks', p. 89. Arguably, in the conflicted emotions of the ending (which may include adolescent ones), Thomas presents the impossibility of describing an indescribable mystery, the incarnation. In rejecting poetic 'word-painting' in a letter of 15 October 1933 to Johnson, he claimed: 'There must be no compromise; there is always only the one right word: use it, despite its merely foul or ludicrous associations; I used "double-crossed" because it was what I meant.'

We see rise the secret wind

Shades of H. G. Wells and Fritz Lang's *Metropolis* lurk in this poem's futuristic sense of the mysteries of the inner and outer universes revealed by science and technology. The city location seems at once liberating and sinister. '[W]retched / Wheel-winders', who currently 'salute the busy brotherhood' (perhaps religious or political leaders), may find freedom in the city's potential as an electric-powered 'godhead' and 'saviour' bearing a 'steel gospel', while technological liberation from oppression and superstition is suggested in the Garden of Eden (or Gethsemane?) updated as an 'orchard / Of lamp-posts and high-volted fruits'. But as the final line makes clear – perhaps too clear for the poem's inclusion in *18P* – the 'electric godhead' is out-ranked by the older, more primordial 'God' it presumes to have supplanted.

Before we mothernaked fall

Like *N4* 'Eight', this poem has minimal punctuation; it is an accomplished, if slightly underdeveloped example of Thomas's fascination with antenatal existence. The *N4* version has an incomplete third stanza, or coda, not included in the version published in *New English Weekly*:

Choose the field of brick and bone
Or the dark well of the brain
Take one away let one remain.
All is foreknown.

Wigginton (2007) notes of this poem (with 'When once the twilight' and 'I dreamed my genesis') that the subject is 'in process, strangely conscious before birth, but as yet unfixed. The space [it] might be said to inhabits is an in-between, or liminal space'. This, in turn, is viewed as an example of Thomas 'occupying, or rather transgressing, the boundaries between Wales and England and within Wales itself' and consequently 'articulating a liminal poetics' which is 'strongly related to the concept of cultural hybridity.'

My hero bares his nerves

Thomas's letters of 1934 and 1935 to male friends jokingly allude to masturbation, but the subject is part of a more serious self-analysis of his (im)maturity. Rather than the bullishness of the 'phallic pencil [that] turns into an electric drill', as Thomas described it to Charles Fisher in January 1935 (*CL*, 208), this poem reflects a complex consideration of the entrapment of both sex and writing in a circle of incomplete identity formation which is at once creative and abusive. As in 'Grief thief of time', a linked poem, the critique includes Thomas's efforts at fathering his own poetic authority. The *N4* version has a final stanza:

Jack my father let the knaves steal off
Their little swag, the gems of life and death,
The lightest bubbles that we breathe
Out of the living grave
And let my hero show his double strength
And all his laughter hidden up my sleeve.

When Thomas revised *N4* 'Five', 'Grief, thief of time', in summer 1935, he took these lines from 'Thirteen' as the basis of the second stanza of the new poem.

Several other poems of the period deal with masturbation; *N4* 'Three' reads like an earlier, clumsier, attempt at this one:

You are the ruler of this realm of flesh,
And this hill of bone and hair
Moves to the Mahomet of your hand.
But all this land gives off a charnel stench,
The wind smacks of the poor
Dumb dead the crannies house and hide.

You rule the thudding heart that bites the side;
The heart steps to death's finger,
The brain acts to the legal dead.
Why should I think on death when you are ruler?

You are my flesh's ruler whom I treason,
Housing death in your kingdom,
Paying heed to the thirsty voice.
Condemn me to an everlasting facing
Of the dead eyes of children
And their rivers of blood turned to ice.

Goodby and Wigginton (2000) and Goodby (2013) find honesty not only in the poem's frankness, but also in its understanding that both writing and auto-eroticism promise a fulfilment, or presence, which can never be granted. It is viewed as deconstructing literary and sexual forms of self-authentication in an exemplary way, the 'page' 'lovelorn' because marked by derivative writing and/or short-circuited sex. Roberts (2009) notes that, just as Thomas's poetic style disrupts the social bonds linking signifiers and signifieds, it here disrupts convention by refusing the socio-symbolic value of the sexual act as approved (because potentially procreative) within marriage.

1, 6, 16 **nerves** = cf. 'The Holy Six' (1937): 'the male nerve was pulled alone' (*CS*, 97). 11 **bares my side . . . heart** = crucifixion imagery (Christ was speared in the side, and Roman Catholicism has a cult of the Sacred Heart), with a hint of the troubadour trope of the proffered heart (cf. note to 'In Country Sleep'). 17 **Praising** = *N4* has 'Turning'. 18–19 **two sad knaves** = Thomas links knave to masturbation because it is another name for the jack in a pack of cards (and so to 'jack off'), as in the deleted stanza. 20 **He pulls the chain, the cistern moves** = cf. letter to Trevor Hughes of Spring 1934: 'Our words – "give me a half-pint, a Hovis, a book by Paul de Kock, and thou, thou old lavatory chain" – are spells to drag up the personified Domdaniel pleasure.' (*CL*, 144–5) ('Domdaniel' is a submarine cave, from *The Arabian Nights*, inhabited by a sorcerer and his disciples, and the passage in Thomas's letter parodies stanza 12 of Fitzgerald's *Rubáiyát*); *N3* 'Twenty Seven' has 'cistern sex'; cf. also Shakespeare's 'cistern of my lust' (*Macbeth* 4:3, 64) and 'cistern for foul toads' (*Othello* 4:1, 63).

The force that through the green fuse

The first three lines of the first, deleted stanza of *N4* 'Twenty Three' are the same as those in the published version of the poem. The remainder of the deleted stanza (with 'storm' deleted twice) runs:

And I am dumb to tell the eaten rose
How at my sheet goes the same crooked worm,
And dumb to holla thunder to the skies
How at my cloths flies the same central storm.

This is followed by the first stanza as we now have it, and stanzas 2 and 3, also in their published form. Stanza 4 in *N4* 'Twenty Three' runs:

The lips of time leech to the fountain head;
Love drips and gathers, but the fallen blood
Shall make her well;
And I am dumb to tell the timeless sun
~~How time is all.~~

The final couplet is as published. Overall, 'Twenty Three' shows the final form of the poem emerging with the rewriting of stanzas 1 and 4 during the fair-copying process.

'The force' helped establish Thomas as the foremost figure of a new poetic movement, particularly when it was reprinted in the *Sunday Referee* in Spring 1934 William Empson (1954) claimed that:

What hit the town of London was the child Dylan publishing 'The force that through the green fuse' . . . from that day he was a famous poet. Thus began the Dylan Thomas revolt against the political poetry of the thirties, with Auden as its most brilliant exponent, in favour of a poetry of magic, religion, guilt or a world of personal relations.

Almost every subsequent commentator on Thomas has analysed this iconic lyric. Its monism, similar to, but stronger than the pantheism of Romantic lyrics such as Shelley's 'The Cloud', derives from Thomas's microcosmic sense of the oneness with natural cycles, intensified in the light of Einsteinian cosmology. Thomas may also have been reading Schopenhauer. Writing to Pamela Hansford Johnson on 21 May 1934, he informed her:

I am tortured today by every doubt and misgiving that an hereditarily twisted imagination, an hereditary thirst and a . . . wet day in a tided town [Laugharne], are capable of conjuring up out of their helly deeps . . . I agree with Buddha that the essence of life is evil. Apart from not being born at all, it is best to die young. I agree with Schopenhauer . . . that life has no pattern & no purpose, but that a twisted vein of evil, like the poison in a drinker's glass, coils up from the pit to the top of the hemlocked world. Or at least I might do. (*CL*, 164)

Bryan Magee, in 'A Conjecture About Dylan Thomas', in *The Philosophy of Schopenhauer* (OUP, 1997) certainly thought so, noting that: 'Not only the theme but also the imagery in detail is too close to certain passages in Schopenhauer for a coincidence to be likely.' However, as James Keery has established, Magee cites a 1958 translation of Schopenhauer, and gives the wrong passage; the one which most resembles 'The force' is this, from the Haldane and Kemp translation of 1886:

He will recognise this will of which we are speaking not only in those phenomenal existences which exactly resemble his own, in men and animals as their inmost nature, but the course of reflection will lead him to recognise the force which germinates and vegetates in the plant, and indeed the force through which the crystal is formed, that by which the magnet turns to the north pole, the force whose shock he experiences from the contact of two different kinds of metal, the force which appears in the elective affinities of matter as repulsion and attraction, decomposition and combination, and, lastly, even gravitation, which acts so powerfully throughout matter, draws the stone to the earth and the earth to the sun – all these, I say, he will recognize as different only in their phenomenal existence, but in their inner nature as identical, as that which is directly known to him so intimately and so much better than anything else, and what in its most distinct manifestation is called will.

(The World As Will and Idea, trans. R. B. Haldane
and J. Kemp, Trubner and Co., 1886.)

That Thomas had recourse to this passage is not as far-fetched as it may seem; it is a well-known one, and often cited in discussions of monism and the interconnectedness of the natural world. In the poem, the interrelationship of speaker and world, and the actions of the processes that make them one, are enacted at the level of word, image and formal structure. Alliteration binds together different categories of object, as do powerful but subtly varied rhythms; 'drives' shrinks to 'dries' to mimic the action it describes; 'veins', 'mouth', 'head' have geographical as well as bodily equivalents.

The cancelled stanza 1 reveals not just that 'The force' owes much to Blake's 'The Sick Rose', but that by splitting 'worm' from 'rose' in his source, Thomas ensured that its images spanned the poem (Stanford, 1954). After establishing an antithetical contrast in the last lines of stanza 1, for example, Thomas reverses the sequence natural image/ bodily image in stanza 2, the reversal increasing the inter-involvement of both realms, and adding 'an increment of meaning through a play on the word mouth' (Maud 1963). Stanza 3 repeats the structure of its predecessors, but metonymically personifies 'the force' as a 'hand'. Stanza 4 deviates still further from the norm, halting the forward thrust of the poem, calming the rhythm as the 'fallen blood' calms the 'sores' of 'love'. The focus on the implications of process is broken, as the speaker generalises about time and love. The final couplet, reiterating 'dumbness', puns on 'sheet' and 'worm' in a powerful and appropriate close.

Of the much-discussed stanza 4, Stewart Crehan (1990) suggests that the 'leeching' may be done by any or all of: *a* an infant mouth at the breast; *b* the poet; *c* the natural cycle renewing itself; *d* time 'like water' homophonically 'leaching down . . . feeding the embryo through the umbilicus or sucking the child from the aquatic womb'. And, as he admits, 'the possibilities do not end there.' The refrain 'And I am dumb' repeatedly poses the dilemma that the human condition is to exist within nature, and its processual 'force', but to be separated from it by self-consciousness, awareness of death, and language. Barbara Hardy (2000) finds the 'oxymoronic' imagery of 'utterance and dumbness' both an admission of real inability and 'a clamant address' which 'tells' about 'not telling', an appropriately non-anthropomorphic way of speaking 'with vegetation, minerals, water, wind, earth, and the dead', and of what happens after death. Ultimately she finds the poem concerns 'artistic language', exemplified in its 'mouth' imagery, which culminates as 'a vast invisible mouth, sucking at the mountain, created by inference from springs and their sources'.

Richard Chamberlain (2002), takes a related approach, viewing 'dumbness' as an expression of Thomas's refusal of 'repressive totalities'; it does not just confess inability, but actively refuses 'to grasp conceptually (and hence reduce and pervert) the singularity of the world', allowing him to 'rejoice in the speaking of . . . silence or shocked inarticulacy'. Dumbness therefore highlights the 'inability to speak, in determinate or conventionally logical terms, truthfully . . . non-assertion is itself the assertion of a necessary truth. [Thomas], even in acknowledging oneness with nature reminds us that he is unable to speak to nature . . . [to] identify with it [in] an act of violent appropriation [and thus] avoids some of the traps of conventional nature poetry.' This ensures that 'the natural image' is not used to underwrite a version of aesthetic ideology which might offer a 'dangerously comforting', falsely organicist solution to the contradictions of existence. The sense of 'deep ecology' resembles Hardy's interest in Thomas's 'greenness', one which goes beyond subject-matter to a sense that untidiness and excess are a form of resistance to dominative logic, anticipating the pastoral as poetic tactic and subject in the late poems.

1 **fuse** = with something of the verbal sense of 'fusing'; **drives** = pushes; perhaps glancing at Freud's *Trieben*, 'drives'; **flower** = 'one who flows' as well as a blossom; in *Ulysses*, Bloom's *nom de plume*, Henry Flower, is similarly ambiguous. 5 **wintry** = with 'crooked' of l. 4 (accented in the *N4* deletions), 'wintry' evokes Shakespeare's 'Crookback' Richard III and his 'Now is the winter of our discontent' soliloquy. 6 **mouthing** = 'The force that drives the water . . . sucks it in . . . the creating and destroying forces are identical' (Maud, 1963). 9 **veins** = cf. George Meredith, 'A Ballad of Past Meridian', 'Another stood by me . . . with breasts of clay, / And metal veins . . . / O Life, how naked and how hard when known!' 11 **whirls . . . the pool** = cf. Donne, 'Elegy 6', ll. 15–16: 'So careless flowers strowed on the water's face. / The curled whirlpools suck, smack, and embrace, / Yet drown them'. On 9 May 1934, Thomas wrote to Johnson: 'I feel all my muscles contract as I try to drag out, from the whirlpooling words around my everlasting ideas of the importance of death upon the living, some connected words that will explain how the starry system of the dead is seen, ordered as in the grave's sky, along the orbit of a foot or a flower.' 14 **hanging man** = the hanging man, being dead, is also now part of the unlistening natural world. 16 **The lips of time leech to the fountain head** = a personified time draws new life from the womb, the fountainhead of new life. 'Leech' is detumescent in 'A saint about to fall', so the penis may also be intended. Either way, 'leech' gives time's feeding on human fecundity a 'repellent, vampiric quality . . . it [could be] the erect penis, filled with blood . . . that seeks vagina and womb' as well as the opposite – 'the female labia . . . suck[ing] in the head of the male member' – with its resultant 'fountain' a 'seminal spurt' (Crehan, 1990). And leech could simply be the animal, of course, the image derived from its use to reduce fevers by bleeding the patient (Wales was particularly fertile ground for leech-gatherers, and by the nineteenth century supplied a quarter of all those used in Britain); so, 'Time, leech-like, lets the blood and reduces the painful feverishness of youth.' 17–18 **Love drips . . . calm her sores** = however 'calming', the imagery remains that of disease, from stanza 1. 19–20 **I am dumb . . . round the stars** = Maud (2003) claims a

privately held worksheet for the poem bears a note in Thomas's hand reading 'am/sêr np 339', a reference to page 339 of *Spurrell's Welsh-English Dictionary* (1925), which contains the entry 'sêr np stars'. This dictionary was in D. J. Thomas's library; Maud argues, plausibly enough, that the final phrasing of l. 20 derives from the Welsh for 'time', 'amser', a compound from 'am' (around) and 'sêr' (stars). See Ralph Maud and Robert Coleman Williams, 'Dylan Thomas and the Welsh language', *New Welsh Review*, 42 (Autumn 1998), 4–6; this article also gives an illustration of the worksheet. 21–2 **crooked worm** = cf. 'The Enemies': 'a crooked worm, disturbed by the probing of the fingers, wriggled blind in the sun', and 'Where once the twilight locks': 'the long worm of my finger'.

From love's first fever

As *N4* 'Twenty Six', this poem ends with the following additional eleven lines:

Now that drugged youth is waking from its stupor,
The nervous hand rehearsing on the thigh
Acts with a woman, one sum remains in cipher:
Five senses and the frozen brain
Are one with wind, and itching in the sun.
Stone is my mate? who shall brass be?
What seed to me?
~~The soldered world debates.~~

How are they seeded, all that move,
With all that move not to the eye?
What seed, what seed to me?

In a letter of early November 1933, Thomas accepted Pamela Hansford Johnson's objection to this ending as 'entirely justified', pleading 'guilty to bathos', and cut them.

For Thomas, as his 'Poetic Manifesto' (1951) stresses, the infant does not 'fall' from some pre-linguistic plenitude; the poem stresses the miraculous potential of language, as division and multiplication evoke a sense not of loss but 'delight . . . [in] language's endless proliferation of an ever more wondrously complex and differentiated world', and in the blurring of categories and identities (Roberts, 2009). The linguistic anxiety of other early poems was more apparent in the original *N4* version's expansion of the masturbatory 'code of night'; as revised, the power to 'knit' words 'anew' overcomes their 'stony', deathly aspect, lending this poem an unusual degree of equanimity. It is also alone in *18P* in its metrical irregularity and lack of a rhyme scheme, adding to its unfinished feel.

12 This line was dropped in *CP52* and restored in *CP88*. 16 **earth and sky** = as in the Greek myth of Gea and Tellus, earth and sky are gendered; here the two 'meet', although at ll. 45–6 we get 'divorcing sky' and 'two-framed globe'. 20–25 **the four winds . . . Green was the singing house** = 'Language . . . is seen not so much as imprisoning the nascent self as awakening it, and . . . stimulating a profound joy through its construction of a relationship between that self and its surroundings.' (Roberts, 2009) The synaesthesia of ll. 21–2 reflects this engagement, as elsewhere in Thomas; e.g. in 'The Tree': 'light was a sound at his ears'. 23 Preceded in *N4* 'Twenty Four' and in the *Criterion* version by the two lines: 'And where one globe had spun a host did circle / The nave of heaven each with his note.' 30 **the voice of hunger** = probably sexual desire. The individual's reconfiguring of 'stony' or 'dead' inherited language is emphasised ('shade' puns on 'shading' as colouring or drawing in a sketchbook: cf. 'Once it was the colour of saying'). 39 **a name, where maggots have their X** = like an illiterate's signature, their bearing witness signifying death (see l. 11 above); another of the criss-crossing 'poles' of the early poems. 42 **many sounding minded** = multiple syntactical possibilities enact the plural condition described here.

* Jack of Christ

N4 'Seventeen', 'Eighteen' and 'Nineteen', dated 25, 26 and 29 September 1933.

These three separate but consecutive poems were typed up under the title 'Jack of Christ', headed by Thomas's handwritten note 'In Three Parts', and sent to Glyn Jones in 1934. A copy in the University of Southern Illinois omits the fourth and last stanzas of 'Seventeen', as do I. Previously published as a sequence in the *Western Mail* on 30 July 1960 (when Jones edited its poetry section) and in Ralph Maud's *Poet in the Making*.

The sequence may reflect Thomas's desire to develop more complex structures at this point in his career. The title, from the last line of Part III, alludes to Gerard Manley Hopkins's 'That Nature is a Heraclitean Fire and of the comfort of the Resurrection': '[Christ] was what I am and / This Jack, joke, poor potsherd, patch, matchwood, immortal diamond.' However, if it concerns (lack of) faith, the poem is not specifically Christian, and the title may also derive from the sense of 'jack' as subaltern, a 'Swansea Jack' (term for a native of Swansea) and 'jack off', slang for masturbation. A primary sense, given his pervasive presence in the early poetry, is Dylan's father, D. J. Thomas, known as 'Jack' Thomas (Davies, 1995). As 'Jack Christ' the term recurs in 'If I were tickled by the rub of love' and 'Altarwise', VIII.

In part I the speaker falls into a barren place 'for lack of' spiritual sustenance, god, or love, which then seems present – the zone thus being defined by an absent-present, paradoxical quality. Their gender is uncertain; they appear male in stanza 4, but refer to their 'dugs' in stanza 5, and the original l. 109 is ambiguous concerning the gender of 'Jack'. While there is a lack of symmetry in the development of the argument, partly caused by the omission of stanzas 4 and 8 of the *N4* version, the phantom otherworld is well established, the characteristic use of double negatives is effective, and on a par with the dream-and-death realms of other *N4* poems (cf. 'I fellowed sleep'), while the narrative of stanzas 5–6, of a spirit who is entombed and stripped of its senses to be paradoxically 'healed' by paying 'the sum of death', perhaps ahead of re-birth, recalls that of poems like 'Light breaks'.

The 'lack of love' and, retrospectively, the overtly sexual imagery of part II, suggests that part I's 'stony hand' and 'palming lads' allude to the auto-erotic (and perhaps to writing), as in 'My hero bares his nerves'. 'Part Two' seems directed at the speaker's own censuring superego as much as any actual father; its plea is to 'let the thieves' who steal semen get on with it; their attempts to satisfy the thirst for sexual experience are 'sad' and counterproductive. Masturbatory 'lust' cannot, in any case, be sharply distinguished from 'love'; more, the lack of love it represents resembles the absence of god necessary to a true faith, and this, in turn, invokes process, by which 'one man must be all and all be one'. Charitable allowance of the knaves' activities will thus eventually allow us to composedly 'yield' to the thieving 'knave of death' and to be reborn from the 'cloudy coast' of the otherworld. Significantly, part II resists the conventional association of auto-eroticism with deathliness and guilt of other *N4* poems. Yet its conclusion is perfunctory, and Thomas eventually decided to mine the poem for 'Grief thief of time'.

Part III develops earlier images of nursing and suggestions of gender ambiguity, in focusing on a 'girl, unlacing' whose trust in her breasts' beauty and nurturing function is exemplary, in a microcosmic way, for trust in the apparently barren universe and its ultimate beneficence.

1 **For loss of blood I fell** = perhaps death; also detumescent (see note on 'leech' for 'The force that through the green fuse', above). 2 **milk and honey** = the Promised Land of Canaan, in the Old Testament, is said to flow with milk and honey. 4 **dry** = both adjectival ('the water which was dry as sticks') and adverbial, as in the idiom 'to drink dry'; an example of Thomas's ability to combine 'colloquial phrase' and 'rhetoric' (James A. Davies, 1998). 9 **humming wraiths** = ghostly bees. 14, 35 **palm, palming lads** = palm (tree) leads to palm as in hand, and 'palming'; while its usual sense would connect it with trickery, sleight of hand, it may also be a euphemism for masturbation (cf. idiomatic 'Mrs Palm and her five lovely daughters'). 23, 28, 30 **womb . . . dugs . . . set his famined hands upon my fat** = indicate a female speaker. 36 **nick** = steal (slang); cut. 37 **Jack** = here D. J. 'Jack' Thomas; but see note above; **knaves** = thieves; the testicles, hanging either side of the Christ-like penis (cf. 'My hero bares his nerves'), which produce the 'swag of bubbles' (sperm) of the next line. 50 **stolen bubbles** = sperm 'stolen' by masturbation; **sad sacks** = scrotums; inept people who give rise to feelings of pity or disgust in others (the U.S. Army cartoon character with the name 'Sad Sack' was not created until June 1942). 43 **silver whistles** = as used by police in Thomas's time; they would blow them when in pursuit of a criminal on foot, in order to summon help. 44 **iron van** = a Black

Maria, used for transporting criminals. 50 **stolen bubbles** = ejaculated sperm 'stolen' from legitimate sexual activity by masturbation or nocturnal emission. 51 **sacked wines** = looted, like the 'swag', but with play on 'sack' as a kind of wine (burnt sherry); the idea is that masturbatory sex is a false satisfaction and only makes sexual cravings more intense. 61 **Where is no god there man believes** = cf. 'No man believes'. 70, 78 **The girl . . . trusts . . . Should the girl doubt** = valorises intuitive trust in the body and in the universe more generally. 74 **unslip** = pun on 'slip' as under-garment (cf. 'shift' in next line). 86–101 **It shall happen . . . Though the flesh fails** = age is inescapable, but we must cleave to the faith that a youthful trust in the universe has endowed us with. 95–9 **milk . . . honey colours** = a return to the milk and honey of 'Part One'. 106–9 even the 'stony-hand' of the masturbator / writer, as long as s/he trusts cosmic process, will be rewarded by being 'star-fathered', and embody the beauty and purity of Christ as the principle of human perfectibility, in line with Unitarian belief. 107 **needles' stroke** = reference to the radium-tipped needles used in D. J. Thomas's cancer treatment in 1933–4; 'surgeon wrist' is interlined in *N4*. 109 **Jack** = 'the bride' is interlined in *N4*.

Light breaks where no sun shines

Its representative quality led to the inclusion of this lyric in the definitive 1930s anthology, Michael Roberts's *Faber Book of Modern Verse*. Roberts's introduction patronisingly describes it as corresponding to 'dream-fantasies of a sexual type' by a poet 'unaware of what is happening in his own mind'. Yet the poem's taut structure, rich suggestiveness and powerful momentum display a mastery of form and content, and have made it a staple of criticism. Maud (2003) discerns a single narrative about 'dead flesh being built up into living flesh by an act of faith', light breaking on the dead body (stanza 1), the sexually dead being raised (stanza 2), tears gushing from a dead smile (stanza 3), the blind gaining their sight (stanza 4) and matching 'enlightenment in thought' (stanza 5). However, the majority view is that the poem presents the forces of growth and death and decay simultaneously. Thus, Emery (1962) claims that 'life' and 'death' processes are presented in alternate stanzas, with the former advancing from conception to puberty, maturity and age to death, the latter moving from decay, to atmospheric absorption and descent (as rain) and springtime revival. By contrast, Davies (2000) views stanzas 1, 2 and 5 as divided into a first part concerned with the living body and a second part concerned with death, with stanza 3 wholly concerned with life, stanza 4 wholly with death. However, these schemas, as their advocates admit, are so fluid as to be reversible in places. Insofar as 'Light breaks' does not so much compare as *identify* the human body with the universe, to the point at which it is almost impossible to distinguish the different aspects of process from each other, it goes beyond even 'The force' to elementalise the body and personalise the cosmos (Davies, 1993).

The stanza form is a good example of Thomas's combination of a standard stress-based prosody (respectively iambic trimeter, pentameter, dimeter, pentameter, dimeter and pentameter) with a strict syllable count.

2–3 **sea . . . tides** = cf. D. H. Lawrence, *Apocalypse* (1930), chapter XVII: 'Man is still a creature that thinks with his blood: "the heart, dwelling in the sea of blood that runs in opposite directions . . . for the blood round the heart is the thought of men."' 9–11 **fig** = the vagina, among other senses, as in Lawrence's 'Figs', *Birds, Beasts and Flowers*; 'before birth, the embryo uncurls like any other fact of physical creation' (Davies, 1993). 16–18 **Nor fenced nor staked . . . the oil of tears** = because the universe's processes are as linked to those of the body as the body's processes are to its own, rain 'is the same response to that process which "divines" (discovers and makes holy) tears of grief behind a human smile' (Davies, 1993). 30 **Above the waste allotments the dawn halts** = Tindall (1962) sees this line as ominously ambiguous, although it may be so at the expense of a conventional (i.e. Christian) interpretation of 'dawn'. Cf. Thomas's letter to Trevor Hughes of June 1934: 'there is still no light, only a new mile of suffering murk added to the horizon, and a fresh acre of wonder at this rotten state that might easily and sweetly be changed into the last long acre where the dead breathe for the first time.'

* I fellowed sleep who kissed between the brains

N4 'Thirty One', dated 27 November 1933.

Although it was the unpublished forerunner to its near-namesake ('I fellowed sleep who kissed me in the brain', to which it also lends the phrase 'grave-gabbing') in *18P*, this poem is a short and shapely lyric that gives a novel twist to some of Thomas's concerns, and it deserves separate consideration. It may reflect something of the relief he felt following the prolonged insomnia referred to in a letter to Pamela Hansford Johnson of 11 November 1933: 'Last night I slept for the first time in months; today I am writing a poem in praise of sleep and the veronal that stained the ravelled sleeve. These twelve November nights have been twelve long centuries to me.' In the poem, the speaker is seduced by a female 'sleep' and 'fathers' dreams; his seductress opens the vast realms of the universe to his sleeping self, but with the suggestion in 'kissed', 'drained' and 'ruin' that the encounter is a nocturnal emission. Although this makes her a kind of Belle Dame Sans Merci, and the speaker ends up in cosmic limbo, the conclusion has a tragic pathos at odds with the more negative, self-punitive treatment of the same subject in poems such as 'When once the twilight'.

2 **her spinning kiss** = taken with 'pit-wombed' and 'pits' in l. 5, the implicit metaphor is of sleep as a descent into a coal mine, or pit, of the unconscious. 10 **salt hairs** = probably pubic; sexual initiation in dream 'unlocks the sky'. 15 **And worlds hang on trees** ▪ The imagery of the last stanza suggests that seduction by sleep leads to the unmaking of selfhood and a temporary return to some elemental cosmos. Like 'grave-gabbing' this phrase was used in a published poem, 'When once the twilight locks'.

See, says the lime

On 25 December 1933, Thomas wrote to Pamela Hansford Johnson 'The last poem I sent you [the one you didn't like] is not very good . . . one day I hope to write something altogether out of the hangman's sphere, something larger, wider, more comprehensible, and less selfcentred (*CL*, 94).' This self-awareness is reflected in the comic playlet he sent her in January 1934, 'Spajma and Salnadny or Who Shot the Emu?' In it, the Thomas character Salnady Moth encounters Spajma (Pamela Johnson) when both are ordering materials for their writing from the Spirit of Poetry (Salnady's shopping list is 'A quick womb, please, two milks, a hangman, a dash of sleep and a pint of wax') (*CL*, 115). 'Milks' alludes to the 'milk of death' image, which Thomas made some use of at the time – it recurs in *N4* 'Twenty Eight'. In 'See, says the lime' it is developed to a greater degree than elsewhere, by making the quicklime, source of the corpse-dissolving 'milk', the poem's narrator. It literalises the 'hangman's sphere' by making the owner of the body it is dissolving a hangman (who imagined a god who could 'undo' death, i.e. was a Christian), now reduced after death in his own lime. The lime / milk reduces the hangman and his 'god / Of death's undoer' by the agency of its 'milk of death' to the natural cycle, proving that 'Death' itself, not any deity, is 'death's undoer'. However, the poem's many ambiguities and disturbingly intertwined graveyard and sexual imagery allow it to be read in a more lurid and apocalyptic sense.

From a letter to my Aunt, Discussing the Correct Approach to Modern Poetry

The judgements in these verses closely resemble those of Thomas's letter to Glyn Jones of mid-March 1934, and reflect his current thinking:

> It would be possible to catalogue most of the reasons for modern obscurity. Some poets, like Gertrude Stein and the French-American Transitionists of Eugene Jolas, have evolved a mathematically precise method of removing the associations from words, and giving language, or attempting to give language, its *literal* sound, so that the word 'cat' becomes no more than a one-syllabled word with a hard consonantal ending; others, like Joyce, have magnified words, lengthened them and animated them with contrary inferences, and built around them a vast structure of unexpected and often inexplicable associations; others, like Auden, have taken their public too much for granted, and have cut out all words that seem to themselves

unnecessary, leaving their poems at the end written in an imaginary shorthand . . . others, like Eliot, have become so aware of the huge mechanism of the past that their poems read like a scholarly conglomeration of a century's wisdom, and are difficult to follow unless we have an intimate knowledge of Dante, the Golden Bough, and the weather reports in Sanskrit; others, like Graves and Riding, have something intellectually new to inform us and indulge in a logical game of acrostics. Then there are the Cummings, so very often short, who, obsessed by the idea of form, chop up their poems into little strips and pin them horizontally, diagonally, & upside-down on the pages. (*CL*, 122)

This bread I break

This poem was much-discussed in the golden years of Thomas criticism between his death and the mid-1970s, largely because it lent itself more easily than many of his poems to a Christian interpretation, at a time when these were more common in academia. Aneirin Talfan Davies (1964), for example, found in it 'a poetic restatement of the reality of the Sacrament of Body and Blood', evidence of a shift during Thomas's life towards 'a Catholic imagery and symbolism', although he admitted that "To what extent [it] . . . signifies the poet's *belief* it is difficult to judge.' M. Wynn Thomas (in Ellis, 2014) notes that 'Thomas's Christ continually cries out against the torture of nature, which He views as a grotesque parody of Holy Communion.' McNees (1992) more or less agrees, but adds that 'Thomas absorbs Christ and priest into himself' and, 'by doubling the personae and confusing their roles . . . is able to articulate the eucharistic sacrament from different vantage points', both mocking a dogmatic belief in transubstantiation by reversing it, and, conversely, 'reinforcing a belief in consubstantiation by granting equality to all the agents and elements involved, natural and divine.'

2 **foreign tree** = sacramental symbolism is common in Thomas's work of the time; cf. 'The Mouse and the Woman': 'He saw her flesh in the cut bread, her blood, still flowing through the channels of her mysterious body, in the spring water.' 6 **Once in this wine the summer blood** = 'wine' in *25P* proofs was misprinted as 'wind' in both *25P*

and *CP52*, but corrected in later printings of *CP52*, *TP71* and *CP88*. However, a new error was introduced in the first edition of *CP14* where 'this' became 'the'; as Seamus Perry charitably observed, 'perhaps the line is jinxed' (Perry, 2014). 7 **knocked** = Tindall (1962) notes: 'a favourite word for sex, birth and heart'; cf. 'Before I knocked'. 15 **snap** = 'break' in *New English Weekly* version.

A process in the weather of the heart

A metapoem, giving an overview of Thomas's vision of the universe as continuous flux and interrelatedness, in which reality is essentially paradoxical. As David Aivaz (1950) noted, '"Process" . . . is the basic theme of all Thomas' poems', and Ralph Maud (1963) took the word as used in this poem to apply as a label to a small core group of Thomas's early lyrics. Jacob Korg (1965) noted the poem's movement in 'a series of paradoxes expressed in insistent stanzaic and syntactic parallelisms [which] asserts the duality of the process of change to which the individual human being and . . . the universe, are subjected,' observing that 'in a world of simultaneous time' living and dead are indistinguishable forms of each other, 'temporary forms of constantly changing matter', and consequently 'two ghosts'. Goodby (2013) argues that Thomas took the word, and some sanction for his process philosophy, from the work of Alfred North Whitehead. 'Quick' and 'dead' are both ghosts in this poem, which emphasises the negative, deterministic side of process.

1 **process** = Thomas is known to have read Whitehead's *Science and the Modern World* (1926) and was interested in popular science and the post-Einsteinian world-view. Whitehead coined his own 'process philosophy' in *The Concept of Nature* (1920) and treated it at length in other works, such as *Process and Reality* (1929). 12 **unangled** = 'unplumbed' in *N4*, alluding to 'The unplumb'd, salt, estranging sea' of Matthew Arnold's 'To Marguerite – Continued'. 13 **seed . . . forest of the loin** = cf. Donne, 'Elegy 18: Love's Progress': 'Thou shalt upon another forest set / Where many shipwreck, and no further get.'

When once the twilight locks

According to Olson (1954) this poem is 'a meditation on the origin of the idea of death'; the speaker 'drowned his father's magic's in a dream', beginning the adult confrontation with mortality through sleep and dream, in which the sleeping-dreaming living and the dead encounter each other (the 'working sea', suggesting Freud's 'dream-work', refers to the unconscious and the realm of death which we access in dream, as in 'I fellowed sleep who kissed me in the brain'). With more emphasis on the poem's dialogic energy, Tindall (1962) and Davies (1986) agree with Olson that stanzas 4 and 5 are to be read as a report, by the 'creature' of stanza 2, of its 'dream' (mentioned at the close of stanza 3); Davies also speculates that the poem 'might be an address by God, the creature being the human being He created', although this idea is not pursued.

2 **long worm of my finger** – cf. 'The force that through the green fuse' for the same finger/worm image. 3 **dammed** = 'Dammed' in *18P* became 'damned' in the 1942 edition, *CP52* and *TP71*; I follow *CP88* in restoring the *18P* form. 18 **He drowned his father's magics in a dream** = the *New Verse* version read: 'He doublecrossed his getter with a dream'. 19 **All issue armoured** = as Tindall (1962) notes, 'issue . . . works equally well as noun or verb. Armour, like any metal, means flesh. The "grave" . . . is also the womb.' Cf. Sir Thomas Browne, *Religio Medici*, II, 14: 'Thus I perceive a man may bee buried alive, and behold his grave in his own issue.' 25–6 **Sleep navigates . . . Sargasso of the tomb** = sleep is able to overcome time; it 'navigates' its tides, and the 'dry Sargasso of the tomb' – what has perished through time – 'gives up its dead' to the 'working sea' of sleep, or dream-work, contrasted with the sluggish sea of what is time- and death-bound. 30 **Who periscope through flowers to the sky** = cf. *N4* 'Twenty Seven': 'I eye the ragged globe / Through periscopes rightsighted from the grave'. Thomas's letter to Trevor Hughes of January 1934 claims: 'The most terrifying figure in history is, to me, the French abbé who became . . . a connoisseur of the grave and a worshipper of his sister Worm . . . [H]is view on the living was through the lenses of the dead – there is a delightful image somewhere which pictures each blade of grass as the periscope of a

dead man' (*CL*, 110). No-one has yet been able to identify the 'French abbé'. **35 suckers** = adventitious shoots which sap a plant's strength; U.S. slang for dupes. **41 carcase shape . . . fluids in his heart** = Moynihan (1966) sees the 'carcase shape' as Christianity, robbing the sleeper of his 'divine blood consciousness' in Lawrentian fashion. *18P* 'carcase' became 'carcass' in *CP52*; I follow *CP88* in restoring the original spelling. **44 a worker in the morning town** = a typically symbolist and archetypal recasting of a social realist image. **45 pickthank** = the pickthank's flattery is that of a self ensnared in fantasy and narcissism.

Our eunuch dreams

One of the most powerful and Blakean of Thomas's early poems. On first publication, in *New Verse* April 1934, stanza 2 of part I ran:

The brides return, freed from the starry knot,
The midnight pulley that unhoused the tomb;
No children break, all flavoured, into light
When love awakes her delver to the worm.

This was rewritten, and other lesser changes were made, before collection in *18P*.

This poem was singled out as 'an appalling affair' by Edith Sitwell in *Aspects of Modern Poetry* (1934), but in reviews of *18P* and 'A grief ago' in 1935 she reversed her opinion of Thomas's poetry. As a result, he wrote to thank his valuable new ally in January 1936, but took care in doing so to dismiss 'Our eunuch dreams' as a 'silly' 'Welsh-starch-itch-trash poem' (*CL*, 238). However, this placatory move was unfair to a poem that arose from a profound understanding of repression. Blake stands behind this aspect of Thomas's work at least as much as Freud, as exemplified in the passage in *Visions of the Daughters of Albion* in which Oothoon struggles, and fails, to awaken Theotormon to 'the heaven of generous love':

The moment of desire! The moment of desire! The virgin
That pines for man shall awaken her womb to enormous joys
In the secret shadows of her chamber. The youth, shut up from
The lustful joy, shall forget to generate and create an amorous image
In the shadows of his curtains and in the folds of his silent pillow.
Are not these the places of religion, the rewards of continence,
The enjoyings of self-denial? Why dost thou seek religion?
Is it because acts are not lovely that thou seekest solitude,
Where the horrible darkness is impressed with reflections of desire?

9 **The bones of men** = skeletons; slang for erections. 12 **one dimen-
sioned ghosts** = we read 'one-dimensioned' literally, which makes
Thomas's point that while the image and photograph are half-true,
dreams are totally false. 19 **kiss or kill** = a childhood game like 'Truth
or Dare' (Davies, 2000). 21 **Which is the world?** = Korg (1965)
observes 'The analogy between waking and sleep on the one hand
and faith and doubt on the other . . . occurs in [Browning's] "Bishop
Bloughram's Apology": "I say, faith is my waking life: / One sleeps,
indeed, and dreams at intervals, / We know, but waking's the main
point with us."' 36 **Suffer this world to spin** = as well as avoiding
the abrupt shift in mood and message half-way through the final line
of the penultimate stanza, Thomas's suggested revision (unused by
Grigson; see *CP14*) emphasises 'this'; 'leave *this* (superannuated) world
to continue as it has in the past' – with a hint of 'spin out of control'
– because we will create a new one.

Where once the waters of your face

A blend of submarine lyric beauty and slippery ambiguity, especially
of the 'green unraveller' figure, is reflected in the critical literature.
Walford Davies (1972) rejected the attempt by Tindall (1962) to read
its imagery 'only in terms of the full-sterile polarity of the womb', but
in doing so he perhaps over-emphasised the degree to which it simply
expresses a renewal of 'childlike delight'. Rushworth M. Kidder (1973)
lists four possible interpretations: *a* an address to a dried sea-channel;
b a poem about birth and mother ('screws' as turnings within the
womb); *c* evocation of a lost love, now only a memory ('the "green

knots" that "sank their splice / Into the tided cord" describes her hymeneal state, green with inexperience'); and *d* a lyric for a very much present lover '"dry" after consummation and soon to revive.' Others could be added; the poem as an address to the self, for example. Goodby (2013), following Davies (1985) discusses the poem as an example of Thomas's use of 'meta-metaphor'; i.e. one which does not return to its real world point of take-off.

I see the boys of summer

Perhaps the most splendid of the Buffalo notebook poems, this one seems to have been composed in two stages ('My world is pyramid' was the result of a similar two-stage process). Part I, written in early 1934, was probably the 'new poem, just completed' Thomas sent to Geoffrey Grigson in late March 1934. After a visit to Pamela Hansford Johnson in London in early April 1934, during which he may have discussed it with Grigson, he appears to have written parts II and III, fair-copying the completed poem as *N4* 'Thirty Nine', dated 'April '34'. This was then sent to Grigson: 'The poem you said you'd read and tell me about is incomplete in the version you have. I enclose the complete poem'.

While critics unanimously praise the maturity and power of this poem, there has been much disagreement over who speaks in it, and over the meaning of part III. In Thomas's lifetime, Nicholas Moore (1948), who approved the poem's different voices, and part III's 'essentially dramatic' nature which 'preserves with great skill the very dislocation it is aiming at', was disturbed by its 'sombre' and 'vicious' images 'with [their] final hint of homosexuality and futility.' Derek Stanford (1954) agreed that a 'note of sterility, of self-destruction, of perversity' was struck throughout, as did Lita Hornick (1958). Elder Olson (1954) found instead a 'pseudo-dramatic dialogue', to be viewed less in moral or expressivist terms than as a struggle between perverse youth and crabbed age, at once external and internal, with the poet interjecting the vocative lines concluding parts I and II. Both Clark Emery and William York Tindall (1962) follow suit, emphasising the Depression–era context of 'ruin'. Tindall is alert to the way that, for all its emphatic rhetoric, the poem is deeply ambiguous, while Emery deviates further from endorsing the authoritative tones of part I by arguing that the poem endorses the boys' rebellion, linking the speaker of part I to Blake's 'Natural Man' and Urizen, and of part II to Ursula in D. H. Lawrence's *The Rainbow* and to his *Fantasia of the Unconscious*.

Ralph Maud's seminal reading of (1963) uses this poem to explain the workings of the process poetic, according to which 'summer'-related images are constantly opposed by those of 'ruin' via the 'essentially fanciful' mechanisms of association and verbal 'breeding', ceaselessly renewing the poem's imagery and momentum. For him, the boys personify the forces of simultaneous growth and decay of process; the poem as a whole has 'a life-cycle theme' and confronts death and the human condition. Walford Davies (1993), however, claims that the poem 'is just as easily spoken by the poet on his own', and his reading is less sanguine; the 'pulse / Of love and light bursts in their throats', ambiguous to Maud – rupture or rapture? – is taken as indicating the triumph of 'conventional morality', preventing the hopeful possibilities of the last line's 'pulse of summer in the ice'. In part II, despite his despair, Davies claims that the speaker realises that birth must happen, 'or *real* death takes over', and 'cynically acts as the spokesman of the "dark deniers"' for the rest of part II. In stanza 7, as a 'boy of summer' already, he attends the birth of new ones, ironically bearing 'a wreath rather a bouquet'. For all this, Davies claims that part II's last line – 'O see the poles of promise in the boys' – registers phallic 'promise'. This possibility, he argues, is restated in the recapitulatory part III, which ends with 'the poles of two circles (womb and the world) touching, as they merge into one at the moment of birth', suggesting at least the potential for renewal. For Don McKay (1986), the boys embody the fact that the best way to serve tradition is by rebellion: 'unresisted systems, they argue, oppress and enslave'. The boys resist these by summoning 'death from a summer woman' and life from drowned and cramped lovers, holding up the sea, dropping its birds, and flooding the deserts. In the last stanza 'the boys move in on myth and ritual', revolting exuberantly, 'crossing' Easter and Christmas, pushing both towards pagan sacrifice.

Later readings often amplify these oppositions rather than resolving them. Stan Smith (2001) is rather Auden-centric – '[the poem] derives its . . . determining trope . . . from "Consider this and in our time"' – but a Dylan Thomas–New Country rivalry is a possible subject of the poem, and he rightly notes that both poems blur youth and age, capitalist and revolutionary. Thomas's poem, like Auden's, 'confuses its addressees and disorientates its speaker', because it describes 'an amoral life force that can never be finally defeated'. Thus, 'The real lesson Thomas draws . . . [is Auden's] rapid telescoping of addresses, which he reproduces in "I see the boys of summer"'. It is not a matter of us and them: we *are* them.' Similarly, George Morgan (1989) grasps the thwarting of resolution into clear-cut oppositions, voices and narratives: 'The two voices finally melt and merge in a cathartic conclusion and fusion of opposites . . . [Thomas's] meaning is not contained in the words of either protagonist but in their verbal and existential jousting and their ultimate resolution'. The boys thus resemble Thomas's other 'hamletic heroes' who try to 'give shape and form' to buried material, often symbolised in spectral form by his father's ghost; '[it] can be seen as a process of re-creation in which the poet engenders his own begetter, is father to the man', achieving realisation when 'rebel sons and the returning father-figure' are joined 'in . . . a union of opposites'. Even so, this does not explain who says what in part III – father-figure, boys, poet, or some as-yet-unknown voice – emphasising the final line's resonant uncertainty.

Only l. 47 breaks the regular syllable count; the pararhyme scheme *aabcbc* rhymes *aa* disyllabically and *bcbc* monosyllabically, with variants in stanzas 5, 7 and 8.

1 **boys of summer in their ruin** = Thomas's friend Bert Trick claimed the poem originated when they were walking along Swansea sea-front; noticing middle-aged men in Corporation bathing-suits on the beach, Thomas described them as 'boys of summer in their ruin'. **boys** = in South Walian speech, 'boy' is often used to refer to men, of any age; **ruin** = echoes W. H. Auden's 'Consider this and in our time' and *The Orators*. 6 **drown the cargoed apples in their tides** = the apple-like breasts of 'girls' are ruined; it was one of the scandals of the Depression era that foodstuffs, including apples and wheat, were burned or dumped at sea to maintain their market prices. 6–7 **curdlers . . . sour the boiling honey** = '"Curdlers" . . . breeds . . . "sour" . . . utilising the alternative meaning of sour: milk *curdles* but honey is made *unsweet* . . . [T]he first image prompts the second, which is, however, not really a continuation of it but something new' Maud (1963). 9 **in**

the hives = the boys reveal the 'frozen' nature of their 'loves' both in the (hive-like) womb and, later, in the way they treat their lovers' 'hives'. 10–12 **sun . . . voids** = '"Sun" . . . suggests "moon"; "nerves" . . . makes the moon a "signal"; and having fed on doubt and dark the boys are possessed of "voids". The signal moon, in keeping with the harvest theme of the first stanza, is the full moon (sign of changing weather); the boys make its roundness a mere zero, an emptiness, so it ceases to be a signal' (Maud, 1963). 13–18 cf. letter to Pamela Hansford Johnson, April 1934: 'Life passes the windows, and I hate it more minute by minute. I see the rehearsed gestures, the correct smiles, the grey cells revolving around under the godly bowlers. I see the unborn children struggling up the hill in their mothers, beating on the jailing slab of the womb, little realising what smugger prison they wish to leap into.' 14 **brawned** = like 'dams' and 'muscling', an unsentimental emphasis on the animal aspect of gestation; **weathers** = suggested by the moon of stanza 2. 21– 2 **lame . . . leaping . . . dogdayed** – 'after negating the harvest and their mothers, the boys now negate themselves', crippling the air itself in the process (Maud, 1963). 25–6 **But seasons . . . a chiming quarter** = 'The real enemy is time, especially clock time, which cuts us up into quarters' (Crehan, 2001), and the boys 'align themselves with diachronic time, avoiding the "chiming quarter" of stasis' (McKay, 1986). 44 **dries and dies** – the shift from 'drives' to 'dries' found in 'The force that through the green fuse' is taken a stage further. 48 **O see the poles . . . the boys** = cf. Auden's 'Consider this and in our time' and a rumoured revolution that will be 'A polar peril, a prodigious alarm.' 50 **Man in his maggot's barren** = cf. the engraved frontispiece to Blake's 'The Gates of Paradise', which depicts a maggot with a baby's face. 54 **O see the poles are kissing as they cross** = cf. 'A Prospect of the Sea', in which, after his first sexual encounter, the protagonist stands 'on a slope no wider than the living room of the world, and the two poles kissed behind his shoulder.' The idea of encompassing, becoming the globe, appears also in 'Altarwise'; also Donne's sermon on Psalm 89: 'Take a flat Map, a Globe *in plano*, and here is East, and there is West, as far asunder as two points can be put: but reduce this flat Map to roundnesse, which is the true form, and then East and West touch each other, and all are one: So consider man's life aright . . . In this, the circle, the two points meet, the womb and the grave are but one point, they make but one station, there is but a step from that to this.' For McKay (1986) this line ascends to 'a meta-metaphysical level, giving us a bird's-eye view of two gestures of reconciliation, kissing and crossing.'

In the beginning

A good example of Thomas's transformation of satirical and blasphemous impulses to more mediated, obviously artistic ones. The final stanza of the original, *N4* 'Fifteen', seems to have provided the cue for a symbolist translation of thought into language and light in the less profane, more rarefied register of *N4* 'Forty', which has a greatly enhanced redemptive role for the word: 'blood was scattered to the winds of light / A secret heart rehearsed its love'. This link between language, blood and love was given greater force in a further revision, to posit a cosmic 'secret brain', and a dispersed, pre-body 'blood' that scatters 'love' to the abstract 'winds of light'.

1, 19 **In the beginning** = 'St John's "In the beginning was the word" was a favourite quotation of [Dylan's]' (Glyn Jones, 2001). 4 **forked** = 'spread' in the April 1934 version; both words have sexual senses. 6 **Heaven and hell mixed** = Thomas followed the Blake of *The Marriage of Heaven and Hell* in regarding contraries as necessary for progress. 9–12 **After came the imprints . . . and left a sign** = as three-in-one, God's, Christ's and the Holy Spirit's deeds are essentially simultaneous and identical ('imprint[ing] . . . the waters' in the course of creation, walking the waves of Galilee, etc.). 11 **crosstree** = cf. *Ulysses*, 'Proteus' chapter: 'sails brailed up on the crosstrees'; **grail** = 'Joseph's grail' in the September version (a reference to Joseph of Arimathea, who collected Christ's blood in a drinking vessel at the crucifixion). 15 **A three-eyed, red-eyed spark blunt as a flower** = euphemistic version of the 'three-eyed prick' of *N4* 'Fifteen'; cf. Leopold Bloom's penis, 'the limp father of thousands, a languid floating flower' in *Ulysses*. 25 **secret brain . . . in the thought** = the 'celled and soldered' brain – a typical cybernetic conjunction – is rooted materialistically 'in the thought', not separate from or subservient to it. 29 **Blood shot and** = *N4* 'Forty' begins: 'And blood was'; **scattered to the winds of light** = cf. Shelley's 'Ode to the West Wind': 'Scatter, as from an unextinguished hearth /

Ashes and sparks, my words among mankind!' 30 **The ribbed original of love** = *N4* 'Forty' has 'A secret heart rehearsed its love'.

If I were tickled by the rub of love

One of Thomas's most powerful early poems, derived in part from *N3* 'Twenty Seven', which lent the themes of bodies 'cursed already by heredity', youth starkly contrasted with age, and the phrase 'herring smelling fevers'. The narrative is marked by a contrast between apparent declarative forcefulness and actual suspension in a counterfactual conditional tense referring to an ongoing present – the 'if I were . . . (then) I' formula. The poem's claims are tautological in form, as Maud (2003) notes; namely, if I were in a situation without fear of x – if I were 'tickled by' it, in fact – I would not be fearful. The tone is darkly ironic, and the poem is both an exercise in bravado and an undoing of that bravado, particularly in stanza 4, an aspect praised by Tony Conran (1997). (Thomas's own reading of the poem for Caedmon, dripping with Jacobean stage-villain relish, brings this aspect of the poem out perfectly.) As elsewhere (cf. 'And death shall have no dominion'), but more blatantly, it is hard to tell whether the mood is conditional ('If I were, I would be') or subjunctive ('I would let be'), and this uncertainty informs the final line: '"Metaphor" for what?', as Maud asks. Rather than simply a 'prayer' for 'engagement with full, contingent humanity' (Davies, 2000), the acute ambiguities of the poem suggest rather that its concluding self-exhortation has more in common with Blake's radical belief that man is the only way to understand the universe (cf. *The Marriage of Heaven and Hell*: 'All deities reside in the human breast'; 'Where man is not, nature is barren'). Foster Damon's *William Blake: His Philosophy and Symbols* (1924), a copy of which was in D. J. Thomas's library at 5 Cwmdonkin Drive, is clear on this point: 'Man originally was, and shall be eventually the whole . . . Therefore the analysis of the universe is nothing but an analysis of himself.'

1 **If I were** = 'One is reminded of Marvell's "Coy Mistress": "Had we but world enough . . .". Marvell follows his subjunctive with "but" and the indicative, "But at my back I always hear . . .". Thomas

similarly modulates into the simple present for a marvellously expressive middle stanza [ll. 29–35] about his predicament as a sexual young adult fearful of old age and death' (Conran, 1997). One way of reading the opening lines is to take l. 3 as being continued in the first clause of l. 3, and l. 2 being continued in its second clause; the syntax enacts the simultaneity of the actions of speaker and girl, in accordance with the process poetic. **2 rooking** = 'thieving and exorbitant' (Davies, 1993). As Moynihan (1966) notes, the boy in 'A Prospect of the Sea' feels the girl he encounters will 'carry me away inside her . . . This is the story of a boy being stolen'; he adds, 'the female who steals is the mother who takes the seed.' **6–7 apple . . . flood . . . bad blood of spring** = the Fall, Flood and crucifixion, respectively. **8, 15 Shall it be male or female? say the cells** = from *N3* 'Twenty Seven'. **16** *N4* has 'Chalking the jakes with green things of the brain'. **22 lovers'** = *N4* has 'lover's'. **23–8 crow's-foot** = wrinkles at the corners of the eye, signs of ageing; **manhood** = 'old age' in *N4* version; **The sea of scums . . . toes** = *N4* has 'The biting days would soften as I struck / Bells on the dead fools' toes'. **29–33 This world is half the devil's . . . smoking in a girl** = 'The dynamic principle of life is brought into startling relief until the whole universe is seen as motivated by the energy of sex' (Huddlestone, 1948). **33 herrings smelling** = with a suggestion of the 'fishy' smell of the vagina (cf. 'Verse Letter to Lauren McIvor and Lloyd Frankenberg', ll. 60–2). **34 nail** = anticipates l. 45's 'Christ . . . on the tree'. **39 the midnight of a chuckle** = cf. Isbrand the revenger's request to Siegfried, 'my midnight of a man', for a song, in *Death's Jest-Book*, III, iii, 302. **40–1 the breast / Of lover, mother, lovers** = in Freudian terms, the mother as the (male) child's first 'lover', followed by the father's prohibition of the mother's body, then by 'lovers' when he becomes an adult. Implicit is the sense that, even in thoughts of the grave and return to a universal mother, desire can never be wholly assuaged. **45 My Jack of Christ** = blurs the identity of Christ, Thomas and 'Jack' Thomas, his father.

All all and all

N5 'One', with one very minor difference from the final version published in *18P*. Though undated in *N5*, Thomas refers to 'All all and all' in a letter to Pamela Hansford Johnson of 20 July in a way that suggests she has already received it, or that it is enclosed with the letter.

Despite the claim by Seamus Perry (2014) that 'I'm not sure anyone has ever cracked "All all and all"', a coherent and convincing explication has been available for over fifty years. As one would expect from its tricksy title, the poem is about totality; there is no comma between the first two 'alls', allowing us to read it as 'Every "all"', with 'and all' simply as an idiom (as in, say, 'Him with his big car and all'). The subject reflects that most totalising of philosophies, Marxism, while the structure derives from Marxism's reliance on the Hegelian triad of thesis, antithesis and synthesis; Thomas was discussing both around this time with his political mentor Bert Trick, and mentions it in letters to Pamela Hansford Johnson. The first and second parts of the poem articulate personal adolescent anxieties and more general ones concerning a universe which seems, as Korg (1957) puts it, 'established to run itself with complete disregard for its inhabitants'. This generates a strenuous attempt to transcend a merely negative sense of the merging of the human and machine, individual and blind process – what Tindall (1962) calls Thomas's 'habitual confusion of metal and flesh' and Ivan Phillips (2003) his 'cyborg symbolism' (cf 'I dreamed my genesis', 'I, in my intricate image'). As Mills (1960) and Goodby (2013) argue, part III builds towards an 'exalted' orgasmic-socialistic affirmation of 'the unity of creation' and mankind.

My world is pyramid

N5 'Two', lacking final stanza of part II, with very minor differences from the published poem.

On 2 August 1934, Thomas sent Pamela Hansford Johnson a poem he claimed would be 'going in New Verse this month', but did not name it. On 5 August, he sent Geoffrey Grigson, the editor of *New Verse*, 'the two poems I said I'd send you'. The proximity of dates suggests that the poem in question may have been the bipartite 'My world is pyramid', which could be described as either a single poem or 'two poems'. Alternatively, Thomas may have sent Johnson only the first part of the poem as a free-standing entity (before it was copied into $N5$), then sent it with a second poem to Grigson, only to realise afterwards that the two could be combined. This would fit Maud's speculation, based on internal evidence, that the last two stanzas of part II were originally the conclusion of a separate poem, the opening five stanzas of which became part I (meaning that the second poem sent to Grigson consisted of the three stanzas of part II beginning 'My world is pyramid') (Maud, 2003).

Although this much must remain conjectural, the $N5$ version was entered between 20 July (the latest possible date of 'One') and 1 October 1934 (the date in $N5$ for 'Four'). The conjecture that Thomas decided to amalgamate the parts of the poem after sending it as two poems to Grigson provides a plausible explanation for the delay in his publishing it, since the poem did not appear in *New Verse* until December 1934 (such amalgamations are not uncommon: cf. 'I, in my intricate image'). In that publication, it contained an additional final stanza, presumably on the missing $N5$ page, which was dropped for *18P*.

The poem's rapid leaps in narrative and subject would accord with a quasi-collage mode of assembly, although much critical ink has been spilled in trying to harmonise its components. Olson (1954), for example, claims that its speaker is 'the secret child' of the final stanza, a 'mask' for the Thomas hero, with the poem's 'pseudo-drama' a debate between parts of the self. Rather than the 'unborn devil' and 'burning fork' of stanza 10 being satanic, however, it is likelier that it is a tricksterish principle, related to the 'dog among the fairies' of 'Altarwise' I, evading heaven's self-righteous spies and 'gossip'.

20 **the wild pigs' wood** = cf. $N3$ 'Thirty Eight': 'This is remembered: the winy wood / Where a wild pig sprang on its mate'. 22 **from** = $N5$ has 'in'. 24 **arterial angel** = 'an image of regenerated man, "arterial" suggesting organic or human and "angel" divine . . . a reference to the Jordan identifies him as Christ' (Hornick, 1958). 25 **What colour is glory?** = Thomas's friend Bert Trick described an occasion on which his young daughter asked this question of Thomas, who, the story implies, saved it for his poem. But cf. D. H. Lawrence's *Apocalypse* (1930), chapter XVI, a key intertext for Thomas's early poetry, which offers an answer and a source for the phrase: 'This, this vivid gold-red was the first colour of the dragon, far, far back under the very dawn of history . . . Ah then the heroes and the hero-kings glowed in the

face red as poppies that the sun shines through. It was the colour of glory; it was the colour of the wild bright blood, which was life itself. The red, racing bright blood, that was the supreme mystery: the slow, purplish, oozing dark blood, the royal mystery' (my emphasis). 31 **pyramid . . . padded mummer** = in Richard Aldington's poem 'A Fool i'the Forest', the narrator declares his hatred for a character called the Conjuror, 'So massively stupid, so pyramidally ignorant, / A symbol of the non-perceptive mind . . . Padded against the shock and stab of truth / With centuries of crusted humbugs.' 36 **parhelion** = cf. note to 'The Mouse and the Woman' and the letter to Pamela Hansford Johnson of November 1933: "There is a beautiful winter sun outside, and by my side the oil-stove shines like a blood parhelion.' 38 **rattled** = *N5* has 'rattles'. 42 **Eloi** = *N5* has 'Eli'. 46–8 **Who seek me landward . . . Atlantic corn** = the Christ-Everyman figure is here also identified with Osiris and Attis, according to Hornick. 50 **On** = *N5* has 'In'.

Especially when the October wind

The late 1932 typescript version was revised in mid 1934 and copied into *N5* as 'Four', dated 'October. 1. '34'.

The poem recalls Stephen Dedalus's meditations on Sandymount strand in the Proteus chapter of *Ulysses*: 'Signatures of all things I am here to read, seaspawn and seawrack, the nearing tide, that rusty boot.' Its speaker, a version of Thomas himself, anxiously considers the extent of his absorption in language, and the degree to which this leads him to see the world in terms of words.

As Harri Roberts (2009) argues, 'Thomas's response to the hollowness of symbolic convention and patriarchal law . . . is not to retreat from language but to engage with it ever more intensely, investing in the materiality of words in a way which aspires to transform them into *things* and so make words *real* and the real *speak*.' Objects signify in a way inseparable from their physical presence (their 'neural meaning'), nor can words simply stand in for them. The final images of a 'coming fury' and 'dark-vowelled birds' refer on the realist level to winter; in their historical context, however, they are ominously apocalyptic and presage war.

1 **Especially . . . October** = 'November' in the 1932 BL MS. 3 **crabbing** = 'miserly [but] its light is sharp enough to cast the poet's crab-like shadow' (Davies, 1985). Cf. *Hamlet*, 2:ii, 205–6: 'for you yourself, sir, should be old as I am – if, like a crab, you could go backward'. 6 **sticks** = Glyn Jones in *The Dragon Has Two Tongues* surmises a link with The Sticks, a grove in Llanstephan mentioned in 'A Visit to Grandpa's'. 9 **Shut, too, in a tower of words** = cf. 'The Orchards', in which 'the word is too much with us' and a pencil is a 'wordy tower' and 'Ears in the turrets hear'. 10 **walking like the trees** = cf. 'The Enemies': 'And the trees walked like men.' 12 **star-gestured children in the park** = may refer to children from the local Deaf Institute signing in Cwmdonkin Park; cf. 'Then was my neophyte'. 13–15 **vowelled beeches . . . oaken voices . . . thorny shire** = for the Welsh tree alphabet, which includes these three trees, cf. 'Altarwise' VII; *bech* (beech), the OE root of 'bechen', was an early form of the word 'book; the thorn was used to make the mock-crown of Christ, the Logos, or Word, of John 1:1. In each case, word and world intermingle. Given the littoral location of the poem, a pun on 'beaches' cannot be ruled out. 16 **water's speeches** = cf. *As You Like It*, 2:2:16–17: 'tongues in trees, books in the running brooks.' Cf. 'Over Sir John's hill', ll. 23–6. 23 **Breaks . . . through the eye** = cf. 'Light breaks where no sun shines', 'The secret of the soil grows through the eye.' 26 **spells** = *N5* has 'meaning spells'.

I dreamed my genesis

N5 'Five', dated '1934', so dating in its final form to October 1934. Conjectured by Maud (1967) to derive from *N3* 'Two'. Cf. *CP14*, p. 274.

The lines Thomas quoted to Pamela Hansford Johnson in his letter of 9 May 1934 ('I dreamed the genesis of mildew John / Who struggled from his spiders in the grave') resemble those found in a draft in one of the 'Walter Bram' exercise books at Austin, which appear to be the germ of the poem:

I dreamed your genesis in sweat of sleep
Breaking from the dark and rotating shell,
From limbs that had the worm upon the shuffle
Let off the creaking flesh.

The working notes with these lines show Thomas in the process of turning it into the syllabic poem of *18P*, and an adjoining page contains the draft of the letter to Hamish Miles describing 'I dreamed my genesis' as 'more or less based on Welsh rhythms.' (The two other poems Thomas says he would enclose with this one were probably 'In the beginning' and 'I fellowed sleep'.) In the classic study of the subject, Katharine Loesch (1982) shows how Thomas adapts the Welsh *englyn* form and pararhymes stressed and unstressed terminal syllables of the first and second lines of each stanza, another technique from Welsh medieval poetry. While it is important to not read too much into resemblances between Thomas's verbal patternings and the twenty-four forms of Welsh *cynghanedd* – they occur in English language poetry where no knowledge of them can reasonably be attributed – their prevalence in his case is too high to be coincidental. Mererid Hopwood (2004) lists examples of three types (also given by T. James Jones (in Hannah Ellis, 2014) in his discussion of translating Thomas into Welsh):

Cynghanedd sain gadwynog = 'Where blew a flower may a flower no more'; 'Weighed in rock shroud is my proud pyramid'.
Cynghanedd draws = 'My world was christened in a stream of milk'; 'Do not go gentle into that good night'; 'Nor heed my craft or art'; 'Though I sang in my chains like the sea'; 'Though the town below lay leaved with October blood'.
Cynghanedd sain = 'When the morning was waking over the war'; 'To the burn and turn of time'; 'Oh as I was young and easy in the mercy of his means'.

In *N5* 'Five', which postdates this phase of the writing, there is an additional stanza, previously unknown, following what is now stanza 2:

All that I owe the fellows of the grave, agents
Of the estated dust, glints
In my rich stream, the will of blood, fortune
In flesh of the provided gut.

This can be compared with the unpublished *N4* 'Twenty Seven',
described by Maud (1968) as 'probably . . . a first draft', which runs:
'All that I owe the fellows of the grave / And all the dead bequeathe
from pale estates / Lies in the fortuned bone, the flask of blood.'
'Twenty Seven' also supplies the opening line of the third stanza
of the final version ('Heir to the scalding veins that hold love's
drop').

In the poem's narrative we may discern a disguised sexual dream
followed by a second, more obvious one, ending in emission. But the
interweaving of other material makes this a complex narrative, best
summed up by Hornick (1958): 'I, in an apocalyptic vision, beheld
(1) the miracle of genesis through sexual union, (2) the miraculous
resurrection of new life from corrupt and dying flesh.'

7–8 **irons in the grass, metal / Of suns** = the admonitions of Isaiah
40:6 and the Burial Service in *The Book of Common Prayer* that 'all
flesh is grass', understood in the light of modern physics. Cf. Sir
Thomas Browne, *Religio Medici*, I:37: '*All flesh is grasse*, is not onely
metaphorically, but literally true, for all those creatures we behold,
are but the hearbs of the field, digested into flesh in them, or more
remotely carnified in our selves'. 10 *N5* has a comma after 'bones';
this matches an equivalent caesura in the other stanzas, and is restored
in the 2016 edition of *CP14*. 17, 21–3, 25–6 **my second death . . .
second / Rise of the skeleton . . . fallen / Twice** = cf. 'After the first
death, there is no other', 'A Refusal to Mourn'. For M. Wynn Thomas
(in Ellis, 2014), reading the poem in the light of Unitarian influence
on Thomas, these lines are the point at which its 'tracking and enacting
[of] the difficult emergence of authentic utterance out of the stifling
grip of verbal habit and deadening convention' is revealed as 'a two-
stage process, the original "nativity" being followed by a "death" that
is eventually conquered by the resurrection of this second Adam into
fullness of life itself'.

I fellowed sleep who kissed me in the brain

N5 'Six', where it is dated simply '1934', but falls between poems dated '1 October' and '26 October'. There are four small differences with the published version, three involving a shift from singular to the plural forms that are one of the more intriguing features of the published version.

The earlier version of the poem, *N4* 'Twenty Two', describes the speaker's ascent 'towards a plane / Set near the stars' where 'the pulse of God / Hammered within the circling roads of fire', and 'the song of God' is 'the singing core'. From it, he observes 'all the laws of heaven / and the mysterious order of the Lord', including meteors, moon and sun. The 'ghostly other', the interlocutor of stanzas 2 and 3 of the later, published version, is also more starkly a 'black ghost' in this original, with a 'mouth of darkness' and 'kiss of death'. In rewriting it, Thomas adapted the opening line of *N4* 'Thirty One' ('I fellowed sleep who kissed between the brain'), and removed its Christian aspect, although the verbal exchanges were scarcely altered (stanza 3 is almost word-for-word stanza 4 of 'Twenty Two').

If 'Twenty Two' recalls the treatment of the religious impulse in 'And Death Shall Have No Dominion', 'I fellowed sleep who kissed me in the brain' stands in a similar relationship to such auto-erotic lyrics as 'My hero bares his nerves'. Both merge the realms of sleep, dreams, death and genetics, and have a vision of the cosmos; this may be why Thomas merged them, emphasising his process poetic at the expense of the religious vision as he did so. Thus, 'ghost' gained more of the sense it has in 'A process in the weather of the heart', and there is an allusion to Darwin. At the same time, the tussle between maternal and paternal aspects of the self noted by Moynihan (1966) remained as a psychodrama. Thus, in stanza 3 the speaker learns from an 'elbow ghost' (the 'black ghost' of *N4* 'Twenty Two') that although his 'father's globe' is below him, he is still in his 'fathers' land'; he leaves it and dismisses the 'dreaming men' / 'angelic gangs', though what he ends up with nevertheless messily combines paternal and maternal, as the oxymoronic 'soily star' and 'worlded clouds' of stanza 5 reveal. Perhaps the 'voice' of the 'living air', the paradoxical nature of language (and by extension, poetry), at once material sounds and abstract sign system, is the one thing which can negotiate the difference between these two realms. Whatever, the final stanza seems to show the price of denying the maternal realm.

The poem is discussed by Korg (1965) and James A. Davies (1998), with Davies finding in 'climbing on the words' a description of provincial escape 'represented by [Thomas's] mother. What he cannot escape is the "'fathers' ghost' of [paternal] literary influence.' Geoffrey Thurley (1974), more imaginatively, discovers 'the Delphic utterances of a Cocteau' in Thomas's 'most deftly ungraspable Surrealist piece', recalling 'the dream scenes of de Chirico and Chagall, with a Celtic fluency of movement'.

4 **'planing-heeled** = echoing the use in *N4* 'Twenty Two' of 'plane' as a flat surface (it means 'aeroplane' here). *CP52* dropped the inverted comma of *18P*; I restore it, following *CP88* **flew along my man** = for an internal or projected self see also 'When once the twilight locks', 'I, in my intricate image' and 'My world is pyramid' (perhaps echoed in Frank O'Hara's 'In Memory of My Feelings': 'My quietness has a man in it, he is transparent / and he carries me quietly, like a gondola, through the streets. / He has several likenesses'. O'Hara was a fan of Thomas's early poetry). 9 **My mothers-eyed** = *N5* has 'All mother-eyed', with 'All' replacing crossed-out 'My'. 11 **My fathers' globe knocks on its nave and sings** = *N5* has singular possessive apostrophe of 'father's' crossed out and replaced with plural possessive apostrophe. This line is cited by Christina Brook-Rose in *The Grammar of Metaphor* as an example of metaphorical over-extension. 'Globe' means 'world', however, and the items are linked by analogy, pun and intertextual linkage. A 'globe' is generated from a circle, or wheel, and a 'nave' is a wheel-hub. 'Nave' is found with 'felloe' (punned on in l. 1) and other wheel imagery in *Hamlet*, 2. ii. ll. 496–9: 'Out, out, thou strumpet Fortune! . . . Break all the spokes and felloes from her wheel / And bowl the round nave down the hill of heaven / As low as to the fiends!' Cf. 'From love's first fever', l. 23, for 'nave'. 16 **mothers** = *N5* has 'mother'. 30 **My fathers' ghost is climbing in the rain** = *N5* has 'father's'. Smith (2001) notes: 'the image of the human subject as some kind of ghost, so frequent in these poems, is ubiquitous in early Auden, quintessentially so in the verse-charade from *Poems*, "Paid on Both Sides", which sees each new-born son as a "new ghost" inserted into the patriarchal culture, "Learn[ing] from old timers what death is, where".'

When, like a running grave

N5 'Seven', dated '26 October 1934'. The *N5* date confirms previous speculation that this is the poem 'of fifty lines so far' mentioned to Pamela Hansford Johnson in a letter of late October 1934. Thomas told Frederic Prokosch he considered it and 'I see the boys of summer' the best poems in *18P*, but it is more turbid and verbally resistant to paraphrase than the latter (*CL*, 235). The opening of the poem is frequently cited in order to illustrate Thomas's surrealism, while David Aivaz (1950), whose pioneering close reading runs as far as stanza 5, takes the poem as a whole to be exemplary of Thomas's 'dialectical method'. However, most critics have avoided it; the usually exemplary Kershner (1976) has just one reference, while Maud (2003) also throws in the towel at stanza 5. Only Clark Emery (1962) and George P. Weick (2004) explicate the whole poem, although there are limited analyses by Rushworth M. Kidder (1973) and Michael Neill (1970).

3 **gear** = as 'clothes' prompts 'naked' in l. 4. 5 **dome** = 'love moves, as if in a funeral procession, from the loins to the head' (Weick, 2004). 6 **like a scissors stalking, tailor age** – Smith (2001) argues that the line 'echoes the cadences of early Auden', who used *Struwwelpeter* in 'The Witnesses', published in *The Listener* in July 1933: 'And now . . . Come the women in dark glasses, the hump-backed surgeons / And the scissor-man.' Cf. 'Twenty-four years', 'Once below a time'. 8 **Cadaver** = a political piece by Thomas for the *Swansea and West Wales Guardian* (6 July 1934) quotes Richard Aldington's *The Fool i' the Forest*, in which hell is the 'heaven of the capitalist': 'It was like a crematorium / Or rather a Kadaver-factory / Where every day / Millions of persons were consumed to . . . black greasy smoke / That whitened to a cloud of banknotes'; **trap** = mouth; snare. 9 **footed tape** = a tape-measure trails from the Scissorman's pocket in *Struwwelpeter*. 12 *N5* has dashes after 'heart' and 'thin', rather than commas; **Cadaver's candle** = cf. 'Light breaks' for candle as penis. 16 **sunday faced** = perhaps idiomatic or proverbial; but see George Meredith's 'The Old Chartist': 'Pray . . . wear a Sunday face'. 31 **sir and madam** = cf. the refrain 'Sir or Madam' in Thomas Hardy's 'Voices from Things Grow-ing in a Graveyard'. 34 **subway bored to foster** = *N5* has 'subway burrowed for the'. 36, 41–5 **tower dome, the tower ending . . .**

leaning scene . . . The actions' end = the 'waxlights' of 'head' and 'heart' are extinguished, but the pun on 'wax' makes this ambiguous. Smith suggests a reworking of the closing lines of 'the most Germanically convoluted of all Auden's *Poems* (1933), "Doom is darker and deeper than any sea-dingle", also about a doomed man on the run': 'Bring joy, bring day of his returning, / Lucky with day approaching, with leaning dawn.' 42, 44 *N5* has commas after 'wind' and 'over', not brackets.

Should lanterns shine

There is no surviving MS for this poem, but the two other poems it appeared with in *New Verse* in December 1935 ('I have longed to move away' and 'The hand that signed the paper'), suggest it may have originated in the missing notebook of July 1932–January 1933, or in *N3* (e.g. the torn-out 'Fifteen' of March 1933). Given its likely date of rewriting and completion in mid or late1934, a fair copy of it could have been written on one of the two pages cut from *N5*. Paul Ferris speculates that it was among those sent to *New Verse* in early November 1934; Thomas's accompanying note to Grigson – 'Do you think it would be better if the enclosed poem were not divided into stanzas? I've tried it that way, but it seemed more obscure.' – does not fit other Thomas poems Grigson was then considering.

Now

N5 'Eight', dated 'December '34', where the first three stanzas have an additional line (eight rather than seven; Thomas seems to have been transcribing an original with eight-line stanzas, but decided to eliminate their last lines at this point; as elsewhere in *N5* the labours of transcription and composition are entangled).

Some critics accept Thomas's claim (made to Vernon Watkins) that this poem 'meant nothing', as far as he knew, and refer to Trevor Hughes's memoir, held in Buffalo:

We had, at one time, been delighted with a burlesque of Gertrude Stein's work which appeared in *The New Statesman*:

There was a young was a young *Was*,
Not *Is*, and not *Will Be*, because . . .

And when, in the tavern, Dylan showed me the manuscript of his poem 'Now', and I read:

Now
Say nay,
Death to the yes . . .

There remained, obviously, only one thing to say: "There was a young was a young *Was*' – a criticism which he accepted with such humour as to persuade me that he had written this poem with little serious intent.

It is with this in mind that 'Now' is described by Davies and Maud in *CP88* as:

the poem in which Thomas pays his greatest tribute to words in themselves, paying such fanatical attention to them in the way they weight a line that referential meaning is ultimately lost in the presentational. The stubborn clarity of repeating the same three words . . . (and thus giving that much theme to the poem) is matched by a stubborn refusal to provide normal syntax . . . Its significance comes from its form and its insistence on form.

But this is to give up too easily. Stein's 'nonsense' always had a purpose, and comments of the kind Thomas made to Watkins were often tailored to his listener's prejudices. As Emery (1962) more accurately observes: 'Since in this poem every Nay opposes a negative or defeatist point of view, it states qualifiedly though gaily Thomas's everlasting Yea'. The details of the scenario, or narrative, are obscure, but there is a shift from near-suicidal introspection, through a rejection of morbidity, to an embrace of the (inevitably failing) universe of process – the 'come-a-cropper rider of the flower' – and a saving sense of unity with process; the movement from the 'dry man' of stanza 1 to the relational self of stanza 5, conveyed (as in 'Ceremony After a Fire Raid') through deliberate confusion of first person singular and plural: 'We make me mystic'.

Thomas once assured Pamela Hansford Johnson that: 'I'm not an experimentalist & never will be. I write in the only way I can write, & my warped, crabbed & cabined stuff is not the result of theorising but of pure incapability to express my needless tortuosities in any other way' (*CL*, 160). But it all depends on what Thomas meant by 'experimentalist', as Goodby (2013) notes. 'A Letter to my Aunt' shows Thomas's respect for experimental modernist writers to be tinged with mockery, but he revered many of them and learnt from them. 'Now' undeniably displays Thomas's love of pure 'sound of shape', yet its syntax *can* be unravelled, and its strange appearance disappears when it is folded up (add the first four lines together to turn each stanza into a standard quatrain). It is, in fact, a jokey fusion of apparent experiment with covert conventionality, and in this sense, it mocks the conventions of traditionalist tameness *and* what Thomas regarded as the pretensions of the avant-garde.

5 **blow the flowered** = *N5* has 'break the buried'. 6 **for** = *N5* has 'who had'. 7 Following current l. 7, stanza 1 in *N5* has the additional line: 'Draw dress on gristle with a cotton fist'. 14 Have = *N5* has 'And', deleted and replaced with ''Have'. 14 Following current l. 14, stanza 2 in *N5* has the additional line: 'Share bone of blood, and medicine the eye.' 19–20 **And this . . . in his ear** = these lines are deleted in *N5* and then rewritten, unchanged, beneath the stanza. 21 **fire** = followed by a comma in *N5*, where it is deleted then rewritten unchanged above the deletion; following current l. 21, stanza 3 has the additional line: 'No master the unarguable crew'. 25, 34 **mystic sun, we make me mystic** = 'mystic' is a key word, and with the pun on sun / (S)son indicates Thomas's belief that process has the same status and force as a religious. 28, 35 **come-a-cropper, two-a-vein** = no hyphens in *N5*.

How soon the servant sun

N5 'Nine', dated 'January '35', and much-revised. The *N5* version disproves the guess by Davies and Maud (1988) that it was composed at Disley in April/May 1935 on the strength of the fact that Thomas forwarded it via A. J. P. (Alan) Taylor to the Oxford journal *Programme*. However, like 'Now', its experimental twin, this poem may well have been taken to Disley and revised there. Making the staid and disapproving Taylor a conduit for one of his two most bizarre-seeming poems would certainly have appealed to Thomas's sense of mischief.

Davies and Maud rightly note the 'careful eccentricity' in 'five intricately rhymed and shaped stanzas' of seven lines, six in the final stanza. Its 'taut, tight form is illustrative of his virtues as a technician', as Nicholas Moore (1948) concedes, and a quirky, growth-in-decay narrative is noted by Moore, Emery (1962) and Maud (2003).

1 **How soon** = as soon as. 3–4 **cupboard stone . . . bone** – as Moore remarks, 'for all its gristly metaphors and sinewy explorations of the familiar identification theme [the poem] reminds one pleasantly of Old Mother Hubbard and Humpty Dumpty'. 4–5 **Fog . . . into meat** = 'Fog' rhymes with 'dog', to strengthen the hint of 'Old Mother Hubbard'. 10 In *N5* this line is an interlinear substitute for an indecipherably deleted line; **cut** = *N5* has 'grave'. 17, 21 **A claw . . . the mouse's bone . . . long-tailed stone . . . the soil squeal . . . the velvet dead inch out** = for mice as Freudian images of sexual threat, see 'The Mouse and the Woman', in which a writer's breakdown is precipitated by a mouse scratching behind a skirting-board: 'nothing on earth could save him, and . . . the mouse would come out . . . working its destruction [it] inched into the light.' 18, 32 **long-tailed, womb-eyed** = epithets unhyphenated in *N5*. 22–35 The syntax is convoluted: perhaps 'This inward sir, the penis, cries: "As soon as I can, on my lower level, do what the sun does on his more exalted one, creating life in the shroud-like flesh, I shall"'. 30–2 **This inward sir . . . womb-eyed** = euphemisms and epithets for the penis. 32 **cries** = the subject of the verb may be any of the penis euphemisms; 'the stump / A leg' is probably the best candidate.

A grief ago

N5 'Ten', dated 'January '35'. Mistakenly submitted to *Life & Letters* as well as *Programme,* Thomas had to find a replacement poem for the first journal (this was 'Altarwise', which he had already submitted to *Purpose*).

Although it deals with sexual determinism, the poem exudes a melancholy tenderness and tentatively explores the nature of the lover as other, and the emotional fall-out from the sexual act.

1 **grief** = cf. Ovid: 'post coitum omnia animale tristis est' / 'after copulation all creatures are sad'. 2 **flower** = pun on 'flour', to give two of the chief ingredients of bread, and so perhaps 'bun in the oven' (slang for pregnant). 2, 9, 13, 17, 25 **She who . . . Who is my grief . . . Was who was . . . she who lies . . . Who then is she . . .?** = cf. *Ulysses*, 'Proteus': 'She, she, she. What she? . . . She lives in Leeson park, with a grief'. 5 **cement** = probably with pun on 'semen'; blatantly sexual images outcrop the generally euphemistic representations of sex, mimicking the workings of the unconscious in Freud's account. 7 **masted venus** = in Thomas's favourite painting, Botticelli's 'The Birth of Venus', the goddess stands, mast-like, in the centre of a sea-borne scallop shell. 11–12 **leaden bud / Shot through the leaf** = Parkinson (1981) notes the yoking of 'ironmongery' with vegetable imagery throughout stanza 1. 22–4 **On field and sand . . . engraving going** = the puffing cherubs and triangular points of a compass rose are a favourite image: cf. the story 'The Map of Love': 'Here, said Sam Rib, two weathers move. He traced with his finger the lightly drawn triangles of two winds, and the mouths of two cornered cherubs.' 26 **The people's sea drives on her** = in addition to the genetic dimension, there is a political suggestion that women's greater role in creating children makes them more at one with 'the people', the masses, and more deeply involved in the future of humanity. 29 **Shape . . . veins of water** = *N5* has 'Shape all her whelps with howling like a water'. 32 **before** = *N5* and Austin MS has 'ere the'. 34 **nitric acid** = used in embalming by undertakers. 39 **So cross . . . eyes** = *N5* has 'So cross her hand through their dead mortal eyes' ('through' crossed out and 'with' written above). 40 **close** = in *N5* this is added below crossed-out 'shut'.

Hold hard these ancient minutes

N5 'Thirteen', dated and located 'April '35 (Cheshire)', and thus copied up at A. J. P. and Margaret Taylor's cottage at Disley. The place of composition (in England) may shed light on the use of proper names, the class and national *frisson* of élite sports (hunting, game shooting, hawking) and the Wales / England dichotomy (Fitzgibbon (1966) may have exaggerated in calling this a 'patriotic poem', but there is more than a grain of truth in it). The 'children', 'men' and 'birds' may also be poems; elicited by 'Time', yet threatened by it, they are urged to 'hold hard . . . in the world of tales', to the 'summer's game' of play; to go with time's flow, knowing they may bring down the 'lank folly's hunter' of the literary world, and be brought down themselves. More important, the seasonal confusion of 'Hold hard' (fox hunting is a winter sport, but co-exists here with spring, 'summer's game' and 'seedy trees') exemplifies the language 'games' of the process poetic, the poem seemingly designed as a context for 'rider rising', 'count(r)y', 'tales' / 'tail', 'fourth' / 'forth', puns on 'vault', 'folly' 'sport', 'spring', 'seedy', 'deer', and so on. These generate rather than serve narrative, in an experiment in how an abstract yet affective complex of words and images – a 'sound of shape' – may become a poem. Cf. Thomas's letter to Glyn Jones of March 1934: 'Narrative in its widest sense satisfies what Eliot, talking of "meaning", calls "one habit of the reader". Let the narrative take that one logical habit of the reader along with its movement, and the essence of the poem will do its work on him' (*CL*, 121). The phrase 'hold hard' occurs with a sexual sense ('hard' as in erection) in Thomas's early writing: cf. the exchange between Jarvis and Beth Rib and Reuben in 'The Map of Love': 'Hold hard. I'll hold you harder. Said a voice, Hold hard, the children of love.'

1 **ancient minutes** = of Thomas's Swansea youth, just a year or two in the past, but now as distant as ancient history. 4 **a folly's rider** = huntsmen often orientate themselves during a hunt by means of a local folly or church spire (cf. 'steepled season', l. 12). 11 **greenwood** = two words in *N5*. 14 **sound of shape** = cf. 'Prologue to an Adventure': 'We are all metaphors of the sound of shape of the shape of sound, break us we take another shape'; 'Altarwise', VII: 'Time tracks the

sound of shape'. 17 **Crack like a spring in a vice, bone-breaking April** = man-traps, used to enforce the notorious Game Laws (banned in 1827); poachers, their victims were the social obverse of the fox-hunting landowners, featured in this poem, who set them. 21 **harnessed** = 'sniper's' in *N5*. 22 **county** = 'county's' in *N5*.

I, in my intricate image

The three sections of 'I, in my intricate image' are numbered as separate poems in *N5*; 'Eleven' (part I); 'Twelve' (part II) and 'Fourteen' (part III). 'I' is dated 'February 1935', and is prefaced by its numeral as if it is already understood to be the first instalment of a multi-part poem. This is borne out by the dating of 'II', 'March '35', and the fact that the numeral 'II', which prefaces it, is written in the same ink as the poem that follows. 'III', however, is initially presented simply as 'Fourteen', without a numeral, and consists of the first three stanzas of part III. On the next page the same three stanzas, prefaced again by 'Fourteen', are written in ink, located and dated '(Disley, May)' and dedicated to the Taylors '(To A & M)' whose guest he was at Disley in April–May 1935. The next page of N5 contains stanzas 4 and 5 of part III in pencil; the next by the same stanzas in ink, with the second of them (i.e. beginning 'Man was the scales') crossed out and rewritten below. On a separate page following this, stanza 6 is written in ink, dated and located 'July '35. Glen Lough'. All three poem-sections are much-revised.

The evidence suggests that Thomas wrote parts I and II of the poem, intending them to be a single item, in London in January–March 1935. In Disley, in April 1935, after entering 'Hold hard, these ancient minutes' in *N5*, he began a continuation of 'I, in my intricate image', entering a three-stanza pencil draft and a fair-copy in ink. Either at Disley or immediately afterwards he drafted stanzas 4 and 5 in pencil, revising them, in ink, probably in Glen Lough, when he also added the last (sixth) stanza of this final section of the poem. The poem's composite origin was reflected in its title in the August–September 1935 issue of *New Verse*, 'A Poem in Three Parts'.

Thomas chose to open *25P* with 'I, in my intricate image', as a *summum* of the creative outpouring of 1933–5, just as he closed the

volume with the equally ambitious 'Altarwise by owl-light'. Yet, while
Alan Young (1975) finds it to be 'one of the most complex and powerfully sustained achievements in modern poetry', its difficulty – unlike
that of 'Altarwise' – has deterred interpreters. Maud (2003), for example,
admits defeat and commends his readers to the 'greater fortitude' of
Emery (1962) and Korg (1965). There is a consensus on some basic
points, however: influenced, it may be, by the ideas of Carl Jung,
Hornick (1958), Tindall (1962), Emery and Korg discern a narrative
of growth, voyaging, and symbolic death by drowning followed by
rebirth, while Young finds 'a quest for self-hood [and] for the secret
of all natural life'. The poem accommodates both interpretations. In
addition, Morgan (1989), Crehan (1990) and James A. Davies (1997)
trace a narrative of Freudian Oedipal revolt, finding Thomas's relationship with D. J. Thomas figured in the Shakespearian allusions of part
III.

The tripartite form is loosely that of the Hegelian-Marxist dialectical
triad of thesis, antithesis and synthesis, as in 'All all and all', with the
helical narrative progression hinted at in terms such as 'spiral' and
'corkscrew'.

1–6 Morgan (1989) finds the twin world of the creative mind set out
here. 2 **brassy orator** = cf. Corinthians 13:1: 'Though I speak to you
with the tongues of men and of angels, and have not charity, I am
become as sounding brass, or a tinkling cymbal'. Smith (2000) detects
Auden's *The Orators* and the 'communist orator' of 'The chimneys
are smoking', who lands 'like a sea-god' at the pier, in a welter of
sub-Hopkinsian inversions . . . [the poem] also develops the theme
of striding to a doom.' 5 **My half ghost in armour** = in 1934 Thomas
told Pamela Hansford Johnson of 'the everyday armour' in which 'the
self, even the wounded self, is hidden from so many. If I pull down
the metals, don't shoot, dear. Not even with a smile' (*CL*, 133). 6
sidle = noun; 'sidling action' (punning on 'side'), from Whitman's
'Song of Myself', where sunset is 'the sidle of evening' (Goodby, 2005).
9–12 in *N5* these four lines are deleted beyond deciphering, and
replaced interlinearly with those of the published version. 15 **harebell**
= flower; organic-metal collocation; hare (animal), bell (cast in metal).
19 **manhood** = replaces indecipherable deleted word in *N5*. 23
shadowless man or ox, and the pictured devil = as well as Von

Chamisso's *Peter Schlemihl* (for which Thomas wrote a film treatment in 1947, *The Man Without a Shadow*), this may allude to the minotaur illustrations by Picasso featuring on the cover of the journal *Minotaure* (Young 1975). Nebuchadnezzar also 'did eat grass as oxen' (Daniel, 4:25, 32, 33), and there may be an echo of the 'valley of the shadow of death' (Psalm 23). 23 **parallel** = replaces deleted word (possibly 'peril' or 'pencil') in *N5*. 25–30, 37–42 shifts of scale and perspective interested Thomas; writing to Johnson in December 1933, he observed:

> Walking, as we do, at right angles with the earth, we are prevented from looking, as much as we should, at the legendary sky above us and the only-a-little-bit-more-possible ground under us . . . We see what we imagine to be a tree, but we see only a part of the tree; what the insects under the earth see when they look upwards at the tree, & what the stars see when they look downwards at the tree, is left to our imagination . . . Think how much wiser we would be if it were possible for us to change our angles of perspective as regularly as we change our vests. (*CL*, 99–100)

26 **green steps and spire** = cf. Marvell's 'Upon Appleton House': 'And now to the abyss I pass / Of that unfathomable grass / Where men like grasshoppers appear . . . And, from the precipices tall / Of the green spires, to us do call.' 30 **weather fall** = perhaps an insect's perception of rain; 'fall' sounds like a barometer foretelling bad weather, but one would see, not 'hear' this. 36 in *N5* this line is 'They walk the globe of grass'. 38 **host at pasture** = suggests a flock of sheep, or still-growing wheat for the eucharist, but also the 'parasite-ridden flesh' (Young 1975). 40–1 **squirrel stumble . . . haring snail** = oxymorons. 44 **Cadaverous gravels** = cf. 'When, like a running grave'. *CP88* has upper case 'c', but the word is an adjective, based on 'Cadaver' (l. 103), and I restore the lower case of *18P* and *CP52*. 47 **petrol face** = 'implacably opaque' for Bayley (1957), but a typical Thomas organic-inorganic collocation. 64 *N5* deletes 'the', with 'a' interlineated above. 65 **whale-weed** = two separate words in *N5*. 80 **bodiless, stick of folly** = *N5* (3-stanza pencil version) has 'denseless' and 'staff of life'. 81–4 *N5* (3-stanza pencil version) has these lines, deleted but not replaced:

Salvation's bottle
Is half glass, half metal;
Be by your one quaff staggered to the pale of death,
Skating the ice that quarrels with the watered cordial.

83–4 And the five-fathomed Hamlet ... the iron mile = *N5* second (ink) version has these lines in reverse order. Cf. Ariel's song in *The Tempest*, via *The Waste Land*: 'Full fathom five thy father lies. / Of his bones are coral made'. Oedipal anxieties are further dramatised by pun; enclosing 'corral' (l. 39) has become beautiful 'coral'. 92 **nicked** = *N5* has 'locked', deleted and replaced (reversing the terms of the cliché). 93, 95 **My, I** = *N5* has 'His' and 'He'. 96 **the crocodile** = Egyptian properties figure similar rebirths elsewhere, e.g. 'Altarwise' IX. 'Crocodile' seems, more generally, to symbolise the armoured self, incapable of empathy or imaginative flight, which it requires a mortal struggle to overcome. 98 **saddler of the rushes** = *N5* has 'straddler of the floods', deleted with final version interlineated above. 99–102 *N5* pencil and ink drafts have the following deleted lines, with 99–101 replaced by the final versions:

Buckling the glass-backed saddle
Time in an hourless house shakes out the skull,
All-hollowed man shrieks for his shifted hide,
Suffer the maul of images on one level.

105–8 **My, my** = *N5* pencil draft 'His', 'he'.

Incarnate devil

N3 'Thirty', titled 'Before we Sinned', of 16 May 1933; *N5* 'Fifteen', dated and located 'July 24. '35', 'Glen Lough', extensively revised. An autograph version of the first two stanzas, plus four lines of the third stanza, exists in MS at Austin, and seems to have been the basis for the *N5* version. Stanza 2 in the Austin and unrevised *N5* versions runs:

When storms struck on the tree, the flying stars
And the half moon half handed in a cloud
Spread good and evil till the fancy fears
All in a fret of weathers made a word,
And when the moon came rose silently windily she was
Half white as wool and greener than the grass.

The stanza is deleted in *N5* and the published version interlineated. The Austin and unrevised *N5* versions of stanza 3 have 'eastern' for 'secret' (l. 13), 'golden' for 'secret' (l. 14), and 'our time that tumbled from the earth' for 'the mighty mornings of the earth' (l. 15). Austin begins l. 16 with 'He', not 'Hell'.

The subject of this poem reflects comments of the kind Thomas made to Trevor Hughes in spring 1934: 'God was deposed years ago before the loin-cloth in the garden. Now the Old Boy reigns with a red-hot pincers for a penis. Here's to him' (*CL*, 145). As in 'Before I knocked', Thomas foregrounds the contradiction of a God who claims to be merciful, but punishes man for his own negligence, a bigger fiddler than the Devil in a plan that involves damning humanity and then engineering its redemption by sacrificing his son. For Aivaz (1950) the poem is, with 'This side of the truth', one of only two by Thomas in which 'morality is a theme', that is, in which it is directly asserted that good and evil are human inventions; elsewhere it is simply assumed. Similarly, Emery (1962) claims that 'it is sex . . . that in the shaping-time of adolescence destroys the innocence of childhood. But it is not a devil but a bearded, Thou-Shalt-Notting Jehovah (invented by the tabu-makers) who . . . enunciated the false distinction . . . that sexuality is hell and asceticism . . . is heaven. And then, himself to blame for destroying the possibility of innocence in sexuality, is given credit for saving the remorseful sinner from the clutches of the Devil. There is in the poem no devil at all.' McKay (1986) develops this insight by claiming the trickster is 'the presiding deity of Thomas's work', and that in his revision of biblical myth,

> it is the devil who performs the trickster's linking and transmitting function [between gods and mortals]. In 'Incarnate devil' Satan is the initiator (or perpetrator) of time itself, stinging the static circle into wakefulness – a dubious gift, perhaps, but an essential one if

man is to be independent from God, the 'warden' who 'played down
pardon from the heavens hill'. Emphasizing the trickster's role on
cosmogony (rather than introducing him as a belated intruder in
the creation story) . . . [acknowledges] . . . the flawed nature of
existence as part of its essence rather than a later aberration per-
petrated by man; diachronic energy is given a place at least equal
to synchronic design; and creative activity is seen as primarily a
subversive exercise.

Do you not father me

Poem 'Three' in *N5*. Its initial version, dated '30 Sept. '34', consists
of three (not four) stanzas of ten (not eight) lines each. This is the
version which exists also in a typescript among the Pamela Hansford
Johnson papers in Buffalo; Maud (1989) was therefore correct in
surmising that it dated from 'around September 1934'. Stanza 1 of
the September 1934 version is identical to that of *25P*, but has the
additional lines: 'Do you not foster me, nor the hailfellow suck, / The
bread and wine, give for my tower's sake?' Apart from initial 'crested'
for 'directed' in l. 13 (where 'crested' is deleted and replaced by 'directed')
the *N5* and Buffalo stanza 2 is also identical to the *25P* version; its
additional lines run: 'Am I not all of you, nor the hailfellow flesh, /
The fowl of fire and the towering fish?' Stanza 3 in *N5*/Buffalo differs
markedly from *25P*:

This was my tower, sir, where the scaffolded coast
Walls up the hole of winter and the moon.
Master, this was my cross, the tower Christ.
Master the tower Christ, I am your man.
The reservoir of wrath is dry as paste;
Sir, where the cloudbank and the azure ton
Falls in the sea, I clatter from my post
And trip the shifty weathers to your tune.
Now see a tower dance, nor the erected world
Let break your babbling towers in the [his!!!]wind.

What *N5* shows is that, in Donegal in summer 1935, Thomas deleted
ll. 9–10 of the first two stanzas, subjected the third stanza to a more

radical rewriting, and added a fourth stanza, creating the poem as it would be published. After entering the new fourth stanza, on the verso of the page bearing the first two stanzas, he dated and located the revision 'July 26 '35 Glen Lough'. There are some signs of Thomas's working on the fourth stanza; he initially tried out 'tower-docked' before deciding on 'destroying' in l. 25; l.26 begins 'You ~~said seaweedy~~, are your sister's sire'; and he tries out 'withershin world' before coming up with 'widdershin earth' in l. 29.

There are several things to be said about the original stanza 3 and its revision, and about Thomas's decision to reshape and extend the poem generally. The first is that the original version of the poem has its own appeal, and stands in its own right. It nicely complements other poems using a tower as a symbol of authorial isolation, such as 'Ears in the turrets hear' and 'Especially when the October wind', and is rhythmically and verbally inventive (the traditional use of 'tower' for the Cross generates some wordplay, and 'azure ton' puns on 'ton', the Welsh for 'wave', as well as alluding to *The Mabinogion* and Dylan eil Ton ('Dylan, son of the Wave'), the source of Thomas's name). However, it curtails the development of the intriguing set of family relationships set out in stanzas 1 and 2, first as rhetorical questions and then in a series of interrogative assertions in the same form; the leap from a Freudian *mise-en-scène* to a Christian one is too abrupt, and muffles the poem's impact. Thomas responded by making the two-stage narrative a tripartite one, having the speaker's parents (the 'she' and 'he' of ll. 17–18) offer their gnomic advice to his adolescent questionings of stanzas 1 and 2, before moving to a conclusion in stanza 4. The parental responses are intended to reassure, but they are complicated by what the tower 'told' in ll. 21–4, and by the speaker's new questions in stanza 4, questions answered by the less distinct 'seaweedy' and 'they'.

Effectively, Thomas clarifies things by emphasising his role as 'Freudian exemplar' (Crehan, 1990) and playing down the encounter with Christ. Thus, Stan Smith (2000) sees the poem as a case of an 'ultimately Freudian paradigm', in which:

conjugations of consanguinity seem like a deliberate meditation on the dilemma of Oedipus, at once father and sibling of his own children, summarised in the line: 'Am I not father too, and the ascending boy?' Adapting Freud, Thomas sees the new, 'ascending boy' overthrowing but in the process becoming the Old Boy – his future ruin as patriarch, thus latent in his present, neophyte state.

This suggests that the real subject is a crisis of masculinity. Maud (2003) misses this Oedipal dimension, but he does unravel the narrative of phallic-tower-as-Cross, *raised* and *razed*, with innocence 'felled' even as the penis is punningly erected. We might say, then, that the claims of the first two stanzas, and their rather narcissistic self-regard, are overthrown in stanza 3 as the speaker is identified with the phallus, which is then said to be as subject as anything else to the creative-destructive forces of process, while stanza 4 (like part III of 'I see the boys of summer') blurs the distinct identities established earlier in the poem to suggest more hybrid and ambiguous states.

11 **bay** = like 'sea', 'shore', 'seaweed' and 'sand', this detail probably derives from Thomas's Swansea location.   23–4 **For man-begetters . . . rise grimly** = cf. Maud, 2003:

What can the 'ringed-sea ghost' possibly be? Could it be a puddle of sperm – a small round salty residue   a ghost dump? Then 'dry-as-paste' would not be a totally unapt apposition, and 'man-begetters' would be the seed that miraculously are rising 'grimly' (another word for 'ghostly') from the wrack.

The seed-at-zero

N4 'Six', dated 'August 29 33', revised and entered as 'Sixteen' in *N5*, dated '2 August 1935, Glen Lough.' The *N5* version includes two stanzas after the final stanza which were dropped for *25P*:

He must stir before the seed
And before the twilight sleep;
Time exploding in the tide,
He must camouflage the sea,
That the pigeon fill her crop
And the star-flanked eagle fly
With the ~~leaden~~ virgin lamb of god.

He must stir before the seed
And before the ~~twilight~~ star-flanked sleep;
Time exploding in the tide,
He must bare the twilight sea,
That the eagle fill her crop
And the iron pigeon fly
~~Will And~~ With the ~~leaden~~ riddled lamb of god.

The rejected stanzas suggest that Maud (1968) was right to claim this poem 'derived its form and some of its phrasing from *N4* 'Six', 'Shiloh's seed shall not be sown'. In this it is also related to *N4* 'Seven', 'Before I knocked', with all three poems owing something to William Blake's 'On the Virginity of the Virgin Mary & Johanna Southcott': 'Whate'er is done to her she cannot know, / And if you'll ask her she will swear it so. / Whether 'tis good or evil none's to blame; / No one can take the pride, no one the shame.'

Walford Davies (2000) observes that the 'suitably unsettling music' derives from Longfellow's *The Song of Hiawatha*, an epic poem in trochaic tetrameters; just as pronounced is the extensive repetition, resembling the effects created by avant-garde writers such as Gertrude Stein.

2 **trodden** = *N5* has '~~trampled~~ trodden'. 6 **stumbling** = *N5* has '~~leaping~~ stumbling'. 19 **Settled** = *N5* has 'Settling'. 20 He = *N5* has 'They'. 31, 38 **scold** = *N5* has 'scald'. 35, 41 **thirsty** = *N5* has '~~starving~~ thirsty'. 39 **high** = *N5* has '~~bright~~ high'. 51 **star-flanked** = *N5* has '~~foreign~~ star-flanked'.

Foster the light

N4 'Thirty-Six' has the opening line 'Foster then light, nor veil the bushy sun'. It was revised in autumn 1934; in a letter to Pamela Hansford Johnson of ca. 23 October 1934, Thomas refers to it as 'some clumsy poem for the Referee', and with the opening line 'Foster the light, nor veil the feeling moon' it appeared in the *Sunday Referee* on 28 October 1934 (this version is given in Maud, 1989). It was further revised at Glen Lough in Donegal, in August 1935, when

Thomas entered it as 'Eighteen' in *N5*. Sending it to Desmond Hawkins for publication in *Purpose*, on 1 November 1935, he urged him not to use 'Altarwise', which he had also submitted, but rather to 'for sweet Christ's sake use the one beginning Foster the Light, nor veil the cunt-shaped moon' (*CL*, 230). It was further revised for *Contemporary Poetry and Prose*, in May 1936.

As Davies and Maud (1988) note, Thomas based the poem on the farewell in his friend Trevor Hughes's letter to him of January 1935 ('Foster the light, and God be with you'). Hardy (2000), however, sees Thomas as less critical of Hughes than they do, referring to the story 'Who Do You Wish Was With Us?' (in which the character Ray is a sympathetic portrayal of Hughes), claiming both story and poem concern the imagination's attempt to impersonalise itself. Certainly, the many revisions reflect Thomas's uncertainty; the *Sunday Referee* version lost the middle stanza beginning 'And father', and changed 'God gave', in the notebook version, to 'One gave'; in 1936 the middle stanza was restored and 'One' became the more questioning 'Who'. In the *N5* and the 1936 versions, a Wallace Stevens allusion appeared, 'meadows' and 'corny bogs' vanished from the second half of stanza 2, while stanzas 3, 4 and 5 were rewritten. Parkinson (1981) notes that the 'controlling syntax' is based on pararhymed words – 'foster', 'master', 'murmur' and 'farmer' (unusual in this verb form) – all of which have something of the substantive about them, and whose syntactical role is ambiguous; and that, together, stanzas 1 and 2 urge mastery, but of a cultivating rather than 'cruel or crushing' kind.

3, 9, 15 **But** = deleted in *N5* version. 4–6 **the snowman's brain . . . on an icicle** = Thomas opposes the philosophy of Stevens's 'The Snow Man' because his own 'egoism' is based on the interrelationship of mind and world and a philosophy of process; it may have attracted him because it requires the unpacking of multiple negatives ('the listener . . . nothing himself, beholds / Nothing that is not there and nothing that is'). 'The poem urges the artist to imagine beyond grief and depression, to do better than the snowman for whom, for instance, the tree – in Stevens . . . pines, juniper, and spruce, in Thomas "each bushy form of the air" – can only be icily patterned and imaged.' (Hardy 2000) 7 **cockerel's eggs** = in *N5* 'cockerel's' replaces an indecipherable deleted word; the collocation is paradoxical, as in riddling folksongs (such as 'I gave my love a cherry'), possibly an image for self-reliance and creativity. Thomas's poems of this period often deal with the self-authoring process, and its implications (as a male writer) for the gendering of creativity. 9 **graft four-fruited ridings . . . country** = 'ridings' are county divisions; but the main sense is sexual-creative. Cf. 'county', 'ridings', etc., in 'Hold hard, these ancient minutes'. 10, 11 **burning, red-eyed** = epithets switched in *N5*. 12 **vegetable** = patient and inexorable. 13 The line originally read 'And father all, nor fail with barren winds.' The change makes the same point more vividly; use awareness of death to spur your creativity. 13–14 The gothic elements echo Thomas's observation to Trevor Hughes that 'faults in oneself' can be 'too easily blamed on the things that go squawk in the night.' 16 **voices** = 'music' in *N5*; **ninnies' choir** = cf. 'angelic gangs', 'I fellowed sleep'. 17 **speak, cloud** = *N5* has 'sing', 'air'. 20 **ring** = *N5* has 'hill'. 24 **cockwise** = 'what Thomas is saying is that, at the moment of death, mortal or sexual, time stands still' (Hornick, 1958). 27 end-line semi-colon is comma in *N5*. 29 **the** = *N5* 'your'.

Grief thief of time

The two stanzas of this poem derive from separate *N4* poems, as noted in *CP14*; the source for stanza 2, part two of 'Jack of Christ', itself derived from a cancelled final stanza of *N4* 'Thirteen', 'My hero bares his nerves', which supplied 'Jack my father', 'swag', 'bubbles', and 'sleeve', as well as giving 'knaves steal off' to the new poem's first stanza. On the page opposite *N4* 'Eighteen' Thomas began a revision, the four lines of which became, with slight changes, the opening of stanza 2. Like 'Altarwise', it seems to be a poem which he part-completed at Glen Lough, but finished on his return to London.

'Grief thief of time' owes much to its sources, but it differs from them in significant respects. By dropping the commas that make 'thief of time' and 'Jack my father' subordinate clauses in the opening lines of its two stanzas, Thomas set himself the task of creating syntactical and narrative contexts which could accommodate the changes; although the theme is unchanged, the syntactical unsettling powerfully torques the way it is expressed and developed.

11 **cast back the bone of youth** = what the old do in the process of idealising the past. 12 **she lies** = that the 'she' of past 'high time' 'lies' in more ways than one is underscored by repetition at l. 14. 15 **let** = allow (may also have the sense of 'hinder', as in *Hamlet*, 1:4, 62). 17 **swag ... in a seedy sack** = sperm in the scrotum 'stolen' from real sexual encounters with a partner, through masturbation or nocturnal emission; the image is that of a cartoon burglar making off with semen in a scrotum-sack marked 'swag'. 20 **twin-boxed grief** = testicles, equating sex with grief: cf. 'A grief ago'. 21 **No silver whistles** = as used by policemen when trying to apprehend miscreants. 23–4 **the undead eye-teeth** = as in 'I, in my intricate image', 'undead' does not mean vampires or zombies, but rather that which is simultaneously death- and life-creating. 25 **rainbow's sex** = probably non-sequiturial, like 'what colour is glory?' in 'My world is pyramid'.

Altarwise by owl-light

A sequence of ten inverted Petrarchan sonnets (i.e. in which the sestet precedes the octet, perhaps taking its cue from Rupert Brooke's 'Sonnet Reversed'). I and II are *N5* 'Seventeen', both dated 'August 35, Glen Lough', followed by Thomas's note to himself 'To be continued at length'. III, IV and V constitute N5 'Nineteen', and are also individually dated 'August 35, Glen Lough'. All five are revised, III, IV and V extensively so.

To Bert Trick in February 1935 Thomas wrote that he had 'just finished two poems which are, I hope, to appear in New Verse, Uncle Geoffrey permitting.' However, the next Thomas poem in *New Verse* was 'I, in my intricate image' (August–September 1935), suggesting that he may have withdrawn the sonnets (probably I and II) because he had extended the sequence. In September 1935 Desmond Hawkins at *Purpose* was sent I–VII, suggesting that VI and VII were composed in late August–September 1935, after Thomas's return from Donegal. At this point, however, he offered I–VII to Robert Herring at *Life & Letters To-day*, suddenly needing a replacement for 'A grief ago', which he had promised Herring but inadvertently published in *Programme*. They appeared in *Life & Letters To-day* in December 1935. VIII was probably written in late 1935 and/or early 1936,

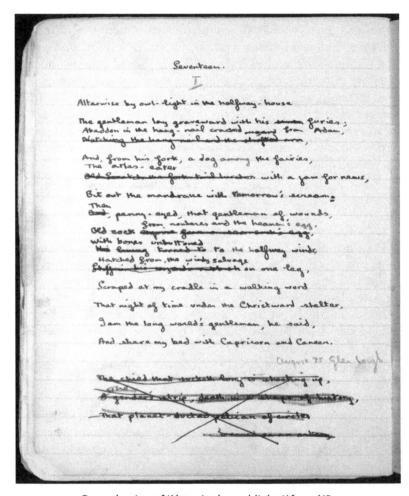

Reproduction of 'Altarwise by owl-light 1' from *N5*.
Courtesy of the Richard Burton Archives, Swansea University.

and was published in Roger Roughton's surrealist-inclined magazine *Contemporary Poetry and Prose* (May 1936). IX and X, perhaps written in May–June 1936, appeared in the same journal in July 1936.

Thus, 'Altarwise' would seem to have taken over a year of sporadic effort, between early 1935 and spring/summer 1936, partly because Thomas was unsure how long it would be. In December 1935 he was still describing I–VIII as 'the first passage of what's going to be a very long poem indeed', while a note in *25P* described all ten as 'the first ten sections of a work in progress'. This is reflected in his ambivalence concerning the relationship between the sequence and its individual components, as reflected in his request that Dent publish each poem on a separate page, 'for, although the poem as a whole is to be a poem in, and by, itself, the separate parts can be regarded as individual poems'. Yet despite this, and its resistance to interpretation, the tone of the sequence is surprisingly consistent, and it does not feel incomplete; the journey begun in I seems to be completed, on a higher level, in the landfall of X, as indicated by the near-anagram of 'altarwise' in 'atlaswise'.

At the time of its appearance, Thomas acknowledged and defended himself against the inevitable accusations of obscurity. Referring to Glyn Jones's review of *25P*, he conceded, and yet obliquely rebutted, charges of verbal density: 'You're the only reviewer . . . who *has* commented on my attempts to get away from those rhythmic and thematic dead ends, that physical blank wall, those wombs and full-stop worms, by all sorts of methods – so many unsuccessful' (*CL*, 272). Informing Jones that he had had to parody his style in 'Altarwise' before others did, he nevertheless parodied 'Altarwise' itself on at least one occasion. William Sansom, in the memoir *Coming To London*, describes meeting Thomas at this time: "'I am the short world's shroud', he said" – said Mr. Thomas, I remember – "I share my bed with Finchley Road and foetus"' (cited in Fitzgibbon, 1987, p. 187). Others joined in; *Comment*, on 19 September 1936, contained a send-up of sonnet VIII by one 'BENJIE', entitled 'After a Poem in (?on) Progress' 'by Thomas Dillon' (see Goodby, 2013). However, neither Thomas's habitual self-deprecation nor the amusement of some of his contemporaries should fool us into believing that he (or they) did not also feel 'Altarwise' to be a serious work, and an important stage in his development as a writer.

Still in part resistant to précis and explication, 'Altarwise' was intended to test the skills of a new élite of poetry readers, the first to be trained up on the writings of Eliot, I. A. Richards, William Empson and F. R. Leavis. It is one of the limit-texts of the 1930s; here, perhaps more than anywhere else, Thomas tried to extend the possibilities of poetry.

Between its publication, and the mid-1970s, 'Altarwise' was usually treated with respect, often judged to be 'splendid in parts', if 'a failure as a whole', as Fraser put it (1957). I, V and VIII, in particular, attracted the lion's share of attention. The first treatment of any length, Francis Scarfe's pioneering analysis of 1942, discerned a 'life-death antagonism' in the work, bound up in a 'double pattern' of Biblical 'mythology' and 'sexual symbolism' involving Satan (death and sin), sex (as life, chiefly Adam), Mary (the justification of sex through child-bearing and suffering) and Christ (victim and blood-offering rather than hero). Marshall W. Stearns (1944) marks the beginning of US New Criticism's interest, particularly in its religiously inclined versions, taking his cue from Scarfe's reading of VIII. This was read as an account of the crucifixion in which Mary witnesses Christ's transcendence of the sexual (death-bringing) body and the conquest of time in the name of eternal love. H. H. Kleinman's book-length study of 1963 marks the apogee of this line of interpretation, drawing comparisons as it does with devotional sequences by Herrick, Donne and Crashaw. Kleinman found 'Altarwise' to be 'a deeply moving statement of religious perplexity concluding in spiritual certainty', following a 'fearful struggle . . . with his God', and was echoed in varying degrees by Kidder (1973), McNees (1992) and Wourm (2000).

Most readings, however, beginning with Olson (1954), have avoided seeking a coherent Christian narrative. In particular, Hornick (1958), Tindall (1962), Maud (1963), Korg (1965), Moynihan (1966), Parkinson (1981), McKay (1985/6), Davies (1986) and Goodby (2013), also avoid viewing the poem as an account of a personal religious crisis. Their differences centre instead on the difficulty of identifying the speakers in the poem, owing to Thomas's deliberate eschewal of diacritical markings. This lack is what allows Parkinson and Davies, for example, to take the resurrected Christ who speaks at the end of I to also be the 'hollow agent' narrator of II; indeed Davies feels he also speaks III, while Emery (1962) takes him to narrate the entire sequence. Several critics have despaired of interpretation.

Moynihan, for example, claimed the poem marks a point where Thomas's language implies so many possibilities that it dissolves all sense in a superabundance of them; Parkinson, likewise, argues that a lack of control over 'pun or ambiguous . . . language' creates insuperable problems: 'When a poem is made up almost entirely of quasi-puns and ambiguous images the result is dense obscurity. Reading . . . becomes an exercise in the mad juggling of permutation . . . and it becomes impossible to separate out and align those meanings that are important for the poem . . . The eternal inter-identification of things becomes merely a mindless roundabout and because everything is like everything else then nothing has any particular identity and images lose their sharpness.'

It did not help the poem's (or Thomas's) reputation that Elder Olson's analysis of 'Altarwise' became something of a byword for over-ingenious critical special pleading. Concluding his otherwise excellent study, he claimed to have discovered no less than six interpretative levels in 'Altarwise', the most important of which concerned the adventures of Hercules and the relationship between the constellation of that name and others. It remains the most notorious case in Thomas studies of what Hardy (2000) calls 'deceptive allusion'. Despite a review in which Maud (1955) pointed out that 'Altarwise' was construable within the process framework applicable to other early poems (as Emery and Kershner (1976) agreed), Olson became a handy stick with which to beat not only 'Altarwise', but all of Thomas's work. This is clearest with Movement writers such as Kingsley Amis (who includes an amusing parody of 'Altarwise' in *That Uncertain Feeling*) and Donald Davie in *Articulate Energy* (1955), for whom it was 'written according to principles which seem to me radically vicious.' David Holbrook (1962 and 1972) redoubled the venom, calling it 'pretentious nonsense', and declaring the opening lines 'disgusting . . . a kind of verbal perversion . . . a damaging sensational necrophilia'. Less aggressively, Beardsley and Hynes (1960) make the conflicting claims over 'Altarwise' a test case for the inadequacies of contemporary criticism; Olson's reading is presented as a classic case of the fourth of their categories of 'misunderstanding poetry', 'The Error of Imposed System'. Their own reading is unobtrusive, but they usefully note that the poem's 'overall tone is ironic or sarcastic, but never unambiguously reverent' and that only in the final lines of X 'is a positive note struck'.

In retrospect, the real problem posed by 'Altarwise', as also by Thomas's other difficult poems, is reflected in comments such as that made in a rather different vein by Davies (1986), who confessed to being 'puzzled as to what use exactly the Christian story is being put . . . by the coexistence of a cocky, sacrilegious note with lines of resounding gravity.' That is, 'Altarwise' lacks the kind of symbolic unity which even high modernist literary texts ultimately offer their readers. The rather flummoxed air common to Thomas critics of this generation stemmed, for Goodby (2013), from 'Altarwise' being the poem in which Thomas most blatantly exceeded the ideological and interpretative horizons of mid-century practical criticism, and the fact that this was making itself felt in the early 1960s, just before the advent of critical theory. Critics formed by Leavisite and New Critical dicta were unable to accept the disjunctiveness of the textures of such works, or able to grasp that, say, the 'hollow agent' of II might legitimately be just that; a paradoxically emptied-out space of subjectivity, which any of the speakers and agents in the poem might enter, and within which they might merge and fuse.

The first critic to make this case was Don McKay (1985/6), who understood the heterogeneous opacity of 'Altarwise' not as a flaw but as a crucial aspect of its meaning. Alluding to Kristeva's and Barthes's idea that modernist writing embodies unconscious energies and linguistic surpluses, he argued that 'Altarwise' was less 'about' some*thing*, or narrated by a some*one*, than the manifestation of a protean 'trickster' principle operating in accordance with a decentred, 'outlaw' logic. McKay sees Thomas the bricoleur predominant in a climate which is carnivalesque rather than devotional, bent on creating 'a sense of illusion and flamboyance, as each item declares itself, like an item in a Mardi Gras parade, momentous and momentary.' Rather than forcing them to symbolically cohere, he claims, their provisional aspect should be embraced, since the poem's purpose is to pull the 'timeless world of mythic pattern' into 'the flux of temporality', neutralising totalising mythic imperatives. With its mutating linguistic logic, 'Altarwise' should thus be regarded as an extreme instance of Thomas's oft-repeated demand that poems should 'work from words' rather than 'towards' them – as, like *Finnegans Wake*, a self-deconstructing, proto-postmodernist work.

I

The *N5* version with its references to 'Old Scratch' (the Devil) and 'wizard' suggests that the 'gentleman' / Christ is highly ambiguous, a manifestation of the processual energies of the universe. While 'Genesis and genitals [are put] into manic alignment' in this opening poem, as Rosenthal and Gall (1983) rightly observe, this should warn against any remotely orthodox Christian interpretation.

2 **furies** = passions; cf. sonnet IX and 'In the Direction of the Beginning', l. 17. *N5* has what could be 'senses', heavily deleted and replaced by 'furies' with a semi-colon. 3 *N5* has: 'C̶l̶u̶t̶c̶h̶i̶n̶g̶ H̶a̶t̶c̶h̶i̶n̶g̶ the hang-nail and the s̶h̶a̶f̶t̶e̶d̶ arm': 'shafted' is deleted twice, the first time to be replaced by 'wizard', which has then itself been deleted. The line as it now stands has been written above. 4–6 **And from his fork . . . bit out the mandrake** = perhaps glances at the journalistic adage that 'dog bites man' is not a story, but 'man bites dog' is. Insofar as 'dog' reverses 'god', also Christ as the god who scatters false ones, as in Milton's 'On the Morning of Christ's Nativity', and victim of God the Father (like the Devil). 5 **atlas-cater** – *N5* has 'Old Scratch the fork-tail lurcher': 'Old Scratch' is slang for the Devil. Cf. Baudelaire's 'Le Voyage': 'Pour l'enfant, amoureux des écartes et d'estampes / L'univers n'est pas égal à son vaste appetit'. 6 **mandrake** – mandragora, plant with a bifurcated root, ascribed powers of fertility in Genesis 30:14–16. It was also held to grow from sperm, and to flourish under gallows as a result of the involuntary ejaculations of hanged men. Cf. the character Mandrake in Beddoes's *Death's Jest-Book*, a Thomas favourite. 7 **Then** = *N5* has 'And', deleted and replaced with 'Then'. 8 **Old cock from nowhere and the heaven's egg** = *N5* has 'Old cock e̶s̶q̶u̶i̶r̶e̶ f̶r̶o̶m̶ a̶ s̶e̶a̶-̶c̶o̶c̶k̶'̶s̶ e̶g̶g̶ from nowhere and the heaven's egg'; **heaven's egg** = cf. Blake, *Milton*, II, l.33, the 'egg-formed world of Los' – what Blake calls the 'mundane shell'. 9 **With bones unbuttoned** = *N5* has 'His living turned', deleted, with final version interlineated above. 10 **Hatched from the windy salvage** = *N5* has 'Stiff in his wizard's rubbish', deleted, with final version interlineated above; **one leg** = cf. the tricksterish Long John Silver, whose name echoes 'long world's gentleman' (McKay, 1985/6). 14 **Capricorn and Cancer** = cf. Sir Thomas Browne, *Urne-Buriall*, which notes the belief in antiquity

that these signs were heaven's exit and entrance; the soul 'came down by *Cancer*' to enter the body at conception and 'ascended by *Capricornus*' at death. Henry Miller, a favourite novelist of Thomas (and dedicatee of 'Lament'), published *Tropic of Cancer* in 1934 and was at work in 1934–5 on its sequel, *Tropic of Capricorn*; Thomas may have known of this. Both novels are, like 'Altarwise', hectic and shattering *Bildungsromans*.

II

Thomas made an initial attempt at the poem at the foot of the preceding page, immediately after 'Altarwise' I. The lines, individually deleted and struck out as a group, run:

The child that sucketh long is shooting up,
A The gender's strip, death in a shape of history,
That planet-ducted pelican of circles
                weaned on an artery

The poem was then begun again on the next clean recto page, the first four lines of which are more or less as the published version.

1 comma of semi-colon after 'history' deleted to make full-stop. 4 *N5* has full-stop after 'strip'. 5–12 **The child . . . and of feathers** = *N5* has this passage, later deleted:

Over these ground-works in a shapeless country
Hairs of your head are but the roots of nettles.
What is the metre of the dictionary?
The devil's grammar and the burning bibles?
The horizontal cross-bones of the buried,
You by the cavern over the black stairs,
Join your live verticals at vein and socket,
And all night long may Jacob to the stars.

The first and second lines of this passage, which were presumably deleted before the others, have interlinear corrections, also deleted, that read:

Over these groundworks in the shapeless lands
Your hairs are but the roots of grass & tree

A bi-directional arrow in the left-hand margin indicates that the two
new lines are to swap places with each other. Thomas then seems to
have decided not to bother with replacing the other deleted lines in
the same interlinear way, and he begins the continuation of the poem
after line 4 as we now have it, starting: 'Child of the short spark in a
shapeless country', continuing exactly as in the published version to
the end. In brackets after the last line he has written 'To be continued
at length', and 'August '35 Glen Lough'.

A version of the concluding couplet appears early in this revision,
and is followed by two questions which were adapted for 'Altarwise'
IV. The revision clarifies the identity of the 'horizontal cross-bones
of Abaddon' and the 'verticals of Adam'; namely, bodies (as skeletons)
of the dead and the living, respectively. The position of 'groundworks'
in the revision also suggests that it refers to the human body after it
has been 'grounded' in acquiring its 'gender strip' and 'shooting up'
(this being ambiguously phrased, so that it could refer to the acquisition
of gender identity in the womb, during weaning, or in adolescence).

III

In *N5* the heading in full is 'Nineteen (Seventeen Continued)' and
III is numbered. It was developed from *N3* 'Twenty Eight', 'First
there was the lamb on knocking knees', a seasonal poem contrasting
youth and age.

The sestet, through pun and ambiguity, explains that Adam, cuck-
olded by the serpent, deceived by Eve, 'horned down' 'three dead
seasons' (of gestation) and the 'climbing grave' of the Fall and Christ's
crucifixion. According to Davies (2000), Christ then describes his
own incarnation: 'when the "dead seasons" (spring, summer, autumn)
on the "climbing grave" of the year had brought the world to winter
. . . Christ dipped himself "in the descended bone" of a human body'.
But the Incarnation occurred in spring, not winter, and spring may
chime 'twice' in one year because it occurs in both southern and
northern hemispheres ('Capricorn and Cancer'). Maud (2003) does
not think Christ appears in this part of the sonnet, either, but his

claim that it is 'Rip van Wink (or forty winks)' seems far-fetched. More probably, the octet's wordplay indicates another zone of criss-crossed identity, with the ram a seedy (male) black sheep, the sole survivor of his flock. Maud claims the speaker of the last two lines are 'the antipodes' themselves.

1–2 **the lamb on knocking knees . . . climbing grave** = unsteady-legged Thomas / Christ child, whose knees knocked in the 'grave' of the womb and on the cross. 3 **Adam's wether** = Adam as wether (often a 'bellwether' because wearing a bell; cf. VI, l. 11; VII, l. 9) and thus the (mis)leader of the human flock (but also Christ, who leads us out of Adam's sin, making 'wether' both object and subject). 4 **mounted** = suggests Eve's seduction by the Devil was sexual, but also that sex itself (the worm as phallus) was responsible for the Fall. 5 *N5* has full-stop after 'toes'. 6 *N5* has 'O̶n̶ ̶E̶d̶e̶n̶'s̶ ̶p̶a̶v̶e̶m̶e̶n̶t̶s̶ b̶y̶ ̶t̶h̶e̶ ̶b̶l̶a̶c̶k̶ ̶p̶a̶v̶i̶l̶i̶o̶n̶s̶', with final version added interlinearly above; **thunderous pavements** = cf. II, l. 13; both apocalyptic and modern traffic noise. 11 **year** = *N5* has 'fold'; **the black ram** = juxtaposes the deadest and most vital parts of the year: the rest of the flock are dead, but the ram (Aries, 20 March–19 April) symbolises spring. 12 **fold** = *N5* 'race', with 'mutton fold' in margin. 13 *N5* reads: 'We rung our laddering changes on the weather', with 'laddering' and 'weather' deleted and changed as for final version. 13–14 **We rung . . . chimed** = 'wether' / 'weather' are the seasons, diametrically opposed in northern and southern hemispheres, ascended or descended to by the 'rungs' of the lines of longitude and latitude; **rung** = 'That fateful pair, Capricorn and Cancer, are *runging* – and this time also ringing – the changes happening to our hero' (Maud, 2003). Nathalie Wourm cites the *Inferno*; Dante and Virgil climb into the southern hemisphere up Satan and towards Purgatory; 'The ladder of hemispheres is . . . a ladder to earthly immortality, [the opposite] to Christianity, which promises spiritual immortality' (Wourm, 2000); **twice spring chimed** = *N5* has 'spring chimed twice', with final version in margin.

IV

In IV Thomas takes a cue from the questions children habitually ask adults about sex, language, and death; their curiosity 'is represented as at once absurd and as an integral part of the life-process' (Dodsworth, 1972). Christ's answers to these, as several critics see them, in the final six lines, go beyond 'egoism' (Davies, 2000), but implicit in what he says is the womb/tomb vision of process.

3 **Pharoah's** = written above a heavily deleted word in *N5*, possibly 'Europa's'. 6 *N5* has the deleted line: 'Questions are hunchbacks. (And the straight dead's No).' 7 **your acres** = 'God's acre' is slang for a graveyard. 9 **needles** – *N5* has 'splinters'. 10 **eye** = *N5* has 'eyes'; **needle** = *N5* has 'splinter'. 11–14 **Love's a reflection . . . cutting flood** = Thomas's autograph note in Edith Sitwell's copy of *25P* at Austin reads: 'Love is a reflection of the features (the features of those you will know and love *after* the womb) which are photographed before birth on the wall of the womb – the womb being surrounded by food; a field being its own field, and the womb being its own food'.

V

In *N5* the two opening lines are heavily deleted, and replaced inter-lineally by the lines as published. Line 1 is indecipherable, but line 2 reads: 'From sleeve of stars trumped [should be "trumps"] up the ten-decked dead.' Eight lines follow, crossed out by two diagonal lines:

The knave-decked sheathes who shuffle in their blades,
And sniper's aces in the joyless pits,
Black-tongued and tipsy from salvation's bottle,
Said the fake gentleman in a [cut] suit of spades;
For loss of blood I fell on Ishmael's hill,
Under the bread-legged mushrooms slew my hunger,
A climbing sea from Asia snatched me down,
And Jonah's Moby had me by the hair;

Thomas then wrote out the entire sonnet as now published, with two variants: 'salt' for 'black', and the deletion of 'hill' for 'plain'. He had to return to the previous page for space to squeeze in the last four lines. 'Glen Lough' is written beneath these.

Critics unsure of the speaker at ll. 7–14 have detected a 'dark night of the soul' suffered by Thomas himself, with 'exile, wandering and desolation' alluded to in images of outcasts and 'waste seas', and the ambiguity created by a lack of speech indicators and the use of 'me' certainly invites a reading of the 'fake gentleman' as an aspect of the speaker. However, McKay (1985/6) claims V 'speaks about, and demonstrates, the craft of illusions – sleight of hand in poker, tall tales in religion and the Wild West', while Wigginton (2007) views it as a 'surrealist collage' and Goodby (2013) argues that the 'sirens' are those of writing, as well as sexual desire.

12 **medusa** = one of the three Gorgons of Greek myth, whose face turned those who gazed on it to stone. Freud explains the myth as an attempt to account for the male erection, calling her 'the supreme talisman who provides the image of castration – associated in the child's mind with the discovery of maternal sexuality – and its denial'; also a type of stinging jellyfish, in accord with the marine imagery of 'Altarwise' as a whole.

VI

For Korg (1965) VI is about language in its 'perverting capacities' and the attempt to sacrifice the impure 'sea eye' and 'fork tongue' to achieve purer expression; at the end the 'celebrated grotesque . . . "ladies" continue "Time's tune" of "heartbreak" as it is called in . . . VII. The final image creates a remarkable effect, at once momentous and enigmatic, vivid and obscure.' Rather less moralistically, the growth of writing is seen as intimately and inextricably bound up with the emergence of (male) sexuality, with all its anxieties, including castration fears.

2 **book of water** = cf. Keats's desired epitaph: 'Here lies one whose name was writ in water', and Thomas's letter of 23 March 1938 to Henry Treece: 'I do not want a poem of mine to be, nor can it be, a circular piece of experience placed neatly outside the living stream of time from which it came; a poem of mine is . . . a watertight section of the stream that is flowing all ways' (*CL*, 329); **tallow-eyed** = typical identification of wax with flesh. 5 **Pluck, cock, my sea eye** = in Greek myth, the sisters of the Gorgons shared a single eye, each 'plucking' it from her eye-socket in order to pass it on; Perseus stole it to learn

how he might kill Medusa (cf. III, l. 12); cf. also Matthew 5:29: 'And if thy right eye offend thee, pluck it out, and cast *it* from thee'. 8 **Old cock** = cf. 'Altarwise' I. 9 **wax's tower** = Korg (1965): '"The fats of midnight" and the "wax's tower" seem to refer, as . . . in "A grief ago", to the act of making love.'

VII

1 **Now stamp the Lord's Prayer on a grain of rice** = the phenomenon was in the news at this time; C. L. Blystone, famed for his ability to write the Lord's Prayer on grains of rice, featured in Ripley's 'Odd-itorium' at the Chicago World's Fair of 1933–4. 8 **scaled sea-sawers** = play on 'scale' (primarily fish-scales and musical scales) and 'seesaw'. 11 **my ladies lend their heartbreak** = they lend their heartbroken / heartbreaking music to (the tune of) Time. 13 **Time tracks the sound of shape on man and cloud** = taking issue with Davie (1955), who misquotes and attacks the last five lines on the grounds that they fail to mime 'the intelligible structure of the conscious mind'. Davies (1986) notes that what is really being objected to is an appositional style, whose syntax creates a sense of simultaneity and identification. But this, he asserts, is justified and necessary, because it is 'the *theme* as well as the style of these sonnets': thus, in l. 13,

> what is being mimed is already a strange and difficult abstract idea – that of the simultaneity of time and space. [It] is Thomas's way of expressing what Time is: Time is imaginable only in terms of the sound and shape of things – things that are not abstract, and that move ('cloud'), fade ('rose'), and melt ('icicle'). Time 'tracks' these things both in the sense of creating the sad music of their mortality (the "sound" or significance of shapes) as on a *sound-track*, and also in the sense of *tracking them down*. The reality of abstract Time is simultaneous and identical with the physical things it destroys.

The imagery preceding the last two lines shows how inseparable any abstract idea of 'Time' is from the processes of gestation and nurture and the maternal body generally. For 'shape of sound' / 'sound of shape' cf. 'Hold hard'; for 'tracking' cf. 'When, like a running grave' and 'I, in my intricate image'.

VIII

One of the most discussed and disputed poems in the sequence, although its vividness should not disguise the fact that, like 'Altarwise' as a whole, it is also concerned with writing; crucifixion as cruci*fiction*. The biggest uncertainty is over who speaks. Scarfe (1942) takes the narrator to be Christ, Stearns (1944) Mary, Tindall (1962) Thomas himself (but identifying at some points with Christ and Mary). Tindall is the most plausible: Christ speaks in the sestet, though he is initially described as 'Time's nerve in vinegar'; 'Jack Christ' later (l. 7) seems equally an external description although 'my' in l. 9 is probably Christ (or Mary). Mary seems to speak in l. 4, but the 'is' in l. 6 reports her in another's voice; even her l. 4 appearance is problematic if the 'Mary / merry' pun is accepted (this would be external description, and a critique of Old Testament Jehovah glad at the death of Christ, as in 'Before I knocked'). Even so, the sense of Mary as witness of the scene, and her temporary membership of the Thomas / Christ subject, is never fully dispelled.

3 the bright thorns I wept = '"I" = Christ (if it means Dylan Thomas the poem loses)' (Scarfe, 1942). 6 **pins for teardrops** = as in Picasso's crucifixion paintings of 1930–2, inspired by Grünewald's Isenheim altarpiece of a tortured, thorn-studded Christ, exhibited in London in 1932–3, and which Thomas may have seen or heard about; the pins are also those that fasten Christ to the cross. 7 **Jack Christ** = cf. 'Jack of Christ', p. 81. 9 **three-coloured** = the rainbow in the three primary colours, as in Milton's *Paradise Lost*, XI, ll. 865–6 and Dante's *Paradiso*. 'Three-footed rainbow' in a typescript at Austin. 11 **all glory's sawbones** = followed by a comma in *CP52*, though not in journal publication, *25P* or *CP88*. Christ as surgeon, but Mary is also the saviour of salvation, if we understand this as a re-statement of her central role. With a comma it is appositive with 'I'; without it 'unsex' can make 'sawbones' its subject. 12 **Unsex the skeleton** = reads 'unsex my skeleton' in Austin MS, suggesting that Thomas initially intended a personal sense of liberation achieved through an unorthodox reading of the crucifixion, 'restor[ing] the Renaissance's sexual reading of Christ's crucifixion as the nuptials of God and Man' (Goodby, 2013) cf. James Thomson's *City of Dreadful*

Night, VIII, 2: 'The unsexed skeleton mocks shroud and pall'; **mountain minute** = no comma after 'minute' in Austin MS. 13 **sun** = Christ; allusion to the darkness that fell at Christ's death, symbolising the abolition of time through his triumph over mortality. This line may mean 'by Christ's submission to the power of time as it is told by children'. 14 **Suffer the heaven's children through my heartbeat** = both 'permit', and suffer in its usual sense (cf. Matthew 19:14). Goodby (2013) observes : 'Like Christ, the artist is . . . able to overcome mortality by defeating time in his work, thus opening the kingdom of the spirit to the "heaven's children", humanity, even as he turns to seed by witnessing this "sun"-like glory.'

IX

The association of Ancient Egyptian imagery with moribund paralysis is familiar from 'Should lanterns shine', 'My world is pyramid' and elsewhere. Tindall (1962) argues that the burial rites also signify the mummification, through writing and printing, of poems. Echoing the different 'bed' of I, l. 14, this image-train culminates in the 'bed' in which a 'forme' of type was placed in a printing-press. According to Rosenthal and Gall (1983), 'the heaviness of the negative is almost overwhelming' by the final line; however, it is with death and burial that renewal become possible; cf. 'I make this in a warring absence' for a similar scenario.

2–3 **Prophets and fibre kings . . . queen . . . priest and pharaoh** = 'All the dead – the royal, the priestly, the scribal ["fibre kings", as papyrus was made from vegetable fibre] – are discovered by Thomas in the process of preserving themselves, as if they had become animated in the archives and pyramid texts (Kleinman, 1963). 8–9 **rants the mask of scholars / Gold on such features** = Kleinman suggests a comma after 'scholars' to clarify syntax (as in l. 11, VIII, Thomas seems to maximise the knottiness of syntax without quite breaking it). 13 **With stones . . . garland** = an example of Thomas's style of 'deceptive allusion' for Hardy (2000), who notes that '["stones of odyssey"] may be read as the Phaeacian ship turned to stone by Poseidon after Odysseus finally lands in Ithaca', although more obvious meanings might make better sense: i.e. 'stones are images of the hard journey, exhaustion and labour replacing funeral rite and laureate praise'; **ash and garland** = 'a hendiadys joining live tree and leafy tribute' (Hardy, 2000). 14 **rivers of the dead . . . neck** = recalls Coleridge's Ancient Mariner, who had an albatross hung around his neck.

X

As Scarfe (1942) noted, this is 'the "Paradise Regained" poem' of 'Altarwise', and it ends by enacting the simultaneous creation and destruction of process. Empson (1954) called 'Altarwise' as a whole 'bad', yet added, citing the last four lines of X:

> but when it is good it is ragingly good . . . I hope I do not annoy anyone by explaining that the Cross of Jesus is also the male sexual organ; Dylan would only have thought that tiresomely obvious, a basis for his remarks. But when you get to the worms instead of the birds able to build something valuable in this tree, and the extraordinary shock of the voice of the poet in his reverence and release . . . when he gets to his nest, you do begin to wonder whether he meant something wiser than he knew.

2 **Atlaswise** = likens Atlas (who had to carry the earth on his back) to the globe-identified Thomas / Christ. 9–10 the question mark at the end of l. 10 suggests we ought to read these two lines as being in the voice of Peter himself; **rhubarb man peeled** = rhubarb is not peeled before cooking, so perhaps peeled by the 'voyage', or – as penis – with the foreskin peeled back. H. H. Kleinman suggests rhubarb as (a) the 'long wound' of the crucifixion and (b) 'the acerb qualities of St. Paul, citing Philip Sidney's usage: 'But with your rhubarb word ye must contend'. 12 **two bark towers** = 'personal Eden and Calvary' (Moynihan, 1966); 'bark', as in tree, but also perhaps because that is what a 'dog among the fairies' would do. 13–14 **the worm builds with the gold straws of venom / My nest of mercies** = McKay (1985/6) notes:

> the serpent or worm [is] the double agent of creation and destruction. The worm is eater of the flesh in poems such as 'The force that through the green fuse . . .' and 'If I were tickled . . .', and it is the creative instrument in others like 'Before I knocked . . .' (the 'fathering worm'), 'When once the twilight', and . . . 'Altarwise' [III].

14 **rude red tree** = 'red' as in 'socialist' ensures that, like *18P*, *25P* closes with a qualified assertion of mankind's utopian potential.

To-day, this insect

A poem which juxtaposes 'space' and 'time' across its first line-break is likely to be concerned with relative states, and this one ultimately concerns its own punning and playful verbal excess emerging as it does at a point when 'symbols' have the usual co-ordinates of reality. Thus, the 'head and tail' play of l. 7 are a typical example of one of Thomas's manipulated clichés: to be unable to 'make head *or* tail' of something is to not be able to understand it; but 'head *and* tail' suggests that the cliché is too polarising. Both hint at a third position, of undecidability and resistance to both faith in 'tales', and to the head's rationalist dismissal of these. As in 'Incarnate devil' and the close of 'Altarwise' X, the serpent is seen as the deconstructive element in the tale/tail of the Old Testament, thereby also relativising the New Testament in an endless process of deferment in which there is no place for absolute truth, as exemplified in the single line segmenting refrains. Desirable yet fixed fictions are undermined, but the poem's as religion is also a fiction, and death is the only 'certain' outcome of all such 'fibs': the one certainty in a relativistic universe is that there is no certainty except ceaseless change and play, and the word 'certain' draws down the 'fabulous curtain' of art in a poem that pushes towards a saturation point of linguistic meaning.

Despite its formal beauty, the inscrutability and dizzying interpretative possibilities of 'To-day, this insect' have deterred commentators. Tindall (1962) likened Thomas's skill in handling the *ottava rima* stanza to Yeats's; Kidder (1973) calls the poem 'ambiguous in the extreme and referential in excess', talking 'not of religion but poems that seem to talk of religion', while Maud (2003) finds it a record of a crisis of faith. Following McKay (1985/6), Rhian Barfoot (2015) offers a pioneering and compelling Lacanian reading. Ultimately, as she notes, the only graspable sense is the poem's playful yet ingenious resistance to paraphrase and biographising. Thus, while McKay (1986), finds a 'firm mythic structure' in the conclusion, with the 'ageless voice's univocality rest[ing] upon the energies of many madmen', suggesting that 'order and anarchy belong to the same poetic and cosmological enterprise', Bigliazzi (1992) seems more in line with the poem's own radical scepticism when she insists that the narrator is immersed in a 'fabulous, obscure world to the last line', and emphasises a fragmentariness which only just pulls out of 'impenetrable Mallarméan obscurity'.

1 **insect** = literally 'cut into', from Aristotle's *entomon* (anticipating 'guillotine', l. 6); anticipates later 'plague', via Biblical plagues of locusts; **the world I breathe** = the 17 March 1936 version has 'plague' for 'world'. 8 **genesis** = capitalised in 1936 version. 9 Tindall (1962): '"insect" is literal insect, poem, or moment of division; "certain" is adverb, adjective or noun ("certainly", a "certain insect" or "certainty"); "plague" may be destruction, an irritant or pest, or a multitude.' For Goodby (2013) 'the chief meaning seems adverbial "certainly": the poem plagues "fables" such as that of Eden, since, for Thomas, a poem is the antithesis of dogma . . . However, like "insect" and "certain", "plague" and "fables" also have at least two potential meanings' and the deliberately ambiguous syntax permits various readings, e.g.: *a* the insect (poem) is certainly the huge number of fables; *b* the insect (poem) expressive of certitude is the curse of fables; *c* the insect (poem) expressive of certitude is the huge number of fables. Of these, *b* seems the dominant, but not the only, sense. 10 **caul** = cf. 'From love's first fever'; homophonic for the serpent's 'call' to Eve. 18 the fabular poem replaces the absolute promises of Christianity with: *a* a promise of certainty; *b* a definite promise; and/or *c*, a certain (kind of) promise (but hinting that death is the only outcome of 'vision'). 23–6 Maud (2003) claims the deconstruction of Eden's 'fable' leaves only Death, who utters the last four lines; 'loving us to death all our stories end up on Death's cross'. 25–6 **All legends' sweethearts . . . the fabulous curtain** = Tindall (1962): 'The timeless Greek' is the poet himself, who is also Christ, 'but his crucifixion is a crucifiction', his creative sufferings hidden from his readers. The 1936 version reads 'A universe of years notched on my criss- / Cross tree behind the fabulous curtain.'

Then was my neophyte

Writing to Glyn Jones at the end of 1936 to thank him for his review of *25P* in *Adelphi*, Thomas added 'personally, I'm sorry you didn't mention the one particular poem in the book – "Then Was My Neophyte" – which I consider the best' (*CL*, 272–3). Thomas was probably being a little mischievous, given the more obviously impressive poems in the volume; however, he was contemplating a change in style at this point, and there are ways in which "Then was my neophyte' anticipates the more flexible lyrics of the late 1930s, even though its womb-locatedness and process-and-religion themes are those of his earlier phase. The poem is also, as Hornick (1958) noted, a Hamletic piece which stages a confrontation between father and 'neophyte' son.

14 **the lane of scales** = hints at the belief that the embryo recapitulated the stages of evolution (i.e. fish), and 'scales' the evolutionary path. 34–5 **threw . . . Love's image** = cf. 'Altarwise' IV, but here perhaps with the sense of future romantic disasters as well as deeper loves (Maud, 2003).

It is the sinners' dust-tongued bell

The poem's general tone and post-coital *mise-en-scène* recalls 'A grief ago'; 'grief' is used four times and is the poem's final word. It is one of the most extreme examples of the way Thomas's early poems proceed by contraries, figuring this in a service at once penitential and sensual, the church's kindled 'black aisle' being sexual as well as funereal. The 'white child in the dark-skinned summer' of stanza 4 may depict sperm climbing the womb-wall, contrasted with the 'child in colour', the poem/orgasm, in a final expression of contrariness ('*Ding dong* from the *mute* turrets'). Stanza 5 seems to say that time is continually abolished (and hence renewed) with the sexual act, which is 'grief', as elsewhere.

13 **There is loud and dark directly under the dumb flame** = the shadow in close proximity to the candle-flame is the line's antithetical point. 16 **christens the cherub time** = an excommunication-like

baptism is performed for a newborn (sexual act / its potential outcome), as the old year ('hourglass'-clutching Father Time) is replaced by the new year (as 'cherub'). 22 **blank and leaking winter** = the poem was written in December 1936.

Two limericks

ii. 'The last time I slept with the Queen': also recorded by Ruthven Todd in 'Dylan Thomas: A Personal Account', unpublished memoir, National Library of Scotland.

From the Veronica Sibthorpe papers

Veronica Sibthorpe (1908–73) was a printer and part of the bohemian scene of the era. A noted cook and connoisseur of wordgames, her London flat was a venue for parties and meals; although disabled, she would set her prosthetic leg (named 'Gilbert') on a stool and hop around her kitchen as she prepared to entertain. The high spirits of her brief amicable affairs with Thomas, in Cornwall in spring 1936, and as her temporary lodger and live-in lover in April–May 1937, are recorded in the two albums which now comprise the Dylan Thomas and Veronica Sibthorpe papers (items 21698E) in the National Library of Wales, and in two of Thomas's letters. The albums consist of around one hundred short texts and drawings by both Thomas and Sibthorpe, chiefly light-hearted and self-mocking: they include a 'To Do' list ('Ring up Bill E.' [William Empson], 'Try to go to party & steal a hat' and 'Get shirts washed'); drafts of articles and letters; Thomas self-portraits with captions such as 'I'm young but I can learn' and 'AM I A POET?'; a cartoon by Thomas titled 'Child surprised by size of cock' by Sibthorpe; several cartoon series, including of a two-headed hermaphrodite named 'Henryenna', one of 'gligs' (imaginary beings) and one mocking peers of the realm (sample caption: 'Insane peer enjoys having been diddled'). There are also surreal drawings (a Kokoschkaesque one of a woman with a globe dangling from her navel is captioned 'Egoistic squeaks!'), and a parody of Joyce's signing-off of *Ulysses* ('Dylan Thomas Zürich – Warsaw, 1929–1937').

For as long as forever is

The MS at Austin is undated, but Thomas had used a form of the first line ('as long as forever & ever is') in a letter to Caitlin on 17 July 1936, and Watkins described it as a poem 'based on images of hunting' which Thomas had shown him 'A year or two before' (*LVW*, 47). The clearer verbal texture and avoidance of heavy stress may reflect a shift away from the densities of the earlier poetry (as also in 'Then shall my neophyte'), indicating late 1936 or early 1937 as the date of composition.

3 **plumed eyes** = cf. 'How shall my animal' 'a bush plumed with flames, the rant of the fierce eye'. 6 **dark** = the Veronica Sibthorpe Papers, the National Library of Wales MSS (NLW) version has 'sea'. 7 **a** = NLW has 'the' for first 'a'. 8–12 **hunted world . . . time's slow riders** = for time as a hunter, see 'When, like a running grave' and 'Hold hard, these ancient minutes'. 11 **By the market . . . townspires** = NLW has 'Through the feather-and-market street by the bled townspires' cf. 'the last whirring featherlands', 'A saint about to fall'. 12 **shave** = Davies and Maud in *CP88* read 'shove' from the Austin MS, but NLW's 'shave' is consistent with the full rhyme used elsewhere in the poem.

I make this in a warring absence

In September 1937 this poem was 'forty lines' long, according to Thomas. On 22 October 1937, it was probably the poem he offered as a 'longish poem' to Julian Symons for *Twentieth Century Verse*. On 25 October he told Vernon Watkins 'my poem is continuing. You shall have it next week.' On 30 October, he wrote to Hawkins again, admitting that he had had to revise the poem: 'I'm now working hard on [it], and it should be complete in some days.' Watkins, who saw it 'at many stages on its way to completion', received the finished sixty-eight line version on 13 November 1937. (Cf. the sailing imagery in 'In the Direction of the Beginning'.)

3 **Harbours . . . slips** = '"slips" is not in apposition to . . . but governed by the subject "minute", and tells us about the departure: apparently

parallel forms diverge' (Hardy, 2000). 6 **pride** = recurring at ll. 6, 13, 17, 28, 41, 59, 62 and 67. 31–6 **I make a weapon of an ass's skeleton . . . jawbone** = 'a magnificent description of raging destructive impulses occasioned by a lovers' quarrel, suggests, by "ass's skeleton" and "jawbone", the "new jawbone of an ass" (Judges 15:15) with which Samson slew a thousand Philistines' (Kidder, 1973). 46–53 **stanza 7** = 'Dylan told me that he had gone down into the tombs of Egypt and must come up in eight lines . . . Of course the wonder he had experienced in reading about the opening of Tutankhamun's tomb is in the verse, and so, too, is the ninth sonnet of "Altarwise by owl-light" . . .' (Watkins, 2013: 62). 53 **In the groin's . . . a man is tangled** To Watkins on 13 November 1937 Thomas wrote: 'It was weeks after writing this that I remembered [Frederick] Prokosch's "man-entangled sea": but I don't think any apologies are necessary, anyway.' The phrase is from Prokosch's poem 'The Baltic Shore'.

In the Direction of the Beginning

In a letter to his agent David Higham of 20 February 1939, Thomas mentioned *TML*, which was to include short fictions as well as poems:

> Church [his editor at Dent's] has, among the mss of the poems, part of a prose piece called 'In the Direction of the Beginning' – a title I originally intended as the title of the whole book. I have, however, been considering this piece, and have now decided to make it part of a much longer work which I want to spread over many months to come. (*CL*, 408)

'An Adventure from a Work in Progress' resembles 'In the Direction of the Beginning', is three times its length, and was published a year after it, and is probably the (unsuccessful) attempt to make it 'much longer'.

'In the Direction' is one of Thomas's limit-texts, on a par with 'I, in my intricate image' or 'Altarwise' in its commitment to composition via image- and word-breeding, pun and sonic structuration. The basic quest-narrative, as the hero maps the world (the woman herself) and moves towards union with her is indistinguishable from the writing of the piece, the aim being to embroil the reader as fully as possible in a language event. George Morgan (1989), in easily the best critical analysis, calls this the 'pre-text'; it is deconstructed by an 'anti-text' in which significance is simultaneously broken down, and linearity and realism disrupted, creating a lexical space in which diverse possibilities are held in dynamic suspension. Simultaneously, he claims, we observe the growth of a 'con-text' in which the nature of the text and its creation is narrated behind the struggle between 'pre-text' and 'anti-text'. This is hinted at in the imagery: the 'cedar-wood' of the boat's mast is that used in making pencils, the 'swinging field' mimics our to and-fro reading of the page, while a series of auto-reflexive puns comment on poetic process; 'bay-leaf' is not culinary so much as a 'leaf' (page) which has to do with a 'bay' (enclosed area of sea), 'eyed arms' are arms of the sea which the reader 'eyes' through the text, and 'blown sea' has less to do with wind than the textualised sea, 'blown' also meaning 'uttered, proclaimed, hinted at' (*OED*). Throughout, images of stone and its varieties ('rock', 'mountain', 'granite', 'sculptured', 'vault', etc.) figure the words of the text, and terms for script, text and sound abound ('scrawled', 'odyssey', 'history', 'index', 'music', 'scaled', 'singing', 'chronicle', etc.). The world described is, literally, the world of the emergent poem, the text describing less its own making than bringing a reader 'to experience the excitement and ungraspability of the imaginative operation itself as it throws up an unceasing variety and richness of mental combinations. It is this . . . which enables the reader, more than with any other poet of the period, to become a co-creator of the work-in-progress.' Cf. *http://revel.unice.fr/cycnos/index.html?id=84*

O make me a mask

Among the four revised notebook poems sent to *Poetry* (Chicago), which was due to carry a 'London Letter' by D. S. Savage subtitled 'Thomas outstanding among the younger poets' in its February 1938 issue. Due to appear in May 1938, they eventually appeared in the August issue.

Maud (2003) finds 'openness', and reads the poem's request for a mask or gag as ironic (because 'made to the loved one in such revealing terms that everything is, in its intention, unhidden and said'), allegedly reflecting Thomas's love for Caitlin immediately after their marriage. However, most critics detect the wariness of the original, and the entering of a plea for greater expressive self-control, protecting the inner self and enhancing its ability to detect the pretence of others. Moylan (1995) unravels the deflective ambiguities manifested in the poem's syntactic and sonic complexities and poetic/sexual anxieties, relating these to 'To-day, this insect', and their shared notion that: 'In the end, the self can only be certain that it doubts itself. But that is something. Although the poet cannot say the truth about who or what he is, he can repudiate his own lies . . . [and] assert a paradoxical claim to integrity.'

As in 'Once it was the colour of saying', Thomas uses truncated sonnet form – twelve thirteen-syllable lines (l. 7 excepted) – with end-line pararhyme scheme *acbabacbdede*.

The spire cranes

Of all the revisions of earlier poems made at this time (1937–8), that of 'IX', from *N2*, seems the least extensive. Comparison with the original, however, allows us to see how far Thomas's adoption of a more conventional form altered the poem's overall impact; sentiment and phrasing are preserved, but the agglomeration of the short *vers libre* lines slows the piece down and lends more prominence to its metaphysical considerations:

The spire cranes; its statue
Is an aviary,
And from the nest
Of stone not straw
He does not let the nightingales   5
Blunt their tawny necks on rock,
Or pierce the sky with diving–
So wing in weed
And foot an inch in froth.
The bell's chimes cheat the sun,   10

And drop in time,
Induced to fall
Like discs upon the water,
Tune for the swimmer's hands
And silver music for his bubbling mouth.   15
But let him keep his faculties.
The spire's hook drops birds and notes,
Each featherless and stony hearted;
The upward birds are choice for you,
And notes that breast the vertical,   20
Or run the corridor on ladder,
Nor tread the cloudy steps like prodigals.

Davies (1985) detects a contrast between the 'carved birds' (early
poems, too crafted and private to escape into the outside world) and
the 'chimes', metaphorised as real birds, that frequent but are not
bound to the spire (the more transparent style evolving in 1937–8).

When all my five and country senses see

3–4 the halfmoon's vegetable eye . . . young stars = for the Renaissance
belief in vegetable, animal and spiritual components of the soul, see
Sir Thomas Browne, *Religio Medici*, I, 39:

> In that obscure world and wombe of our mother, our time is short,
> computed by the Moone; yet longer than the dayes of many creatures
> that behold the Sunne, our selves being not yet without life, sense,
> and reason, though for the manifestation of its actions, it awaits the
> opportunity of objects; and seems to live there but in its roote and
> soul of vegetation: entring afterwards upon the scene of the world,
> wee arise up and become another creature . . . obscurely manifesting
> that part of Divinity in us, but not in completement and perfection,
> till we have once more cast our secondine [embryonic sac], that is,
> this slough of flesh, and are delivered into the last world, that is,
> that is . . . that proper *ubi* [here] of spirits.

Thomas also echoes Blake's term 'vegetative eye', the organ of the
'single vision' of Newtonian science and Enlightenment rationalist
thought, to which he opposed his own 'four-fold' spiritual vision.

4 **handfull zodiac** = Thomas's spelling, 'handful*l*', may emphasise fatedness in hinting at the proverbial 'to be a handful', difficult to control.

Not from this anger

Sent to Vernon Watkins on 21 March 1938 with 'O make me a mask' and 'When all my five and country senses', like them this is a variant on sonnet-form: two stanzas of seven lines each, with end-line para-rhymes *aababcc aacabbbc*. In a letter to Watkins of 1 April, Thomas responded to his interim comments: 'Before your letter came I had cut out the ubiquitous "weather" from the anticlimactic poem and am revising it.' By then, however, the poem had been sent to Chicago.

How shall my animal

One of Thomas's most dynamic and inventive works of the late 1930s, this poem's originality and energy are reflected in a tortuous gestation. It was probably the piece Thomas referred to in a letter to Desmond Hawkins of 16 March 1938 as 'meant for your stupendous number', but which 'died, twisted in its mysteries', and which he was 'trying now to bury . . . in another poem'. By 21 March 1938, Thomas deemed it fit to send to Vernon Watkins – in a letter which referred, in another context, to the line from *N1* '42' 'I build a flying tower, and I pull it down' – and described it as a poem he had 'spent a great deal of time on' (on 1 April, this was put at 'months'). It still had to be further revised before being sent to Henry Treece on 16 May 1938.

Early critics tended to see the 'animal' as a foetus, or read the main narrative line in terms of the sexual act, concluding in climax (Gene Montague, 1968). But Montague also discerned that the 'sexuality is metaphoric [for writing]', and later critics, including Davies (1985), Maud (2003), Goodby and Wigginton (2000, 2013), have emphasised its concern with the creative act, with Davies stressing its expressivist (Romantic), Goodby and Wigginton its autonomous (modernist) aspects. In the poem, the struggle to externalise the animal is cast in gendered terms, but these deconstruct each other; the poet/animal is both genders, and its creation-realisation is an androgynous process, as elsewhere in Thomas's poetry.

The paradox of the poem, then, is to agonise over the killing of the 'animal' while countering the killing (although never fully justifying it) with the vitality and formal beauty of the lyric that results from fishing it up from the psychic-linguistic depths it inhabited. The process(es) occur in language which may be read in terms of the inadequacy of the male sexual quest, psychoanalysis and biomorphic process; the difficulty of grasping the unconscious is imaged through surreal and playful shape-shiftings (snail, octopus, lion, horse, turtle, crab, fish, bird). These are Ovidian, but a Welsh source may be the tale of Gwion Bach, in which the young boy Gwion accidentally tastes three drops from a magic potion being brewed by the witch Ceridwen, and performs a series of startling animal transformations in his attempt to escape her, before she devours him, and he is reborn as the *ur*-bard Taliesin.

1 **animal** = creature, but also 'anima', Latin for the soul, and (in Jungian psychology) the female aspect of the male. 16 **haybeds of a mile** = cf. D. H. Lawrence's 'Love Among the Haystacks'. 20 **bowels turn turtle** = used in Djuna Barnes's *Nightwood* to describe loss of sexual desire. 22 **parched** = perhaps pun on Welsh *parchedig* 'reverend', a religious title (cf. 'After the Funeral'), or simply a sermonising, self-righteous male voice. 26 **Tongue and ear in the thread** = in 1934 Thomas argued for 'poetry that . . . comes to life out of the red heart through the brain', attacking casual reading styles for 'lack of aural value' and the 'debasing . . . an art that is primarily dependent on the musical mingling of vowels and consonants' (*EPW*, 166). 29–31 **Nailed with an open eye . . . bowl of wounds . . . clap its great blood down** = Maud (2003) sees the 'bowl' as the 'skull' of stanza 1; Montague reads the passage as a sexual struggle. 36 **sly scissors . . . Clack through the thicket of strength . . . in pillars drops** = the allusion to the cutting of Samson's hair develops 'temple-bound' (l. 26) and punningly alludes to his toppling of the pillars of the Philistines' temple; cf. 'Deaths and Entrances'. 38 **a bush plumed with flames** = as well as the burning bush of Exodus, may also allude to the tale of 'Peredur Son of Evrawg' in *The Mabinogion*: 'On the bank of the river he saw a tall tree: from roots to crown one half was aflame

and the other green with leaves.' 43 **whinnying** = originally 'blowing'; the replacement was suggested by Watkins.

After the funeral (In memory of Ann Jones)

In February 1933, Thomas's description of his ambivalent response to the death of his aunt Ann to Trevor Hughes was self-consciously literary:

> As I am writing, a telegram arrives. Mother's sister. . . is dying. . . . Mother leaves. The old aunt will be dead by the time she arrives. This is a well-worn incident in fiction, & one that has happened time after time in real life. . . . After Mother's departure [to see Ann in Carmarthen Hospital] I am left alone in the house feeling slightly theatrical. (*CL*, 30)

His appalled contemplation of this response (a 'foul thing') is caught in the poem he tried to write at the time, N3 'Six', which began 'After the funeral, mule praises, brays / Shaking of mule heads betoken / Grief at the going to earth of man . . .', and concluded:

Another gossips' toy has lost its use,
Broken lies buried amid broken toys,
Of flesh and bone lies hungry for the flies,
Waits for the natron and the mummy paint
With dead lips pursed and dry bright eyes;
Another well of rumour and cold lies
Has dried, and one more joke has lost its point.

A revision of the poem was sent to Vernon Watkins on 28 March 1938; then, after telling him that he was 'completely rewriting [it]' on 1 April, Thomas sent Watkins the poem in almost-final form, noting that the 'facile &, almost, grandiosely sentimental' ending of the previous version 'now becomes the new brackets'.

Its history suggests the later poem was a palinode, aimed at correcting the first with a ringing affirmation. But we should not overlook the sophistication and self-awareness that temper the callowness of the 1933 letter to Hughes. Life takes forms prepared for it by 'fiction', and reality itself can be seen as 'theatrical', tropes which suggest at least some understanding of the paradox that in achieving the detachment necessary for writing, the poet may egotistically sever himself from the lives most people lead (a theme for Thomas as late as 'In my craft or sullen art'). This does not save the 1933 poem, which is why Thomas inscribed his awareness of the problem in its successor, framing his melodramatic adolescent posturing within its opening lines. Only after this is done may Ann be eulogised; but this does not mean that the 'theatrical' aspect of the original response has been banished on the grounds of humanist 'sincerity'; the later poem wrestles with, but does not renounce, histrionics, and the speaker mounts the stage of her hearth in order to create Ann's monument.

'After the funeral' has attracted extensive critical discussion, and is widely regarded as the first major fruit of Thomas's turn away from the early process style, announced later in 1938 in 'Once it was the colour of saying' ('Things rather than ideas of things have begun to detain the poet' (Tindall, 1962)). T. H. Jones (1963) sees it as the first clear sounding of 'the notes of exultation and celebration' which dominate his later poetry, while Aneirin Talfan Davies (1964) claims Ann is treated as a 'Protestant saint', discerning 'two contrasting and recurring images, one of dryness, the other of life-giving waters'. In line with his reading of Thomas as moving towards a Catholic pantheism, he calls it his 'last Nonconformist utterance . . . from now on the preacher was to give way to the priest.' Moynihan (1966) demurs, finding all other images and contradictions to be incidental to the primary water – life identification. Barbara Hardy (2000) draws several of these strands together in viewing it as both Thomas's most Welsh poem, and the one that links the earlier and later aspects of the 'green' strain in his work. Thomas's nature is not, now, elemental, but pastoral, and Ann resembles a dying but regenerative nature god, such as Attis or Osiris, or – more literarily – Lycidas or Adonais, in the tradition of the English pastoral elegy, with overtones of Welsh poetry in its the 'ecstatic metamorphoses of Christian church into wild green nature'.

7 boy who slits his throat = may also be a sort of pledge to Ann, alluding to the children's 'pledge' in games (in South Wales, but possibly elsewhere) in which the child held up his/her finger, having licked it, and chanted the following, or a version of it: 'See this wet, see this dry, [having wiped the finger on a sleeve or whatever] / Cut [or Slit] my throat and hope to die.' 12 **I stand** = the poem's first main verb. 14 **hooded fountain** = Thomas's Aunt Ann is visualised in a way which recall's 'Salem' (1908), a famous painting by Sydney Curnow Vosper (1866–1942). An iconic depiction of Welsh Non-conformist virtue, this shows an old woman (Siân Owen, Caradoc Evans' aunt) in traditional Welsh costume, wrapped in a shawl and holding her Bible, making her way from chapel after a service. Thomas's evocation is, like the rest of the poem, both ironic and loving. 22 **wood-tongued virtue** = virtue which lacks eloquence, since if the tongue of the bellbuoy in the following line was wooden it would make no sound; however, Ann's poet-nephew, the poet who was the mere tongue-tied 'boy' of 1933, will now be her eloquent bard. 32 **cramp** = of death, but also of narrow, puritanical religion. 36 **These cloud-sopped, marble hands** = 'mocking the conventional belief in heaven' (Ackerman, 1991); but Ann's hands are emblems of the rigours and privations of her entire existence.

O Chatterton and others in the attic

Although written in Laugharne, details in the poem echo a letter by Thomas of fifteen months before, written from the house his parents had retired to in Bishopston in Gower; they may originate in one of Thomas's self-deprecating comic routines (see below).

15 **tripper's knicker in the gully** = cf. letter to to Emily Holmes Coleman, a London-based American writer and Thomas's erstwhile lover, of 29 March 1937: 'It's a Welsh bank-holiday, a very special day, and soon I shall join the cold picnic-parties on the cliffs, drink beer in the 'bus-depôt, find a tripper's knicker in the gully, be a pocket Chesterton on the rolling inn-roads.' 22 **Love's a decision of 3 nerves** = writing to Trevor Hughes in January 1934 Thomas identified the need for 'a new consciousness of the old universal architecture' (cf. 'Praise to the architects'), and self-mockingly quoted Ezra Pound's 'Fratres Minores', in which poets complain 'in delicate and exhausted metres / That the twitching of three abdominal nerves / Is incapable

of producing a lasting Nirvana'. The '3 nerves' are the plural subject of 'love's questions' in l. 23. 41–2 **women figures** – cf. 'woman figure without fault', 'The hunchback in the park'.

On no work of words

1–2 **bloody / Belly of the rich year** = for red leaves as blood see 'Especially when the October wind', 'Poem in October'. 3 **poverty and craft** = the Thomases were living in dire poverty at the time when this poem was written. 11 **woods of the blood dash down to the nut of the seas** = images that reflect the Darwinian perspectives of Thomas's 1930s poetry; the speaker calls on his blood to de-evolve, back to the sea-water which was the basis for the blood of the first primitive life-forms, if he fails to make use of his poetic talents; the scientific frame counterpoints, but does not annul, the poem's Biblical references.

The tombstone told

'Thirty Six' in N3 was expanded from one stanza to three in the September 1938 revision.

The rewriting made it much less 'Hardy-like' than 'Thirty Six'. The idea of events in the outside world projected film-like on the wall of the womb occurs in 'Then was my neophyte' and 'Altarwise' IV. This poem collapses times together in order to link the long-dead woman, Thomas in his mother's womb, and his adult self, a simultaneity characteristic of the process poems. It is, like 'After the funeral', another poem of the period which anticipates the transparency of Thomas's later style, creating a certain jarring effect; later Hardyesque graveyard pieces (e.g. 'In the White Giant's Thigh') unpack its implications and realise its potential more satisfactorily.

2 **two surnames** = her maiden and married names; she was married, but died before the marriage was consummated. 14 **Through the devilish years and innocent deaths** = to Vernon Watkins's objection to the notebook version ('Through the small years and great deaths'),

Thomas replied: 'I agree with your objection to "small"; "innocent" is splendid, but "fugitive" & "turbulent" are, for me in that context, too vague, too "literary" (I'm sorry to use that word again) too ambiguous. I've used "devilish", which is almost colloquial.' (*CL*, 376). 21 **hurried** = 'winding' in *N3*, remaining so in *Poetry* (Chicago), *Seven*, and *Voice of Scotland*. 27 **bellowing** = dismissing Watkins's objections, Thomas said: 'No, I still think the womb "bellowing" is allright [*sic*], exactly what I wanted'; although it is what Thomas called 'a stunt rhyme', the word contains 'bellows' and 'below'-ing, both apposite in the context.

A saint about to fall

Conception is as much this poem's subject as birth, as Maud (2003) argues, with two 'falls'; in stanza 1 from the 'heaven' of the sexual-orgasmic act, and in stanza 3 from the womb into the world.

In stanza 1 the 'saint' is its father's seed, imagined praising the 'song' of the sexual act, specifically in the form of the about-to-erupt 'etna' of the father's erection. As it moves towards spilling over the edge of heaven, it says farewell to its home and hymns the sexual act in eucharistic terms, followed by the 'spitting vinegar' of ejaculation and the enviable 'flames and shells' of orgasm. Stanza 2 begins with the orgasmic act and its detumescent aftermath; male self-centredness is interrupted by the mother asking the incarnated 'saint' to 'wake in me', and this begins the second part of the poem, in which the foetus is told 'what a world it will see'. Stanza 3 deals with gestation and birth; it continues the hortatory tone, asking the saint to deceive the Saturn-like, offspring-devouring terror of the time it enters, and to 'wail' injustice at those whose loss of selfhood has turned them into things (their 'I's / 'eyes' 'already murdered'). The desperate ambiguity of 'wake in' is now intensified in 'raise' / raze, 'lapped' (protected, but also 'lapped up', devoured), 'stocked' (well-prepared and put in the stocks) as the birth is imagined. The big question the poem asks is: how can one bring a child – 'Bull[y]' it – into the 'rough seas' of a world of such misery and violence? There is no answer apart from the brilliant enactment of the fusion of historical trauma and joy at birth (Thomas told Watkins that the words 'Cry joy' were the most important in the poem): the exit from the womb is an 'iron' one, and its oiled 'bolt' and 'flick of the thumb' approximates the readying of a gun for firing.

7 **his father's house in the sands** = Thomas and Caitlin were at this time living in a house in Laugharne, beside the sandy beaches of the Towy estuary. 16 **vinegar** = given to Christ on the cross (Thomas may also have in mind the idiom 'vinegar strokes' for the final thrusts of the penis in sexual intercourse). The intermingling states are enacted by a syntax which reads in both directions and puns (e.g.: 'quick' as 'quickly' and 'living'). 26–34 **O wake in me . . . brains and hair** = lines perhaps addressed by the mother to the child (with the father returning to speak at l. 35). 49 **Bullies . . . you so gentle** = for 'bully' as a verb for birth, cf. 'If my head hurt a hair's foot'. 51 **A thundering bullring** = allusion to the Spanish Civil War, then entering its final phase before the defeat of the Republic by Franco in early 1939.

Twenty-four years

One of the birthday poems that form a distinct sub-genre in Thomas's oeuvre (cf. 'Especially when the October wind', 'Poem in October', 'Poem on his birthday'). Michael Neill (1970) gives the best reading of the imagery, although his general attitude to Thomas is disappointing; William Rowe is better, seeing Thomas's as a vision of life as 'sheer exuberant loss' opposed to the 'common-sense idea of [it] as an accumulation of experience' (Goodby, 2003). At the heart of the poem, as Goodby describes it, is the image of a young man going out on the town on a Saturday night with money in his pockets and the hope of getting lucky with a girl ('the sensual strut'). Davies (1993) adds, 'The last line transforms the melodrama of the poem into a note of resignation, with a subtle suggestion of value ("advance") and the irony of having a poem about death end with the verb "to be" – "as long as forever *is*"!'

2 (**Bury the dead . . .**) = to Watkins's suggested improvement, in his letter of 20 December 1938, Thomas replied: 'sorry about that bracketed line . . . but, until I can think of something else or feel, it will have to

stay. I thought your alternative line clumsier & more bass-drum (rather muffled, too) than mine . . . If ever I do alter it, I'll *remember* your line'. 3 **I crouched like a tailor** = a favourite Thomas image, as discussed by Neill (1970); cf. 'I see the boys of summer', 'Once below a time'. The letter of 24 October had observed: 'In the first version I had "like a stuffed tailor". I think "stuffed" is wrong, don't you?' 5 **meat-eating sun** = cf. Hamlet in *Hamlet* 2:2, ll. 183–6: 'For if the sun breed maggots in a dead dog, being a good kissing carrion – have you a daughter? . . . Let her not walk in the sun.' John L. Sweeney (1946) notes 'the Welsh festival of "meat-eating" (*ciga*) celebrated when a bullock was slaughtered . . . and the Freudian concept of energy, the "hunger energy" symbolized by the sun.' 6 **sensual strut** = cf. 'After the funeral', 'the strutting fern'. 8 **town** = points the contrast with Milton's Christian vision of the future, which involved a grander, heavenly city.

Once it was the colour of saying

Vernon Watkins was sent this 'Cwmdonkin poem', as Thomas described it, on 29 December 1938; Thomas responded to his comments on 8 January 1939, writing:

> I shan't alter anything in it except, perhaps, the 'close & cuckoo' lovers. The 'dear close cuckoo' lovers is a good suggestion. I can't say the same for 'halo for the bruised knee and broken heel' [presumably Watkins' alternative l. 11] which is esoterically off every mark in the poem.

More than any other poem in *TML*, this one marks the stylistic turning-point of 1937–8, its first half revisiting Thomas's precocious boyhood and his room at 5 Cwmdonkin Drive, while the second hazards a guess at the future. Maud (1989) suggests that Thomas was reworking a piece from the lost notebook of July 1932–January 1933; if true, it would suggest that the farewell to the lush, romantic style of 1931–2 found in *N1* and *N2* is being conflated with that to the process poetry of 1933–7. This would account for the fact that, in its most obvious sense, 'the colour of saying' actually increased in certain ways after 1938. Reworking a 1932 poem in order to represent a move in the opposite direction to the one being signalled was an appropriately paradoxical gesture, as was the self-mocking use of 'Voyelles' as a model.

1 **the colour of saying** = as well as 'Voyelles' (translated by Thomas's friends Edgell Rickword and Norman Cameron), this phrase echoes Joyce's *A Portrait of the Artist as a Young Man*: 'He drew forth a phrase from his treasure and spoke it softly to himself: – A day of dappled seaborne clouds. The phrase and the day and the scene harmonized in a chord. Words. Was it their colours?' 3 **a school** = as James A. Davies (2000) notes, this was Clevedon College, lower down the hill than the Thomas's house, 'a small private school, mainly for girls, occupying a field in treed grounds that were sometimes grazed by "coughing sheep . . . [that] plague my life".' It has been replaced by Clevedon Court, a cluster of modern houses on a street which makes another entrance into Cwmdonkin Park. Further up the hill, opposite number 5, is a small enclosed reservoir, the remains of a larger one that once extended into the park. 4 **black and white patch** = continues the image-train begun with 'soaked' in l. 2: the 'colour of saying' was like an overturned ink-bottle 'soaking' his writing-'table', with 'black and white' poems (often about girls) on the 'field' of paper. The soaking/capsizing imagery in turn leads to 'seaslide' and 'drowned'. 5 **gentle seaslides of saying** = very early poetry (the poems of 1933–7 are anything but 'gentle'). 6 **cockcrow** = treacherously (like Peter's renunciation of Christ three times before 'cockcrow'). Like 'colour' and 'gentle', 'charming' seems rather vague, but it can also mean drowned as if by a magic spell, or 'charm'.

Because the pleasure-bird whistles

The implicit metaphor here is the idiom 'food for thought'; the year of 1938 contained terrible examples of this, the poem says – the Third Moscow Show Trial, Franco's impending victory in Spain, the Anschluss, and the Munich Agreement – but it did not digest them. World war now looms as a result. The poem is self-critique and a sincere if oblique commitment to explore the links between suffering and art more fully in future, as many of the poems of *TML* and the War would.

13 **bum city** = bad, as in a letter to Vernon Watkins of 20 December 1938:

> I've just come back from three dark days in London, city of the restless dead. It really is an insane city, & filled me with terror. Every pavement drills through your soles to your scalp, and out pops a lamp-post covered with hair. I'm not going to London again for years; its intelligentsia is so hurried in the head that nothing stays there; its glamour smells of goat; there's no difference between good and bad. (*CL*, 392–3)

'If my head hurt a hair's foot'

In a letter to Vernon Watkins of 3 March 1939, Thomas informed him that proofs of *TML* had arrived, but that he wished to include this just-finished poem: 'Please, can I have a quick criticism. It's deeply felt, but perhaps clumsily said.' Some changes were made before publication in *Poetry* (London) in April 1939.

In his BBC reading of it in 1949, Thomas defended the poem against charges of obscurity; however, they were repeated by Robert Graves in the Clark Lectures he gave at Cambridge in 1955, when Graves offered one pound to anyone who could make sense of the poem's first stanza (but refused to pay up when M. J. C. Hodgart did so) (Brinnin, 1961).

6 **game** = as in colloquial 'to be game for' something. 7–10 **I'll comb ... ghost with a hammer** = metaphors drawn from mining and a miner's leisure pursuits: poaching, cock-fighting, boxing, the fairground shooting-range. 21–2 **Now to awake husked of gestures ... To the anguish and carrion** = J. H. Martin, in a letter to the *TLS* in 1964, claimed that Thomas had told him in 1936 of an aleatory composition method he practised when he was at a loss for a line; he would 'try ... on for size [words] from the top lines of various books, often Djuna Barnes's *Nightwood* within the draft of a 'general scheme of a stanza'. Martin offered no examples to substantiate Thomas's claim, and it seemed to be a typical example of the kind of leg-pulling answers Thomas used to give to gullible listeners. However, in 1968 Gene Montague

found *Nightwood* allusions and echoes in 'After the funeral' and 'How shall my animal'. Following his cue, I checked other poems of the time against Barnes's novel, and discovered a word-cluster lifted from it which Thomas had used to generate these two lines in '"If my head hurt"' (cf. Goodby, 2011, 2013). The *Nightwood* passage in question reads:

> Night people do not bury their dead, but on the neck of you, their beloved and waking, sling the creature, *husked of its gestures*. And where you go, it goes, the two of you, your living and her dead, that will not die; to daylight, to life, to grief, until both are *carrion*. (Cf. Djuna Barnes, *Nightwood*, London: Faber, 1936 repr. 2012, pp. 79–80)

joy like a cave = the copy of the poem sent to Watkins held in the BL (MS 52616) has 'calm like a cave'; 'calm' was replaced so that it could go to the penultimate line. **24 grain** = sperm and ovum, 'symbol for man in general'; **grave** = womb as well as tomb, 'man's origin as well as his destination' (Hornick, 1958). **26 dust-appointed grain** = the 'grain'-like sperm and ovum have an 'appointment' with 'grain'-like 'dust'. **29–30 The grave . . . and the endless beginning of prodigies suffers open** – in the 3 March version the poem's final line ran: 'And the endless, tremendous beginning suffers open', over which Thomas agonised: 'is the last line too bad, too comic, or does it just work? Have you any alternative for the adjectives'. To Watkins's 'quick criticism' he replied: 'I agree with every word you wrote abt my poem. The 2nd person speaks better than the first, & the last line is false. I haven't been able to alter the first part, & will have to leave it unsuccessful. The last line is now: "And the endless beginning of prodigies suffers open."' Maud (2003) sees 'prodigies' as an 'optimistic word', but its older sense of 'terrifying' and 'portentous' seems more appropriate for a birth in 1939.

Poem (To Caitlin)

Although it shares its central conceit and symbolic language with the revised and collected version of 1945, this earlier version of 'Unluckily for a death' is a substantial poem in its own right, and the marked differences in lexis, phrasing and tone – largely, as Watkins noted, a shift from a processual towards a religious one – usefully illuminate the changes in Thomas's style between 1939 and 1945.

The siren-like 'dust-drenched two' are a 'puffed phoenix', and a 'widow'; they call on the speaker to 'shoo up the light . . . to heaven' or 'sing underground' with the 'passionate dead and gone / In the burial holes of enticement' – that is, to falsely transcend or submerge the self by valorising the spirit at the expense of the body, or vice versa. The 'very enjoyable mood' of the writing is evident in the poem's fluid movement and brilliant phrase-making, and in its rejection of the 'phoenix' and 'widow' it marks a further step away from the darker aspects of the process style and towards the greater amplitude of the later work. As with other ode-like poems of 1938–40, such as 'How shall my animal' and 'A saint about to fall', the handling of complex form paves the way for post-1944 works such as 'Poem in October' and 'Over Sir John's hill'.

The poem is formally unusual in several ways; first three stanzas are 14 lines long (sonnet-length), the last 15, with a syllable-pattern of roughly of 7, 7, 13, 6, 10, 10, 10, 6, 9 (or 9, 6), 10, 10, 13, 8 (8 in stanza 4's additional final line). Each stanza opens with *abcd* (except 1, which runs *abca*) and permutates the four end-rhymes, introducing others up to *e* (stanza 1), *g* (stanzas 2 and 3) and *f* (stanza 4) (e.g. in stanza 1: *abcabdcacdeaee*, rhyming death-wreath-mouth-broth; stone-gone; briared-occurred-forehead; enticement-constant; lyrical-rails-fossils).

13 **sheeted** = Vernon Watkins suggested 'withered', a proposal Thomas rejected: 'it cuts across the poem and does not come out of it' (*CL*, 434). 16 **burly body** = cf. 'On no work of words'. 37 **In an imagining of tumbled mantime** = Watkins proposed an alternative to this line; Thomas replied:

> I think you are liable . . . to suggest alterations or amendments for purely musical motives. For instance, 'Caught in a somersault of tumbled mantime' may (and I doubt it) sound more agreeable – we'll leave out any suggestion of it sounding inevitable because it is, however good the implied criticism, a group of words outside the poem – to the 'prophesying ear' than 'In an imagining of tumbled

mantime', a line I worked out *for* its sounds and & not in spite of them. My criticism . . . in this case is that your 'ear' is deaf to the logic of my poem;

'Caught in a somersault etc etc
Suddenly cold as a fish'

is an ambiguous tangle, very like nonsense.

Thomas added: 'your criticism often works towards the aural better-ment (ugh) of details, without regard for their significance in a worked-out, if not a premeditated-*in-detail*, whole' (*CL*, 434). 49 **fiery wheel** = *King Lear*, 4:5, l. 40. Cf. 'All all and all'.

To Others than You

2 **bad coin in your socket** = revealingly adduced as an example of 'word-tumbling without gravity or point, or point of fun', by Grigson (the presumed target of the poem) in his essay 'How Much Me Now Your Acrobatics Amaze' (Tedlock, 1960). 5 **brassily** = brass is proverb-ial for impressive-seeming but shoddy or fake goods. 8 **sucked** = in a P.S. to his June 1939 letter to Vernon Watkins, Thomas notes: 'The word I used too much – sucked – is here bound, I think, to be.' 10 **memory worked by mirrors** = like this poem; in his broadcast 'A Few Words of a Kind', Thomas described poetry as 'worked by mirrors' (*CL*, 434). 15 **desireless familiar** = Thomas's postscript in the letter to Watkins noted that it was 'a phrase used in my "Orchards" and what caused me to write the poem', and a letter to Dent of 25 May 1939 shows that he had been proofing this story for publication in *TML* on that very day. In the story, the phrase has positive con-notations: 'They sat in the grass by the stone table like lovers at a picnic, too loved to speak, desireless familiars in the shade of the hedge corner.' 17 **While you displaced a truth in the air** = the Watkins letter notes: 'The best thing is, as you'll perhaps agree, the simple last line of the middle bit'. 18–21 The final quatrain shifts to the plural, and insists that the speaker is not naïve – he knows his friends have faults, but in this case the 'friend' has actively deceived him.

When I woke

The finished poem seems not to have been sent to Vernon Watkins, unlike many at this time. Davies and Maud note in *CP88* that in his copy of *Wales* (for June 1938) Thomas tested out several lines, one of which is 'When I woke, the dawn spoke', but this only gives an earliest possible date. The summer of 1939 is likelier than 1938, and the context of the impending war is clearer in the first version, published in *Seven*, than in *DE*:

Shaking humanity's houses:
Wake to see one morning breaking:
Bulls and wolves in iron palaces:
Winds in their nests in the ruins of man.

Bulls, wolves and eagles' (?) nests seem to symbolise fascist Spain, Italy and Germany in these final lines; too portentously, perhaps, resulting in their later replacement.

20 **sparrowfall** = the small bird is contrasted with the huge, unpoetic (and un-biblical) mammoth. 29–30 **shells** = as in 'I see the boys of summer', these are the military as well as the marine variety.

Once below a time

Written during Thomas's writing of the autobiographical stories of *A Portrait of the Artist as a Young Dog*, and an example of the more discursively autobiographical poems of the late 1930s. Part I develops the tailoring conceit of 'Twenty four years', in a way which moves it in the direction of both surrealism and the comic self-description of the radio broadcast 'Return Journey' (1946) as 'a bit of a shower-off; plus-fours and no breakfast . . . a bombastic adolescent provincial bohemian with a thick-knotted artist's tie made out of his sister's scarf . . . and a cricket shirt dyed bottle-green; a gabbing, ambitious, mock-tough, pretentious young man'. The central conceit of flesh as clothing is common in Thomas (cf. 'Twenty-four years', p. 107) and in Metaphysical poetry (cf. George Herbert, 'Mans medley').

8 **snapping rims of the ashpit** = 'the snapping [dentate] rims of the ashpit [of love]' (Maud 2003). 19 **bear** = a pun on 'bare' (see l. 49), 21 **kangaroo foot of the earth** = D. H. Lawrence's poem 'Kangaroo' stresses the kangaroo's 'down-urge', whereas Thomas here emphasises his youthful defiance of gravity. 24 **Up through the lubber crust of Wales** = Thomas responded to Vernon Watkins's criticism of this line: 'I agree . . . but have, so far, done nothing about altering it. Gaels is good, but that sounds to me facetious. Actually, although I thought the pun out quite coldly, I wanted to make the lubber line a serious one, and I'm glad that you like it apart from its joke' (*CL*, 496). 37, 40 **Columbus on fire, Cold Nansen's beak** = similar extreme territories and sea-journeys feature Thomas's most experimental fictions: e.g. 'In the Direction of the Beginning'. 47 **Never never oh never to regret the bugle I wore** = Thomas told Watkins: 'I didn't much like "I do not regret the bugle I wore" but its omission makes the end too vague. I'll either retain the line or alter it', later adding: 'For "I do not regret" . . . I have put "Never never oh never to regret the bugle I wore"' (*CL*, 497).

There was a Saviour

Although no version of this poem is extant in Thomas's letters to Vernon Watkins, they discussed it in early 1940, as Thomas's letter of 6 March 1940 attests. Watkins evidently felt it was one of his best poems, probably because there is an explicitly religious theme. In essence, the poem complexly accuses and shares in the guilt of those who made the War possible by perverting Christian ideals for selfish ends, particularly in exploiting the natural desire of the young for leaders and role models. Davies (1993) detects only a religious theme, although Moynihan (1966) notes that 'This [final line] is a form of impassioned humanism, to which Thomas's revolt turned at this point, but it is not a faith in, nor even a praise of the faith of, the savior "rarer than radium".' Goodby (2013) shifts the emphasis still further, focusing on the poem's fusion of religious with psycho-political and sexual tropes, while Nowottny (1962), offers one of the most thorough and subtly insightful Practical Criticism-based readings of any Thomas poem, identifying and discussing the verbal structures and tropes of the poem in a virtuoso critique.

For Nowottny and Goodby, the displaced aggression of the saviour's followers is what leads them to identify with the deity for reasons akin to those that produced identification with Hitler or Stalin. Such displacement and escapism brings one to the benighted state of the 'brothers' of stanza 4, and liberation from their plight – as in the process of political radicalisation which led the British population to embrace the Beveridge Report – requires acknowledging past hard-heartedness. This alone, it is claimed, can release the solidarity, empathy and sexual loving-kindness that will erode the stony barriers barring us from the house of love 'exiled' within ourselves and others. In this way the poem probes the psychosocial and even economic origins of the war and, taking its cue from poems such as Blake's 'London', uses building imagery to figure the repressed self and the institutions reared upon it.

7–8 ll. 7–8 establish a formula repeated in stanzas 2 and 3: '*something human* / In the *buildings* of [*some expression of*] *human feeling*': that is, '[t]he "we" of the poem and the "saviour" . . . are presented in human terms but between them there intervene buildings' (Nowottny, 1962). 12 **hindering man** = to a suggestion of Watkins's, Thomas replied: 'I'll think of "stupid kindred", which is right, of course, in meaning . . . but kindred seems a little pompous a word: it hasn't the literal simplicity of hindering man.' 'Hindering' is from Blake's marginalia on Lavater's *Aphorisms on Man*. These distinguish sin from 'acts' of energy: 'To hinder another is not an act; it is the contrary; it is a restraint on action both in ourselves & in the person hinder'd, for he who hinders another omits his own duty at the same time. Murder is hindering another. Theft is hindering another . . . But the origin of this mistake in Lavater & his cotemporaries [*sic*] is, They suppose that Woman's Love is Sin; in consequence all the Loves & Graces with them are Sins.' 14, 19 **we . . . you** = Nowottny notes: 'The shifting pronouns and oddness of their usage makes it reason-able to infer that the "we" and "you" are somehow the same and yet different', and that 'it is being forced upon our notice that this is a poem about continuous identities with a changing outlook, taken at various points in a continuum running through the poem'. 14 **murdering breath** = cf. Swinburne's 'Hymn to Proserpine', in which a Roman pagan acknowledges Christianity's triumph: 'Thou hast conquer'd, O pale Galilean; the world has grown grey from thy breath'. 20–23 **O you who would not cry . . . shell** = a list of the things the brothers did and did not do in turning to false religion to evade their involvement in human suffering. 21 **On to** = changed from 'on' in *Horizon* version to emphasise that they were above the 'ground', immune to the suffering of those below them. 23 **laid your cheek . . . a cloud-formed shell** = Nowottny detects an allusion to Keats's 'Bright star' sonnet: 'Pillow'd upon my fair love's ripening breast'. 28–30 **O we who could not stir . . . near and fire neighbour** = the brothers' self-indictment is of attitudes which underwrote the government's appeasement of fascism and hard-heartedness towards the unemployed in the 1930s. 35 **Brave deaths . . . never found** = with allusion to the 'lost' children of Blake's *Songs of Innocence* and *Songs of Experience*. An earlier draft had 'Deaths of the only ones, our never found', but Thomas told Watkins: 'you're right as can be and somehow I must make "death" the second word . . . in that particular "death" line you showed to me the one big misbalance in the poem' (*CL*, 502). 39–40 **Exiled in us . . . all rocks** = we activate the open, unaggressive and androgynous sexual love isolated within us and which can overcome the ossified psychic and social structures we have been imprisoned in; **armless . . . love** = cf. 'A Prospect of the Sea': 'the arm of an empire broken like Venus'.

The Countryman's Return

Thomas took pains over this poem, and was happy for it to be published in 1941, but he probably considered it too demotic to be collected in *DE*. It is an experiment in a kind of semi-surreal, largely urban mode, which we might regret he didn't do more with (Philip Larkin was sufficiently impressed to include it in his 1973 *Oxford Book of Twentieth Century English Verse*). It has affinities with the bantering wartime verse-letters to friends, while the scenes described in the second and third sections recall the unfinished novel *Adventures in the Skin Trade*, on which he was working at this time.

Buffalo MS B434F1 consists of a London Film Institute Society programme of 21 April 1940 on which a version of ll. 25–76 was pencilled by Thomas. It is too close to the version Thomas sent in a letter to Vernon Watkins to have been recalled from memory, but nevertheless differs from it on several minor points, and so may have been an attempt at revision which Thomas afterwards either mislaid or decided not to use (no changes were incorporated into the published version) (*LVW*, 86–8). Some of the differences between the versions are noted below.

32 missing from B434F1 33 **propped** = may have a theatrical connotation, as in 'The hunchback in the park'. 51 **queen** = B434F1 has 'quean' (slut), which makes better sense. 54–5 B434F1 lacks these two lines, and begins l. 56 with 'cautious' for 'dark'. 66–8 omitted in B434F1. 72 **Dean Street** = in Soho, London; a centre of the film and advertising industry, home to several pubs, clubs, theatres and hospitals, including the Lock Hospital for venereal diseases (the word 'Lock' was a euphemism at this period for venereal disease). 77 **Cut** = the poem cuts, film-like, from London to the countryside in its last section. 91 **dirtbox** = London; Thomas is describing the need to dispose of any evidence of debauchery in the capital when he returns home.

Into her Lying Down Head

Like 'After the funeral', 'If my head hurt a hair's head' and several other poems of the time, this poem was influenced by Thomas's recent reading of Djuna Barnes's *Nightwood* (1936). Thomas's 'note . . . in my copybook', copied out with the poem when he sent it to Watkins (*CL*, 362), closely echoes a speech by the novel's most seedily spellbinding character, the visionary Dr Matthew Dante O'Connor:

> For what is not the sleeper responsible? What converse does he hold, and with whom? He lies down with his Nelly and he drops off into the arms of his Gretchen. Thousands unbidden come to his bed . . . The sleeper is the proprietor of an unknown land. He goes about another business in the dark – and we, his partners . . . cannot afford an inch of it . . . For the lover, it is the night into which his beloved goes . . . When she sleeps is she not moving her leg aside for an unknown garrison? . . . We are continent a long time, but no sooner has our head touched the pillow, and our eyes left the day, than a host of merrymakers take and get. *Nightwood*, pp. 86–7.

The poem's concern is with the jealousy provoked by dream 'betrayals' of this kind, inextricably enmeshed as they are with actual sexual memories and fantasies.

Biographical approaches refer to Caitlin Thomas's abuse at the hands of Augustus John, who had raped her when she was modelling for him as a fifteen year-old, and whose mistress she was when she first met Thomas in April 1936. Although relations between all three were cordial enough after Dylan and Caitlin's marriage in July 1937, John's shadow is highly likely to have fallen between the couple; the poem's 'thief of adolescence' seems too accurate a description of his role to be coincidental.

Stanza II presents sex, in caricature terms, as a violation of the female, recalling the sexual activity preceding sleep as a 'raping wave'. This may reflect a general sense of the sexual act as a form of violence against women (cf. 'The seed-at-zero', 'My world is pyramid'), exacerbated by the speaker's envious sense that while his partner is being 'enjoyed' by her dream-lover, he has 'no lovely part' in their doings. In this sense, the caricature of phallic masculinity presented here seems less his partner's dream, or the reality of their own sexual relationship, than a masochistic projection, in which both are victims of her past. Indeed, the luridly 'superhuman' quality of the images make them read like *male* imaginings of *female* fantasy, and may even be darkly humorous; thus, Tindall (1962), notes that the poem shares some aspects of the scenario it describes with *Ulysses*: 'Mr. and Mrs. Bloom preside over the house of Thomas. The intruder who threatens it is as "furnace-nostrilled" as any of Mrs. Bloom's twenty-five suitors . . . and as comic.'

The poem has 'wide implications' (as Thomas informed Watkins), as well as personal ones, and its 'beast' is 'always anonymous' partly because it may lurk in every sexual subconscious. Barbara Hardy (2000) stresses this aspect in her reading of the poem as a 'highly original, strange, love lyric', which is simultaneously 'one of Thomas's best nature poems'. In it, his perpetual concern with 'the unity of being' finds expression in the images of sand, shell, bird, stone and grass, which in stanza III are used to magnify the 'needs, desires and severance' of the estranged couple. These image the natural world's amoral detachment, as part of a larger vision which humans are shown to be unable to attain, even though 'the nonhuman phenomena can be described . . . by the human creature standing on the threshold of their existence, doing his best to invent a language for his empathy, allowing them to refuse to be subordinates, instruments, and symbols.' Maud (2003) and Goodby (2013) remind us that while the female figure is objectively perceived as 'innocent', the poem concludes with the speaker inconsolably 'torn up' by her behaviour.

Its contorted psychodrama is embodied in the poem's structure. Thomas told Robert Herring: '[it] may look very sprawly, but it's really properly formed', and Vernon Watkins that he had 'never worked harder on anything, maybe too hard: I made such a difficult shape too'. So hard was the pattern to maintain that the last ten lines of the June 1940 version abandon it completely (see below).

5 **Noah's rekindled now unkind dove** = a 'dove of peace . . . bred dialectically from "enemies"' (Maud, 1963); it returns not with an olive twig, but a 'man'. 18 **rode and whistled** = See Marvell's 'Damon the Mower', who 'with his whistling scythe, does cut / Each stroke between the earth and root.' 22–3 Circe is a chapter title in *Ulysses* (cf. *CP14*, and the cancelled l. 20 which refers to 'Circe's swinish, coiling island'). 27 **baskets of snakes** = cf. George Meredith, 'Modern Love', 'The strange low sobs that shook their common bed, / Were called into her with a sharp surprise, / And strangled mute, like little gaping snakes, / Dreadfully venomous to him.' 33 **Oceanic lover** = 'vast and womb-projected' (Tindall, 1962). Cf. 'Love in the Asylum', 'oceans of the male wards'. 37 **white gowned** = innocent and night-gowned. 38 **middle moonlit stages . . . tiered and hearing tide** = the man hears his partner's groans as if she is an actor and he is the audience; the tiers of the auditorium resemble waves; pun on 'teared' (tearful). 45–6 **foul wingbeat of the solemnizing nightpriest . . . always anonymous beast** = cf. the sexual Black Mass of 'It is the sinners' dust-tongued bell', and the 'beast who follows / With priest's grave foot' of 'I make this in a warring absence'. Cf. Meredith, 'Modern Love': 'He felt the wild beast in him betweenwhiles.' 47–9 **Two sand grains . . . Singly lie with the whole wide shore** = cf. 'We, lying by seasand' and the stories 'The Enemies' ('the grains of sand on far-away seashores would be multiplying as the sea rolled over them') and 'The Map of Love' ('two-loves-in-a-grain of the million sands'). Cf. Meredith 'Modern Love', 'Here is a fitting place to dig love's grave; / Here where

the ponderous breakers plunge and strike, / And dart their hissing tongues high up the sand.' 51 **domed and soil-based shell** = 5 June 1940 version reads: 'And out of every helled and heavened shell'. Thomas asked Watkins: 'Is this too clumsy? I like it but it may be'. Though perhaps keen on the 'helled' / held pun, and the rhyme on 'shell', he decided on non-religious alternatives for both the ample and earth-tethered aspects of 'shell', as whispering sea-shell, or shell of the self (cf. by contrast the 'cloud-formed shell' as a falsely idealistic concept of Christ in 'There was a saviour'). 52–6 **one voice in chains ... dissolving under the water veil** = 'dissolving', however, challenges the idea that such roles are fixed. 60–9 The 5 June 1940 version reads:

> From the madhouse and menageries
> Of jealous night uncage the grain and bird:
> The love of women and men
> Scrapes and sings denied in them,
> The filth and secret of death is sweeter with the sun than these
>   inconstancies,
> A loveless man mourns in the sole night.
> Betrayed will his love betrayed find an eye or a hair to hate?
> Will his lovely hands let run the daughters and sons of the blood?
> Will he rest his pulse in the built breast of impossible, great God?
> Over the world uncoupling the moon rises up to no good.

In *Life & Letters Today*, l. 5 of this section read: 'Damned damned go down or caress to death the sun-sized bridal bed's cruellest brood'. As a whole, the passage implies that the woman's death is preferable to her nocturnal faithlessness; this disappears in the revision. 60–2 **A blade of grass ... O she lies alone and still** = Hardy (2000) adds: 'We finally return to the human creatures, in a total and profound presentation of two points of view, the amoral view of nature, and the human sexual and social suffering which can't reach that larger natural view as it suffers.' 67 **A man torn up mourns in the sole night** = the speaker / Thomas; with pun on 'sole' / 'soul' and its dark nights.

Deaths and Entrances

An MS exists in Austin of Thomas's workings on this poem dating from the point when he had completed the first two stanzas and was working on the third. One sheet, headed 'Deaths & Entrances' in pencil, contains the first two stanzas typed out, with minor corrections in pencil, a first (four-line) attempt at a third stanza below it, and the line 'The hyena in the face that was her smile' is written below this. A second sheet, with the underlined heading in pencil 'Third Verse 1st Draft', extends the stanza to seven lines with an attempt at the next two, after which Thomas has drawn four horizontal lines to represent the lines yet to be written, and written out the 'hyena' line from the typescript sheet as the stanza's final line. The workings are continued on three more sheets, with two further examples of Thomas's intentions for the line, confirming the claim made by Gwen Watkins (2005) that the poem originally ended with a 'hyena image' drawn from Djuna Barnes's *Nightwood*. The worksheets also confirm the importance of stanza shape to Thomas, and his reported habit of working from a cluster of pre-existing phrases, some (or all) of which had been assigned a place in the matrix of the poem before the link sections had been written.

'Deaths and Entrances' concerns the impending Blitz, which Thomas may reasonably have felt would bear out Donne's claim that 'This whole *world* is but an *universall churchyard*, but our *common grave*', a sentiment common in Jacobean writing (cf. John Webster's *The Duchess of Malfi* [IV, ii, 162–5], another Thomas favourite: 'I know death hath ten thousand several doors / For men to take their exits; and 'tis found / They go on such strange geometrical hinges, / You may open them both ways'). The worksheets reveal that the 'your' of the published version began as 'she', and this backs up the sense most readers have that the poem also deals at some level with Dylan and Caitlin Thomas's turbulent marriage.

Critics have noted the poem's successive engagement with: *a* 'near' friends and family threatened by bombing; *b* 'strangers', probably on the side of the speaker (such as RAF pilots); *c* Luftwaffe pilots, conflated with Death. Emery (1962) and Maud (2003) believe a different *single* figure is successively addressed: a close friend; a 'stranger' who is an enemy bomber (or Christ-figure); Thomas himself. The different schemas reflect the dangers of imposing a causal or univocal narrative on the poem's slippery referents, tortuous syntax and evasive personal pronouns (the Donne texts Thomas echoes, for example, suggest that the 'globe . . . water thread' imagery of stanza 2 may be amniotic, and indicate that an embryo is one of the figures being addressed).

The slipperiness stems in part from Thomas's repugnance at his potential complicity in killing, and the demonising of Germans *en masse*. In 1939 he told Rayner Heppenstall that he 'wanted to know what my friends . . . are going to do when they are told by the State to fight not their enemies', and the double negative hints at the ethical questions behind the poem and its manner of raising them, blurring boundaries between self and other, friend and 'enemy' (*CL*, 480). In the spirit of the seemingly oxymoronic title ('deaths' is not an antonym of 'entrances'), the poem's polarities undo themselves, with 'near' inhabiting 'far' and 'stranger' 'friend' at every point. (Thomas noted that in *DE*, the poems' 'deaths' and 'entrances' 'keep their individualities and lose them in each other', and that is truest of this poem above all the others (*CL*, 396).) Death is omnipresent, both feared and necessary, even desired, as 'enemy' and 'immortal friend', but resembles a 'son' / the Son; and, as in 'Into Her Lying Down Head', Thomas explores the contradictions of his and others' situation via the dubiously triumphant figure of Samson.

1 **incendiary eve** – of the bombing of British cities by the Luftwaffe. 12 **many married London's estranging grief** = the city, linked with so many places, is now isolated, but with a glance at Thomas's marital 'grief' of the time. 15 **locking, unlocking** = imagery of imprisonment is pervasive in the wartime poems. 18 **dive up to his tears** = a quasi-paradox, since you normally 'dive' 'down', not 'up'. The imagery resembles Paul Nash's painting *The Battle of Britain* (1941), a pilot's-eye view of a 'thunderclapping' dogfight and 'water thread' Thames winding to a watery 'globe', whose surface is 'entered' by shot-down aircraft, although the poem was written before it was painted. Cf. George Herbert, 'Marie Magdalene': 'Though we could dive / In tears like seas, our sinnes are pil'd / Deeper than they'; **male sea** = originally 'tall stream' in Austin MS. 20 **strode** = 'drove' in Austin MS. 21 **wind his globe out of your water thread** = the 'globe'-like amniotic sac and umbilical cord, which the 'polestar neighbour' (Death, the

Germans, even Christ) threatens to wind into *his* 'globe'. 23 **cry** = 'sound' in Austin MS, deleted with line to possible alternatives ('noise', 'note', 'shout', 'with all wild cries') in the margin. 31 **In the watched dark, quivering** = Austin MS has 'In deepest dark inches'. 36 **Samson** = a victim of his own sensual appetite and female wiles, who destroyed himself in destroying his nation's enemies – a heroic suicide (cf. 'I make this in a warring absence', 'How shall my animal', 'Into her Lying Down Head' and 'Ballad of the Long-legged Bait').

On a Wedding Anniversary

An earlier version of this poem appeared in *Poetry* (London) on 15 January 1941, and it was collected in his US-published *New Poems* of 1943. Thomas sent it, with others, to Baron Howard de Walden on 24 December 1940, noting that they were 'done during the last six months'. This is the text of that earlier version, from the MS in Austin.

At last, in a wrong rain
The cold, original voices of the air
Cry, burning, into a crowd,
And the hermit, imagined music sings
Unheard through the streets of the flares;   5

The told birds fly again
From every true or crater-carrying cloud
Riding the risk of the night,
And every starfall question with their wings,
Whether it be death or light;   10

The sky is torn across
This ragged anniversary of two
Who moved for three years in tune
Through the singing wards of the marriage house
And the long walks of their vows.   15

Now their love lies a loss
And love and his patients roar on a chain;
The sun's brought down with a shout.
Three years dive headlong, and the mice run out
To see the raiding moon.   20

Returning the corrected proofs of *DE* to A. J. Hoppé at Dent's on
18 September 1945, Thomas noted: 'The poem on page 32 is substantially altered. In form, it is now three stanzas of four lines each.' He
condensed the twenty lines of the original to twelve, largely by deleting
the first two stanzas (but saving the phrases 'wrong rain' and 'crater-
carrying cloud'), eliminating the imagery of 'voices', sun and moon,
mice (symbolic of sexual crisis: cf. 'The Mouse and the Woman') and
'told [foretold] birds' of the bombers.

Parodies from The Death of the King's Canary

Because *The Death of the King's Canary* was co-authored with John
Davenport, it cannot be categorically proven that all the poems in it
are by Thomas, although 'Request to Leda', and 'The Parachutist', which
he read at the Oxford University English Club in November 1941,
certainly are. This event was recorded by Philip Larkin, then a student.

> [he] made hundreds of cracks and read parodies of everybody in
> appropriate voices. He remarked: 'I'd like to have talked about a
> book of poems I've been given to review, a young poet called Rupert
> Brooke – it's surprising how he has been influenced by Stephen
> Spender . . .' There was a moment of delighted surprise, then a roar
> of laughter. Then he read a parody of Spender entitled 'the para-
> chutist' which had people rolling on the floor. He kept this up all
> night – parodies of everyone bar Lawrence – and finally read two
> of his own poems, which seem very good. (*Selected Letters of Philip
> Larkin: 1940–1985*, London, Faber, 1992, p. 28)

The use of the phrase 'scalecophidian void', a phrase from *N3* 'Twenty
Four', in 'Lamentable Ode', suggests that it is by Thomas (we know
he took the notebooks with him to Davenport's country house in

Gloucestershire, since he left them there, and had to ask Davenport to locate them when he wanted to sell them). Stylistic and other clues allowed readers of the time to work out the targets: 'Fergus O'Hara' is probably F. R. Higgins, 'Robert Gordon' Norman Cameron, 'Wyndham Nils Snowden' W. H. Auden, 'Edmund Bell' Edmund Blunden, 'Sigismund Gold' Humbert Wolfe, 'Sir Frank Knight' Sir John Squires, 'John Lowell Atkins' T. S. Eliot and 'Hilary Byrd' Cecil Day Lewis.

Ballad of the Long-legged Bait

On 8 January 1941 Thomas wrote to John Davenport: 'Today the pipes burst, and Caitlin, in a man's hat, has been running all day with a mop from w.c. to flooded parlour, while I've been sitting down trying to write a poem about a man who fished with a woman for bait and caught a horrible collection.' Written in the first quarter of 1941, the 'Ballad' is Thomas's longest poem, and one of his most impressive, with the 152 worksheets held at Buffalo constituting the fullest MS record for any poem, and revealing arduous labour and great invention. It has much in common with the prose pieces 'An Adventure from a Work in Progress' and 'In the Direction of the Beginning', which also take the form of sea-borne sexual-spiritual quests. Writing to the novelist Graham Ackroyd on 24 September 1948, Thomas described 'Ballad' as 'brash, barging & violent'; he didn't want its title used as a chapter title in a comic novel by Ackroyd because it was 'a serious sexual adventure story', and a 'serious, if chaotic, poem' (assured of Ackroyd's basically serious purpose, it seems Thomas later relented).

The piece begins in the voices of a series of speakers – 'sand' and 'bulwarks', 'looking land', 'dwindling ships', buoys, and fisherman's boat. They tell of the fisherman casting off from land and then baiting and casting off a 'girl alive', hooked through the lips. Once in the sea, she 'longs among' the sea-creatures; he becomes storm-tossed, but happy at her amorous behaviour until she starts celebrating 'huge weddings in the waves'. When 'the seal 'kisse[s] [her] dead' the fisherman's 'tempter under the eyelid' vanishes, 'Lucifer . . . is lost' in the 'vaulted breath' of the bait, while 'Venus lies star-struck in her wound.'

Though stripped of his earlier desire, he reels in a chorus of 'long dead' monitory 'fathers' attached to the girl's hand with the message that he must 'Kill Time'. Now God himself 'clings' to the girl's hair and 'weeps' and the fisherman's rod 'bend[ing] low, divining land', pulls him into a land composed of the body of the bait and his home town, where he is led to the 'ox-killing house of love' as his boat 'dies down', the bait is 'drowned' in 'hayricks', the anchor 'dives through the floors of a church' (perhaps symbolising marriage), sun and moon wish him 'goodbye' and 'good luck', and he finally finds himself 'at the door of his home', 'long-legged heart' in hand.

Olson (1955) and Emery (1962), cued by 'the wanting flesh his enemy' (l. 91), find in 'Ballad' a 'meditation on the possibility of salvation through the mortification of the flesh'. However, the death of the tempter and the events that follow are not told with a sense of triumph over sin and sex; rather, it seems the fisherman feels he has given in to sin and regrets his loss. Parkinson (1981) and Moynihan (1966) also detect a fall from Eden, but with the fisherman brought low by 'marriage, pregnancy and fatherhood', a victim of female guile. For Tindall (1962), more positively, Caitlin is the bait, and salvation is 'from the amniotic sea of his adolescence'. Olson, Emery and Moynihan all think the italicised stanza describes an actual birth, and base allegorical readings on this assumption. Certainly, this moment resembles others (e.g. in 'A grief ago') where conception provokes the appearance of ancestors. However, Parkinson's case for it being a metaphorical formulation by the 'old men', who sing 'forebodingly of the cycle of reproduction and death of which sex is only the prelude', is very plausible. As she notes, the catch is not 'unwelcome', as the earlier critics claim, nor a child, nor is the bait herself 'Time'. Moreover, if the poem presents a sower of wild oats tamed by marriage at one level, by the end of it he is also 'alone', with 'an air of expectancy of return to the sea' (Maud, 2003).

Jungian readings naturally view the fisherman's quest as one for integration; this also excludes too much quirkily brilliant detail, but in making the bait his *anima*, they rightly note that the two are identified with each other ('long-legged bait' > 'long-legged heart'). This suggests parallels with other marriage-related poems of the time, in particular 'Into her lying down head', with its male projection of a woman's fantasy partners, perverse courting and savouring of betrayal, whale-rivals, and sense of the innate violence of sex which almost matches the cruel piercing of the bait's lips with a phallic hook. It is also significant that after the bait's death, the fisherman's own fantasies, or 'tempter under the eyelid', vanishes; the implication may be that she was a product of his desire, perhaps a fantasy figure, 'killed' for cavorting with his rivals. By Thomas's Blakeian frame of reference, the poem must be critical, to some extent at least, of the equation of women with 'Sin' at l. 110.

In general, like other poems of 1939–41, 'Ballad' seems more transparent than his previous work, but offers new challenges; it confuses agency and speaking subjects; uses repetition in more subtle ways; and juxtaposes house and family with the insatiability of desire for which the 'long-legged heart' is a perfect image. Who catches whom, or what? Tindall (1962) and *CP88* identify the phrase 'Dylan & Caitlin', scrawled on one of the Buffalo worksheets, as proof of autobiographical intent; however, the hand in which it is written is closer to Caitlin's than Thomas's. As so often, it proves impossible to impose a singular narrative upon a poem's richness of verbal event.

Title: information about 'Samson's Jack', the Gower megalith which supplied the working title for the poem, can be found at: *http://www. megalithic.co.uk/article.php?sid=4501* 6–8 **anchor . . . by the top of the mast** = cf. 'In the Direction of the Beginning' and 'An Adventure from a Work in Progress', both also about the voyages of boats manned by and symbolic of the (male) author in pursuit of a vividly sexual female figure. 32 **hilly with whales** = cf. 'Into her lying down head'; Thomas told Tindall (1962) that 'whales mean [male] rivals'. 49–52 Goodby (2013) notes 'the lines are heavily alliterated . . . and slip between high frontal vowel sounds and lower, more palatalised ones, in order to mimic the slide from wave crests to troughs, realising the fisherman's seasickness.' 122 **cast** = cf. Ecclesiastes 11:1: 'Cast thy bread upon the waters: for thou shalt find it after many days.' 146, 174 **insect-faced . . . Insects** = a slippery symbol in Thomas; here, it seems to mean something like wizened and incredibly primeval respectively (cf. 'fossil', l. 144). 216 **long-legged heart** = Tindall (1962) notes that the line 'weds the final to the unfinal', and that the heart includes 'both his wife and himself', and 'may be clutched, offered, displayed, contemplated, or about to be thrown away; and since a hand is what a poet writes with, "hand" is the last word, fittingly. A poet's heart is in his hand . . . [t]he comic, the tragic, the ironic, the humorous and the pathetic pace the scene.'

Love in the asylum

The 'girl mad as birds' may reflect Thomas's view of his and Caitlin's relationship; in 1936 he had told her: 'There is, in the eyes of the They, a sort of sweet madness about you and me, a sort of mad be-wilderment and astonishment oblivious to the Nasties and the Meanies' (*CL*, 271). However, several details complicate this reading. The final line is adapted from *N3* 'Fifty one' ('the frail / First vision that set fire to the air'), in which the transience of a 'living vision of the truth' leads to its memory being jealously guarded by 'arrow-eyed senses' long after its potency has faded. Similar imagery (birds, stars, asylum, etc.) is found in 'The Mouse and the Woman' (1936), in which a man writes a woman into existence, kills her off because he cannot deal with her sexuality, and goes mad (cf. also 'On a Wedding Anniversary'). Tindall (1962) claims the poem mimics the story, with the difference that the 'madwoman' made by the 'madman' helps him to achieve 'vision' and, Genesis-like, create a world – he is a successful, rather than a failed, madman. Hardy (2000) also finds a god-like madman-poet, but less benignly; for her the poem 'mime[s] a mad language', and accordingly 'the feathery armed girl with her distress and nympho-maniac desire . . . may be a product, rather than an instance, of erotic delusion'. The final line is, then, not so much a creative *fiat* as 'a megalomaniac delusion of the ordinary madman who knows he is God, and of the mad arsonist making his light and starting a fire by striking a match'.

The unusual form alternates hexameter and dimeter lines (often combinations of iambs and anapaests), grouped in tercets, with full and consonantal rhyme patterned *abc abc abc cde cde cde*.

12 The Buffalo MS has 'Oh possessed by stars'; probably changed to avoid repetition of 'stars' when Thomas decided to use the line from *N3* 'Fifty One'. 13 **narrow trough** = Buffalo MS reads: 'She lies in the narrow trough and she walks the dust'. 14 **raves** = The Buffalo MS has 'moves' as an earlier attempt. 16 **at long and dear last** = an

example of hendiadys, a figure used for emphasis; a conjunction is substituted for a subordination, so that two words are linked by 'and' instead of the one modifying the other. Hardy (2000) notes: 'Thomas is probably the modern poet most fond of [this] Virgilian and Shakespearian figure . . . which here sounds aptly odd, new, simple, and yet logical, as it separates epithets, revises meanings, and distinguishes categories . . . in mutating a common expression.'

On the marriage of a virgin

A good example of the numerous stages a Thomas poem could go through. Its forty-two-line notebook version was subject to interlinear alterations, many of which were then incorporated in a twenty-nine-line revision copied on the opposite page in *N3*, titled 'Dog-in-a-manger' and 'For A Woman Just Married ~~On The Marriage Of A~~', and dated 'Revised January 1941'. This, in turn, was revised inter-linearly. In summer 1941, Thomas made yet another revision (not extant in any MS), copying stanza 1 in a letter to Vernon Watkins of 21 June 1941 and sending him the whole poem, now sonnet-length, on 4 July (Maud, 1968, gives a full account).

Sweeney (1946) noted how the poem's 'complimentary conceit based on the attribute of miraculous virginity' was a typically con-flicted Metaphysical one 'drawn from pagan and Christian miracles of love'.

1–5 Waking alone . . . was miraculous virginity = Sweeney (1946) notes that the blend of 'sensual and metaphysical elegance' closely echoes the image-sequence in stanza 3 of Marvell's 'The Gallery':

[Thomas] has reworked the sensual and spiritual color of Marvell's imagery. Dawn, 'thighs', the miracle of manna (replaced by the 'loaves and fishes'), and the dove symbol have the same order of appearance . . . He has put the sensual reference, 'thighs', in a central position, and has made it a central point of rhyme into which the dominant sound is struck from 'light', 'nightlong', 'iris', 'sky', 'light-ning' and 'hide'. In the pattern of spiritual reference 'manna' has been converted into the New Testament symbol of the Sacrament which it prefigured.

3 **golden** = 'shining' in the stanza 1 sent to Watkins in June 1941. 4 **leapt** = 'rode' in the Watkins stanza.

The hunchback in the park

This poem retains some important features of *N2* 'LVVV', its source. Thus, it incorporates the first three lines verbatim, retaining and altering five other lines, and keeping many details to do with the park, 'woman figure' and hunchback. In his 1943 radio piece 'Reminiscences of Childhood' Thomas described both Cwmdonkin Park and the hunchback, claiming he could recall the face of the latter more clearly 'than the city-street faces I saw an *hour* ago.' In its subject-matter, then, this lyric begins the mining of the personal vein which would produce many of Thomas's best-known poems, among them 'Poem in October' and 'Fern Hill'.

For all its apparent clarity, however, it also broaches complex questions beneath which lurks LVVV's bald statement concerning the female muse figure: 'It is a woman and it is a poem'. Jon Silkin (1997) notes that Thomas suppressed LVVV's wordplay ('mister . . . mistier') in his rewriting, and that memory is made anticipatory of Thomas's poetic calling. He argues that the park is an imaginative space which the artist must leave in order to re-enter the 'real' world, leaving his creation behind in order to preserve its autonomy and freedom, while the raw materials (memory) which fuel his creation retire with him. Barbara Hardy (2000) similarly stresses the importance of the hunchback as a figure for the poet, complicating the poem's invitation to read its successive clauses as simply additive and impressionistic. This is in any case resisted by Thomas's disguising of the poem's conventional grammar, generating uncertainty which causes shifts of viewpoint between narrator, former selves and the hunchback. The use of 'propped' hints at theatrical props and the park as an imaginative theatre, linking the poem to a general concern in *DE* with the wartime theatricalisation of everyday existence (Goodby, 2013).

While often understood as a Wordsworthian poem of personal reminiscence, 'The hunchback in the park' uses nostalgia less for its own sake than as a device for drawing its readers into a visionary lyric comprised of receding planes of reality and illusion, and to involve them in a paradox: a composite speaker imagines the park and its contents as the imaginings of the hunchback, with these including the speaker's own earlier selves. Even so, the hunchback's attempt to create, from his deformity, a perfection able to transcend his nightly expulsion, makes him emblematic of the artist asserting the permanent value of the imagination in a benighted world. Speaker, birds, trees, hunchback, 'woman figure', park-keeper and boys figure a continually lost and renewed Eden. However, as so often in Thomas, there is a countervailing current; while rhyme is generally irregular elsewhere, 'park' and 'dark' enclose the opening and concluding stanzas.

3 **Propped** = this is an observation in the voice of the narrator viewing the scene; it describes the derelict state of the hunchback but also his and the park's status as imaginary, theatrical ('props') constructs. 8 **chained cup** = for chains in *DE*, cf. 'On a Wedding Anniversary', 'Into her lying down' head', 'Among Those Killed', 'Fern Hill'. 10 **I sailed my ship** = the only mention of 'I'; a self which pre-dates that associated with the 'truant boys'. 11 **Slept at night in a dog kennel** = the dog image is repeated at l. 25, emphasising the hunchback's abased condition; in its final appearance, all the objects in the park, and the boys themselves, go with him 'To his kennel in the dark', suggesting that the kennel is a symbol for mortality itself. 35 **That she might stand in the night . . . in the unmade park** = cf. Parkinson, 1981:

> The full import of the earlier lines which visualize the trees and water entering the park . . . manifests itself now, for the poem is not about the hunchback's poverty, the boys' cruelty or play, but about the hunchback's problem of being locked out of the park at night and . . . dealing with it. The park is 'unmade' in contrast to the woman, i.e. it is merely real, not formed by the hunchback's fantasy. Her fantastic existence is, however, for him, more real than objective reality.

Among those Killed in the Dawn Raid was a Man Aged a Hundred

The MS in Austin is accompanied by a statement by its donor, Charles de Lautour, explaining the poem's origin in a newspaper article about the death of a centenarian in an air-raid on Hull which he and Thomas read while working for Strand Films, in Bradford, in 'about 1940–41'. The old man's death is presented as a release from the 'locks', 'chains' and 'cage' of bodily ageing, a release into 'funeral grains' and vegetal regeneration, figured in biomorphic imagery which recalls that of Graham Sutherland and other wartime artists. Its visual extravagance is also a reminder of how Blitz writing 'returned repeatedly to versions of Surrealism as an explanatory mode' (Mellor, 2011), as the Daliesque image of an 'ambulance' drawn through the sky by a 'wound' hints. Readers expecting humanist homily have reacted in sharply opposed ways to the apparently grotesque incongruity of the sester's linguistic display; thus it is a 'most excellent jest' (Emery, 1962), a witty mockery of war's futility, and a heartless *jeu*, 'fanciful . . . pure trifling [with] no imagination' (Olson, 1954). Tonal undecidability may be the point; for Steve Vine, the destabilising of the discourse of mourning is a linguistic performance offered as a substitute rite, an 'ironic imagism' in which the 'language of celebration . . . parodically compounds irony with affirmation'.

2 **he died** = Davies (1993) notes that Thomas emphasises this event as 'a natural process', not as a social or personal tragedy. 3 **The locks yawned loose** = locks (and bolts, chains, cages, etc.) are common in *DE*; literally they secure the doors of homes and lives from being blown open by the bombs; metaphorically, they reflect the repressive constraints which, through death, empathy, solidarity and soul-searching, are being dissolved by the war. 7 **the craters of his eyes grew springshoots and fires** – anticipates the poem's final image. Mellor (2011) suggests the appositeness of 'craters' to Thomas's process-informed vision:

bombsites contain absolute doubleness. They are inherently both a frozen moment of destruction made permanent; as much as they capture the absolute singular moment, the repeated cliché of the stopped clock . . . they also act as a way of understanding a great swathe of linear time previously hidden or buried.

8 **keys shot from the locks** = cf. Donne, 'Death's Duell': '*God the Lord* . . . hath the *keys of death*, and hee can let me out at that dore'. 11 **Assembling** = of the version he sent to Vernon Watkins on 15 July

1941, Thomas noted: 'I am a bit dubious about "Through ruin" in the third line of the sextet. Originally I had "All day".' A letter of a week later makes clear that Watkins supplied the improvement: 'Thank you for "Assembling". Of course.' 14 **a hundred storks perch on the sun's right hand** = 'Death unlocks the imprisoned spirit of an old man by the violence of its coming and frees the stored life force' (Huddlestone, 1948). The sun / Son pun reverses and paganises Biblical protocol, according to which Christ sits 'on the right hand of God' (Mark 16:19). 'Storks' may pun on 'stalks' of regenerative growth.

*A Dream of Winter

This poem was published in the January 1942 issue of the magazine *Lilliput*, one tercet stanza under each of eight winter-themed photographs. It was included, *sans* photographs, in *The Doctor and the Devils and other stories* (New York; New Directions Press, 1966, pp. 207–8), but never reprinted in the UK or in any collected or selected poems before I republished it in 2015 in *P.N. Review* 226, 42:2 (November–December 2015, p. 5) and the 2016 paperback edition of *CP14* (again *sans* photographs). The story of how the poem was brought to my attention by Allan Wilcox, with additional information, is given in *P.N. Review* and *CP14* (2016). Due to the exigencies of the publishing industry it is not included in chronological sequence in *CP14* (2016), but appears as a separate item preceding the rest of the poems in the volume.

In it original incarnation in *Lilliput*, 'A dream of winter' is introduced by a short paragraph below the first photograph:

Out of thousands of winter pictures we chose these eight because they seemed to us to have a curious dreamlike quality. We showed them to the young poet, Dylan Thomas, and asked him if he would like to write some verses to go with them. Here are the pictures and here is his poem.

The photographs, in sequence, are of: (1) a crescent moon over a hillside trees in mist (by 'Brandt'); (2) a man silhouetted standing on a frozen lake, holding an axe (about to hack at the ice) ('Fox'); (3) a steam-breathing polar bear on an icicle-fringed promontory in a zoo enclosure ('Darchan'); (4) three men descending a misty hillside at night ('Brandt'); (5) a frost-etched statue of a classical female figure, bare to the waist, in a park ('Brandt'); (6) a canal between factories reflecting a distant light ('Fox'); (7) three ice-pick alpinists wearing crampons ascending a glacier ('Brassai'); (8) a man holding an umbrella standing in snow beside a busy, slushy London street ('Glass').

Thomas himself referred to the poem in a letter to John Sommerfield of 6 January 1942: 'Glad you liked my winter verses, very quickly produced from my tame Swinburne machine' (*CL*, 557). As so often, he was being too modest. Although not as densely wrought as other wartime poems written for publication, perhaps because it was a commercial commission, 'A Dream of Winter' is nevertheless syntactically intricate and verbally striking; it plays imaginatively with its photographic images, but may be read as a stand-alone work with its own logic and distinctive soundscape. Its stylistic significance lies in the fact that (like its immediate predecessor 'The hunchback in the park', of six months before), it anticipates in many respects the style that emerged fully fledged in 1944. It shows, that is, that Thomas' style altered in late 1941, and thus did not do so as a result of having to write more 'accessibly' for film and radio, in 1941–4, as is often claimed.

The end-rhyme scheme, modelled on *terza rima*, is *abacbcdedfefghg thijkjlkl*, mixing single and double rhyme, full rhyme and pararhyme.

4, 6 fish-trodden churches . . . sandgrains skate on the beeches = as elsewhere in his writing – see note to 'Prologue to *Collected Poems 1934–1952*' in *CP14* – Thomas alludes to the tale of the legendary kingdom of Cantre'r Gwaelod (Lowland Hundred), now sunk in Cardigan Bay. It first appeared in the medieval *Black Book of Carmarthen*, but Thomas may have come across it in *The Misfortunes of Elphin* (1829), a novel by a favourite author of his, Thomas Love Peacock. Cantre'r Gwaelod has other Celtic counterparts, including the Breton Ker-Ys, with which it shares details such as submerged tolling church bells. Both images take their cue from the accompanying photograph (number 2, above) in a characteristic way, by confounding dry land and water, ground level and height (cf. the beeches / beaches pun), as elsewhere in the poem (e.g. l. 18: 'The Ark drifts on the cobbles').

4, 16 Drowned beyond water . . . Drowned fast asleep beyond water = cf. 'The grains beyond age . . . by the unmourning water', 'A Refusal to Mourn the Death, by Fire, of a Child in London'.
9 The Great Bear = puns on the English name of the constellation Ursa Major (the adjacent photograph is that of a polar bear).

* *The postman knocks. By Cain, he knocks once more!*

Verse letter to Donald Taylor, sent from Blaen Cwm, and dated 'Tuesday' [August 1945], this is part of a longer letter asking for advance travel expenses ahead of a meeting with Taylor, the head of Gryphon Films, in London later that week. Its fantasies of requests from powerful and glamorous Americans shows that, at this relatively early point, Thomas already had his heart set on a trip to the USA, as well as revealing his awareness of US culture. For more elaborate evidence of his sympathies with, and knowledge of, US culture, see 'Letter to Loren in *CP14*, written after his first visit to the USA in 1950.

1 Cain = James M. Cain, author of *The Postman Always Rings Twice* (1934) made into a film starring Lana Turner and John Garfield in 1946. The opening line is modelled on that of Alexander Pope's 'Epistle to Dr. Arbuthnot'. **7 Bob Martin's** = de-worming tablets given to dogs; they would be ground up into the dog's food. **11–12 unseen / Blush** = reference to the lines 'Full many a flower is born to blush unseen / And waste its sweetness on the desert air', from Thomas Gray's famous 'Elegy Written in a Country Churchyard'. **12 hippocrene** = cf. Keats's 'Ode to a Nightingale' ('the blushful hippocrene'), conflated with 'Elegy'. 'Hippocrene' is water from the springs at the foot of Mount Ida, sacred to the Muses, hence a symbol of poetic inspiration. **13 Truman** = Harry S. Truman: US President after 12 April 1945. **14 Lease-Lend** = the 1941 agreement between Great Britain and the USA by which the British leased overseas military bases in return for war *materiel*. **15 Betty Hutton** = US film actress (see 'Letter to Loren'). **16 Gypsy Lee** = Gypsy Rose Lee, famous US striptease artist (see 'Letter to Loren'). **17–18 MacArthur, / Hecht, and Wilder** = Charles MacArthur, Ben Hecht and Billy Wilder were Hollywood screenwriters. **19 Miss Colbert** = Claudette Colbert, US film actress. 20 **Sam-stamped** = the US Mail postmark on the letters; from Uncle Sam, a figure personifying the USA.

Lie still, sleep becalmed

An earlier version of this sonnet, which Thomas sent to T. W. ('Tommy') Earp in April 1944, exists in identical MSS held at Ohio and Austin:

Lie still, you must sleep, sufferer with the wound
In the throat, burning and turning. All night afloat
On the silent sea we have heard the sound
That came from your wound. Your wound is a throat.
Under the mile off moon we trembled listening   5
To music pouring like blood from the loud wound
And when the bandages broke in a burst of singing
It was to us as the music of all the drowned.

Open a pathway through the sails, open
Wide the gates of the wandering boat   10
For my journey to the end of my wound,
The voices cried when the bandages were broken.
Lie still, you must sleep, hide the night from your throat,
Or we shall obey, and ride with you through the drowned.

The published version of the poem is a dialogue between a 'we' (lines 1–8, 13–14) and a 'sufferer' (lines 9–11), although Thomas typically omits markers that would indicate the speakers. The more transparent draft version is preferred by Conran (1997), who feels that Thomas erred in replacing 'bandages' with the less realist 'salt sheet', and deplores what he views as a general shift towards 'gratuitous lyricism'. However, it is perhaps a sign of the poem's deceptive slipperiness that what he calls 'the really disastrous change . . . to throw the attention away from the "sufferer with the wound" on to the poet himself [in] line 11' is a misreading; the draft has 'my', not 'the', wound . . . It could even be addressed to a lover tormented in sleep (cf. 'Into her lying down head'). Broadly speaking, the changes increase the slipperiness of an already ambiguous poem, as the several meanings of 'salt sheet' show, further confusing its 'we' and 'you', and wrapping anxieties about a father and the war within longer standing ones to do with wordshed as bloodshed, the poetic gift as a wounding and fear of silencing.

4, 7, 12 **salt sheet** = cf. 'The force that through the green fuse'. Burial at sea involves being wrapped in a sail with rope ('sheet') before being committed to the 'salt' sea, and there may be a further buried pun on 'shroud', which is also a term for a rope on a sailing ship. 9–11 **Open a pathway . . . to the end of my wound** = D. H. Lawrence's 'The Ship of Death'; **wandering boat** = cf. Shakespeare, Sonnet 116: 'It [love] is the star to ev'ry wandering bark.'

From Wales – Green Mountain, Black Mountain

The script of this film is full of evocative and poetic detail: miners who 'go down like ghosts in black' to a 'blind, propped underworld', dockers who 'load the ships to slide into the mined and death-sprung waters', and worshippers who 'talk among the poorer gravestones with their gifts of valley-soured flowers'. This passage, its one excursion into verse, shows Thomas as the social-realist poet he chose not to be, comparable to Idris Davies and W. H. Auden (there are echoes, here and in another Thomas script, *Our Country* – see below – of Auden's script for the GPO Film Unit's *Night Mail* (1936)).

Ceremony After a Fire Raid

The poem begins with 'myselves' bearing witness to the fact of the newborn child burnt to death with its mother in a raid, and establishes an imagery of fire and water. ('Blood' here chiefly meaning lost potential progeny, since at this stage, the lament is for the child's unborn 'sons', rather than her.) In Part II, Eden is a 'skeleton' buried under the child's 'head stone', even if, as the speaker acknowledges, the discourse of Christianity cannot be 'silent' within his ceremony; indeed, it now subserves the new religion of the dead child, the 'chronology' of her death being irrelevant 'in relation to other deaths, real or mythical,

because what the atrocity [of her killing] represents is decreation'
(Davies, 2000). The knowledge that Christian discourse will shape the
girl's ceremony, despite its radically non-Christian content, determines
the imagery of part III and its apocalyptic burning of the churches
and cathedrals which are the embodied forms of the religion that has
failed the child. The strong charge of *Schadenfreude* and 'Blitz sublime'
spills over from destruction into a new version of the Eucharist whose
liquid symbolism, renewed from part I, puts out the fire (Goodby,
2013). The imagery of the final lines recall Thomas's use of the Biblical
and Bunyanesque trope of the punishment of the sinful city elsewhere
(cf. the story 'Prologue to an Adventure'), as he presents himself in the
guise of a prophet of the regeneration of British cities – slum-clearance
accomplished with the aid of the Luftwaffe. See Goodby (2013), who
reads this section of the poem in the light of what Mikhail Bakhtin
calls the 'generative principle', the response of the collective carnivalesque body to the depradations of military might and war.

4 **tireless** = the death has manifested itself as a single, traumatic event,
but it is actually ceaseless in its operations. 14 **a star** = bomb; in
shocking contrast to the star of the Nativity. 15 **centuries** = cf. Thomas
Traherne's ***Centuries** of Meditations*, with its ecstatic account of childhood (cf. note to 'Fern Hill'). 19 **Give** = present in the *Our Time*
printing and the MS of *DE*, this single-word line was dropped when
the poem was reprinted in the anthology *War Poets* (1945); Maud
(2003) speculates that this maimed version was used for *DE*, and thus
for *CP52*. Happily restored by Davies and Maud (1988), the error
was unaccountably re-introduced in Derek Mahon's Faber selection
of 2003. An earlier MS read: 'Give / Over your death'. 23 **the dust
shall sing like a bird** = cf. 'A Winter's Tale', with the nightingale that
'flies on the grains of her wings' and 'dust of water . . . telling'. 34
the adorned holy bullock = cf. Keats's 'Ode on a Grecian Urn': 'Who
are these coming to the sacrifice? / To what green altar, O mysterious
priest / Lead'st thou that heifer lowing at the skies / And all her silken
flanks with garlands drest?' 40, 54 **little skull** = cf. Thomas's story
'The Burning Baby': 'I want the little skull, said a voice in the dark.'
49 **in my service** = in my ritual, the use to which I put the 'legend'.
52–3 **Child who was priests and servants . . . singers** = cf. Keats'
'Ode to Psyche': 'So let me be thy choir . . . thy voice, thy lute, thy

pipe, thy incense sweet . . . Thy shrine, they grove, thy oracle, thy heat / Of pale-mouthed prophet dreaming.' 59 **nurseries** = for plants and children ('plant' in Welsh means 'children'; the singular is 'plentyn'). 78 **The sundering ultimate kingdom of genesis' thunder** = thunder is common in Thomas (cf. 'Shall gods be said', 'A saint about to fall'), and may allude to the ambiguous thunder at the end of *The Waste Land.*

Our Country

This film-script, Thomas's best after *The Doctor and the Devils*, is an experimental piece, written in a fluid modern verse style, and a good example of the lyrical documentary form pioneered in the 1930s, most notably in Auden's *The Night Mail*. It opens with establishing shots of the two chief cities of the United Kingdom, Glasgow and London, before following the travels of a sailor on shore leave through England, Wales and Scotland. At the end of the film he finds a new ship. His part was played by a real merchant seaman who had been torpedoed three times and who was on sick leave; he returned to active service after making the film. The other main character, his girlfriend, was played by a real Sheffield factory worker spotted in the street by the director, John Eldridge, while she was talking animatedly to a friend (Ackerman, 1995). For once in his script-writing work, filmic demands did not precede verbal ones; Thomas wrote the script before shooting took place. Perhaps as a result, it echoes his poetry of the time, especially 'Ceremony After a Fire Raid'. It is significant that in trying to escape the demands of propaganda, Thomas embraces pastoral, the genre that dominates his later writing. His chief worry, eclipsing those he had over the cuts made to the film, concerned proposals (later dropped) to give copies of the script to those attending the premiere (*CL*, 588). However, the script stands up in its own right, and sheds much light on how the competing impulses to both communicate and avoid propaganda shaped Thomas's wartime poetry.

Last night I dived my beggar arm

An autograph copy (entitled 'For Ruth') given by Ferris (1977), with
two pairs of alternative words, runs:

Last night he/I dived my beggar arm
Into her breast that wore no heart
For me/her alone only the deep drum
Telling her heart

That her luminous, tumbled limbs   5
Will plunge his betrayal through the sky
So the betrayed will read in the sunbeams
Of a death in another country.

Your breath was shed

Pamela Hansford Johnson's memory of the earlier version this poem,
mentioned in Thomas's letter to her of 2 May 1934, was that at this
stage it had the title 'The Candle' and began:

Thy breath was shed
Invisible to weave
Around my carven head
A carven eve.

A notebook in the Veronica Sibthorpe papers held in NLW (MS
21698E) contains a variant consisting of the first two stanzas only:

White breath was shed
Invisible to dark,
About the bright undead
Black for my sake
A scented trail
Intangible to them
With wolf's loud tooth & tail
And cobweb drum.

Vision and Prayer

Maud (2003) speculates that 'Vision and Prayer' was begun before 1941, but no other critics mention the possibility, perhaps because the poem's visual aspect, distinctive among even Thomas's varied and ingenious stanza forms, is so striking. It takes to an extreme his interest in the shape of poetry on the page, and the debt to shape-poems by Herbert and other Metaphysicals, and the significance of that debt, has provoked much discussion. This has ranged from the similarities with the quincuncial lattice prefacing Sir Thomas Browne's *The Garden of Cyrus* to Korg's (1965) suggestion that the stanza-shape of part I may 'reflect the idea of "opening" [obstetrically and spiritually] which prevails in it', while in part II he finds the 'convergence of forces or reversal suggested by the stanza form corresponds with the conflict of impulses which is its subject', the poem's movement of 'withholding [being] followed by the yielding of assent'. What is undeniable is that each of the shapes (negatively) defines the other, something Thomas was interested in at a verbal level, and this probably enacts the relationship between 'vision' and 'prayer'. Sweeney (1946) adds that the progression from one to nine syllables per line in I may establish 'the calendar measure of beats from one to nine [months]', 'symbolizing physical birth', this being inverted in II 'to center on the individual "I" . . . in the final stanza', so that 'The burning blessing of the Sun is a vision of spiritual rebirth in the son.' Thomas was less happy with II than I; to Vernon Watkins he wrote: 'I am so glad . . . that the diamond shape of the first part no longer seems to you to be cramped & artificed. I agree that the second part is, formally, less inevitable, but I cannot alter it, except, perhaps, in detail' (*CL*, 593).

The poem appears to present a two-part conversion narrative, in which the speaker resists, and then finally succumbs to the Christ-child; there are analogues in Herbert, Hopkins and, by Thomas's own admission to Watkins, Francis Thompson's 'The Hound of Heaven' ('Yes, the Hound of Heaven is baying there in the last verse'). In stanza 1 the speaker asks the identity of the child being born in the 'next room'; in stanza 2, listening to the birth-pangs, he chafes at his own confinement, imagining the child explosively emerging to break down the wall between them. Terror at this sees him in stanza 3 imagining himself 'run[ning]' to avoid the 'cauldron' of the child's kiss. At the

Christ-like child's throne (stanza 4), imagining himself in his sheltering but terrifying presence (stanza 5), the speaker declares he 'shall waken' to a vision of the Day of Judgement, as the 'bidden dust' of the dead from the time of Adam will rise up from the 'world' (stanza 6) and he 'dies' in its pain. Part II consists of three prayers, the second and third of which are linked by a couplet spanning stanzas 10 and 11, which sums up the essence of the dilemma: that death and lostness is what humankind is fitted for, not the terrifying demands of salvation. The prayers end at stanza 11, with the 'amen' described by Maud (2003) as 'bitter'. But in stanza 12, the sun / son makes answer; the sinner who would escape Christ, or father unaware of his love for his child, has been hunted down by his love, 'lost in the blinding / One'.

This précis suggests why Christians and non-believing critics alike – for example, Raymond Garlick (1973) and Ralph Maud (2003) – are able to see the poem as a genuine conversion narrative. Others, however, such as Tindall (1962), are more sceptical, noting Thomas's habitual lack of belief (but not religious feeling), and noting this poem's kinship with 'burning baby', parturition and 'holy child' poems going back to 'Before I knocked', and reawakened around the time of the birth of Llewelyn (like 'If my head hurt a hair's foot', 'Vision and Prayer' also expresses the notion that birth can be undone). The final impression left is deeply ambiguous: if the poem records a conversion, is it a radical humanist one (as in 'There was a saviour') or a genuinely mystical experience of dying into and being reborn in Christ? If about neither, to what degree can we align it with the births of Llewelyn (1939) and Aeronwy (1943)?

4 **in the next room** = Cf. Sir Thomas Browne, *Urne-Buriall*, IV: 'A Dialogue between two Infants in the wombe concerning the state of this world, might handsomely illustrate our ignorance of the next, whereof methinks we yet discourse in *Platoes* denne, and are but *Embryon* Philosophers.' 9 **thin as a wren's bone** = '[W]hen I asked the poet himself . . . he laughed and said that all he meant . . . was that the wall dividing him from the birth room was so thin as to be non-existent' (Aneirin Talfan Davies, 1964). 49 **cauldron** = was 'caldron' in *CP52* and *CP88*; changed to its standard spelling in *CP14*, as for 'I make this in a warring absence' and 'Ceremony After a Fire Raid'. 103, 177–82 **In the name of the lost . . . in the name / Of no one /**

Now or / No / One to / Be . . . = 'An extreme example of . . . the rhetorical negative . . . where the poet prays in the name of the wrong people . . . But he is praying, in their unholy or nonexistent names, for the *opposite* of what he wants', because he ends up praying in the name of 'no-one' (Maud, 1963). That is, the double negatives produce a highly qualified faith statement. 106 **the burial song . . . birds of burden** = echoes the opening of Shakespeare's 'The Phoenix and the Turtle'; **burden** = play on 'beasts of burden', also 'burden' as repeated refrain in a song or poem. 186, 187 **interpreted evening . . . known dark** = as in 'discovered skies' ('How shall my animal') and similar collocations elsewhere in Thomas, a natural phenomenon subject to human ratiocination. 194 **Christens** = makes like Christ, as well as the usual ritualistic sense.

Poem in October

The topography of the poem, with its transfigured seaside town and hill, alludes to Thomas's first residence in Laugharne, in 1938–40. While the suggestion made by Lynette Roberts that it was almost complete by 1939 seems unlikely, and Vernon Watkins's claim that 'originally the first line read "It was my twenty-seventh year to heaven"' forgets that Thomas's twenty-seventh birthday was in 1941, after he had left Laugharne, the general point they make – that it is a birthday-and-place poem – is accurate enough. As Charles Mundye (2014) has suggested:

> perhaps Thomas was saving it for the more resonantly rounded whole-number birthday, or perhaps he wanted the culture rhyme with the opening of 'Le Testament', the greatest poem by François Villon, another poet, drinker, and rogue: 'En l'an de mon trentiesme eage / Que toutes mes hontes j'eus beues' ['In the thirtieth year of my age / when I had swallowed up my shame'].

If 'Poem in October' contains no evidence of Villonesque drunkenness or criminality, Laugharne's appeal to Thomas as a somewhat wild, beyond-the-pale place is well-attested; in 1939 he described it to Watkins as a 'little Danzig', because (like the Polish original, at the end of a 'Polish corridor' across German territory) it lay deep within an alien – Welsh-speaking, more law-abiding – rural hinterland. The poem distinguishes itself from the constraints of the traditional place-and-memory poem, with its striking shape reflecting the effort of perfecting a new style – one in which, for the first time, syllabic metrical principles wholly dominate those based on stress. It consists of seven ten-line stanzas with a 9 12-9-3-5-12-12-5-3-9 syllable pattern, broken only in ll. 55–6; an end-line pararhyme scheme *abacabcbac* is set in stanza 1 and varied thereafter.

19–20 **And the gates of the town / Closed** = the walls of medieval Laugharne had western and eastern gates. Thomas may also allude to the garden gates which 'were at first the end of the world' in Thomas Traherne's *Centuries of Meditation*, 3:3, which describes his ecstatic childhood vision of the created world (see note to 'Fern Hill', pp. 215–16). At this point the speaker ascends Sir John's hill, which overlooks the town.

Holy Spring

The origins of the poem a 'long time ago', and the 'lot of work' expended on it, both mentioned in Thomas's accompanying letter to Vernon Watkins of 15 November 1944, are not connected; the debt to one of its sources 'Out of a war of wits', 'Ten' in *N3* (see above) is very slight; all the compositional struggles date from autumn 1944, and these are attested to by the existence of several other versions of the poem. *CP88* notes vaguely that 'a manuscript offered for sale in a House of Books catalogue is said to differ greatly from the version finally published in *Horizon*', and gives a transcript of another version, from the Gilvarry collection (which has its first line as title rather than the Blakean-sounding one of the published version), offered for sale in 1988:

> O out of a bed of love
> When that immortal hospital made one more move to soothe
> The cureless, counted body
> And ruin and his causes
> Winging over the gunpowdered sea assumed an army   5
> And walked into our wounds and houses,

I climb to greet the war in which I have no heart but only
    That one dark I owe my light,
Call for confessor and wiser mirror but there are none
    To purge after the planed rough night   10
And I am struck as dumb as cannonfire by the sun.

Praise that springtime is all
    All all in a flower fire of peace and songs after the evil
Leaves of the clanging fall
    O prodigal sun the father his quiver full of green trees   15
Praise to the blood of days
    That uncalm still it is sure alone to stand and sing
Dumb by the chanted blaze
    By the mother and showering voice of the mortal spring
Hail and upheaval of the judge-blown drowned of the sun,   20
    If only for a last time.

The poem takes the form of two twelve-line stanzas, with alternate short lines (trimetrical or tetrametrical) and long lines (hexameters or fourteeners), except for the opening lines of stanza one. Counting the opening single-syllable lines of each stanza, the rhyme scheme for each stanza is *aabcbcbdede* and *aabaabacdcd*.

4 **counted body** = numbered, as in the Bible (cf. 'Deaths and Entrances', 'Ballad of the Long-legged Bait'). 'Cureless' (curate- or *curé*-less) also means 'without a priest for the cure of souls', hence the need for a 'confessor' in l. 10. 5–7 **ruin . . . houses** = Thomas's own homelessness and poverty in 1940–1 are alluded to here (cf. 'On a wedding anniversary', 'Into her lying down head'). 11 **god stoning night** = Gilvarry's 'planed rough night' plays on (aero)plane / plane for smoothing wood; night was paradoxically 'roughened' by the German aeroplanes and their bombs. 12 **as lonely as a holy maker** = according to Stan Smith (2001) an allusion to Thomas's 'deepest terror – being silenced'. 13–24 Smith reads stanza 2 in terms of anxiety at being struck dumb and internal struggle:

The prodigal son, in collusion with the mother, judges and drowns the father, cancels his singing. But this son is not principally the boy Dylan. In the poem's palimpsest of complexes, Oedipus has given way to Chronos. The rebellious 1930s prodigal has taken on the chronic anxiety of the 1940s patriarch, 'fathered' (that is, turned into a father) by the birth of a son who is a rival for the mother's love. Judged and found wanting, the father stands alone in the possession of a 'toppling house' and, Chronos-like, contemplates the symbolic infanticide of the rising generation.

13–20 **No / Praise . . . but blessed be hail and upheaval** = negating the unqualified 'Praise' of the Gilvarry version permits a more nuanced claim; renewal is natural, hence not a cause for 'praise', which is reserved for the process of change itself. 14–15 **radiant shrubbery** = as bomb-crater vegetation symbolises regeneration in 'Among Those Killed in the Dawn Raid', and more generally in Blitz writing (Mellor, 2011). 17 **weeping wall** = from the Wailing Wall; cf. 'spelling wall' in 'How shall my animal'. 18–19 **My arising prodigal / Sun the father** = the Christian doctrine of incarnation is implicit, and God's prodigal sacrifice of his only son. Sweeney (1946) notes the 'prodigal' pun was used by Shakespeare in *Timon of Athens* ('a prodigal course is like the sun's but not like his recoverable'), and by Henry Vaughan in 'Regeneration' ('The unthrift Sunne shot vital gold / A thousand peeces') and 'The Pursuite' ('The lost Sonne had not left the huske / Nor home desir'd'). 20 **blessed** = possible play on Fr *blesser*, to wound (cf. 'Poem on His Birthday').

A Winter's Tale

One of Thomas's most ambitious later poems, pioneering his use of the pastoral genre in his later work.

The narrative is structured through the manipulation of tenses and film-like cutting and panning: stanzas 1–2 (present tense) tell of the tale being borne to the poet, in the 'river wended vales' where it first occurred, with the winter twilight; in stanzas 3–11 (past tense) the tale itself starts being told in its medieval setting; the hermit kneels, weeps and prays 'from the crest of grief' for a mystical deliverance from the 'time dying flesh' which will be both loving union and annihilation, anticipating his fate at the end of the poem; at this point, in stanzas 12–13 (present tense) the reader is addressed directly, urged to 'Listen', and told that an earlier, spring-like life seems reborn in the past landscape; in stanza 14 (past tense), the door of his hut is 'glided wide' on a 'she-bird' who rises from the snowy ground; in stanzas 15–16 (present tense) there is another address to the reader, urged now to 'Look', as the figures in the reborn landscape move; though dead, they 'exult', it seems for the 'love' of the hermit's prayer; now in stanzas 17–22 (past tense) the she-bird seems to sing and praise his devotion and the 'sky of birds' in her voice 'charms' him to pursue her as she flies off across the winter-bound countryside; then, in the passage running final line of stanza 20–penultimate line of stanza 21 (present tense), the reader is asked to 'Listen *and* look' at the bird sailing the snowy 'sea' and, among other things, the 'joy beyond / The fields of seed and the time dying flesh astride' (the hermit had prayed in a negative way for deliverance from this in stanza 15, and that transcendence is now presented by the she-bird in a positive form); from the final line of stanza 21 to stanza 22 (past tense) the 'door' of the hermit's death is 'glided wide' and 'the tale ended'; in stanzas 23–4 (present tense) the animated 'spring weather' village scene dies back into the snowy landscape; and finally, in stanzas 25–6 (past tense), the tale culminates with the man and she-bird dying in sexual union, which is death (hypothermia) or delusion, but also an ambiguous assimilation of the man into the bird and phoenix-like ascent to new life. The opening frame of the poet in his own time remains unclosed, suggesting identification between himself and the hermit / 'she-bird' in their union.

The poem is notable for its variations in sentence-length – long and syntactically involved for the action, abruptly declarative for the dramatic asides – and a more overt use of allusion than in earlier poetry. One intertext is Thomas himself; thus, 'bread of water', via 'long-legged bread', is one of several echoes of 'Ballad of the Long-legged Bait'. Plentiful use of internal- and end-rhyme, and repetition of key phrases (e.g. 'hand folded snow'), together with the timeless properties of the tale ('spit', 'pot', 'byre', etc.), help create a fairytale or folk-tale ambience and a ritualistic, hypnotic tone. Symbolism, such as that of the eucharistic 'cup' and 'bread', is pervasive. The hermit and the snowy landscape are also suggestive of the poet confronting the blank page. The new and different complexity (intercutting addressee, place and time rather than making metaphoric and associative leaps) may be why Thomas told Vernon Watkins he thought the poem was a failure, albeit one he liked.

As a result of its size and ambition, 'A Winter's Tale' has provoked extreme reactions. For Huddlestone (1948) it was Thomas's 'most sustained piece', 'certainly one of the finest poems of this century', like 'the biblical *Song of Songs*, in that its interpretation may be taken on three levels. literally as the love story of magic fairy-tale character; as an allegory of romantic, but profane love; or as an allegory of sacred love.' W. S. Merwin (Tedlock, 1960) also believed it to be 'one of the great poems he has written', and speculated that it was based on an actual myth or legend. Emery (1962) follows Huddlestone, but with more emphasis on process, drawing a comparison with the story 'The Visitor', in which Peter, near death, experiences a vision of process. The poem is likewise said to consist of 'the . . . delusions of a dying man', with the 'continuing function of his dynamic stuff in the material universe' presented in medieval vision form of 'centaur-dead' horses, oaks, maypole dancers, etc., although 'the reality of the [concluding] marriage state' is 'attritional but fecundating decomposition'. 'Exulting' (l. 73) is thus earth's response to the hermit's invocation of process in his prayer and his own joy (in his vision of spring) at the answer to it. The she-bird *is* process, 'neither moral nor purposive, but holy in the Blakeian sense'. Korg (1965) and Moynihan (1966) largely agree, with Moynihan noting a use of assonance and alliteration to choreograph the poem, mimicking the sound and sensation of falling snow in the opening stanzas, the attentiveness demanded in the spring vision sections, and so on. Tindall (1962), however, feels the poem's craft ultimately outweighs 'story' to produce a 'deliberate, calculated and essentially cold product of great skill'.

Later commentators have tended to follow Tindall in being suspicious of the poem's intricate and foregrounded contrivance. Seamus Heaney (1992 and 1995) claims it is too verbally 'soft-contoured', a 'Disney fantasia', 'more a case of "vended Wales" than "wended vales", so like a tourist board landscape is it.' Goodby (2013) argues that Heaney misreads the poem as rural realism gone wrong, rather than as the fantasy or vision its title tells us to expect, and that his comments reflect the empirical prejudices of the post-1970s British poetry mainstream. He links 'A Winter's Tale' to the 'paragrammatic' form of pastoral Thomas developed from 1944 on, 'based on repetition, verbal exfoliation and a miscegenatory incorporation of the English poetic canon'. Finally, James Keery finds it to be an exemplary New Apocalyptic work, owing much to D. H. Lawrence's *Apocalypse* (1930), and 'drenched' in the book of Revelation, as evidenced by 'countless' 'lexical parallels':

In the 130 lines [they] include 'tribes' (7:5); 'graves' (11:9); 'bride' (18:23); 'harp' (5:8); 'trumpets' (9:14); 'horses' (19:14); 'The woman-breasted and the heaven-headed / Bird' (17:3 'the woman, and . . . the beast which carryeth her, which hath the seven heads') and 'paradise' (2:7).

Three additional contexts are: *a* the 'unimaginable / Zero summer' of the opening of T. S. Eliot's 'Little Gidding' (1942); *b* twelfth-century Welsh poems about hermits and winter landscapes (recently made available in Kenneth Jackson's translations in *Studies in Early Celtic Nature Poetry* (1935)); *c* the exceptionally harsh winter of 1944–5, reflected in contemporary reports of the fierce battles taking place in the Ardennes and along the Eastern Front.

2–4 snow blind twilight . . . cup of the vales . . . hand folded flakes = phrases which will be repeated, with variations, throughout the poem, to create hypnotically self-echoing cadences (e.g. 'hand folded air', 'snow blind love'). **5–10 breath . . . cold . . . owl . . . folds . . . Flocked . . . sheep . . . told** = the 'The Eve of St. Agnes' comparisons include a 'Beadsman' near death, Madeleine likened to a 'ring-dove', and ambiguous sexual 'solution sweet'; Keats's 'Bright Star' sonnet may also contribute towards the snowy landscape, while Emery (1962) claims Thomas may also have recalled Tennyson's ascetic rejoinder to Keats's sensuousness, 'St. Agnes's Eve', combining and reacting against each of them. **13 As the food** = cf. Revelation 7:17: 'For the Lamb which is in the midst of the throne shall feed them.' **14 scrolls of fire that burned** = 'Apocalyptic', as in Revelation 6:14: 'And the heaven departed as a scroll when it is rolled together' (Tindall, 1962). **17 firelit island** = 'clearly "the isle that is called Patmos"' of Revelation 1:9 (Keery). **18 white as wool** = cf. Revelation, 2:14: 'His head and *his* hairs were white like wool, as white as snow; and his eyes *were* as a flame of fire.' 42–3 **the bread of water . . . high corn . . . harvest** = cf. 'On no work of words'; also, the manna in Keats's 'Eve of St. Agnes' and 'La Belle Dame Sans Merci'. 48–9 **always desiring centre . . . bride bed forever sought** = the snowstorm and landscape symbolise the birth and consummation of a desire to escape the human condition, as elaborated in ll. 51–5. Cf. 'the wanting centre', l. 128. 54–5 **the fields . . . flesh astride** = 'white seed' is sperm and flesh as well as snow. 69–70 **A she bird rose and rayed like a burning bride . . . scarlet downed** = Moynihan notes: 'as is customary in fairy tales and legends of wish-fulfilment, the man follows the bird', citing Kierkegaard's discussion of the motif in *Fear and Trembling* – a book Thomas is likely to have read. The burning baby of the Blitz elegies and 'Poem in October' also inform the 'she-bird'; cf. also Robert Southwell's 'The Burning Babe' (1595), who appears 'in hoary winter's night' to the poet 'shivering in the snow'. 71 **the dancers move** = cf. T. S. Eliot, 'East Coker', part I, in which dancers also signify harmony. Thomas's figures are carnivalesque and 'wanton', by contrast with Eliot's peasants, whose sexuality is likened to that of beasts, as John Ackerman points out (Ackerman, 1991). 72 **moon light** = the whiteness of moonlight not only makes it possible to see a green landscape as a snowy one, but also to imagine that the snowy fields are green ones under moonlight. 84 **all the elements . . . rejoiced** = 'all the fallen world rejoices, for in the prayer and the bird who came in answer . . . all nature sees its redemption' (Moynihan, 1966). In non-Christian terms, 'elements' are the chemical elements the man will become in dying and entering the most fundamental level of process; **slow fall** = play on 'snow fall'. 126 **brought low** = the negative aspects of the hermit's transfiguration are inherent in the exalted aspects; they are not simply balanced against each other, but presented as a painful paradox. 128–30 **folds / Of paradise . . . flowering** = 'flower', like 'whirl- / Pool', echoes 'The force', emphasising the she-bird as process, both killing snow and saving heaven.

The conversation of prayers

It was G. S. Fraser (1958) who first noticed Thomas's apparent use in the poem of the Catholic idea of the 'reversibility of grace': 'God, in his inscrutable mercy, can give the innocent the privilege of suffering some of the tribulations which have been incurred by redeemable sinners'. While Fraser did not claim that Thomas was thereby endorsing this doctrine, others have argued that the prayers cross because the child is 'not caring', and so deserving of a vision of 'one who lies dead'. This ignores the marked compassion for children in *DE* and confuses the boy's *dreams* with his *prayer*. More plausible is Emery's suggestion that the child and the man may be Thomas's younger and older selves (Emery, 1962). Yet if, as in 'This side of the truth' (included with this poem in Thomas's letter to Vernon Watkins of 28 March 1945), the poem assumes an amoral universe which treats the two prayers, distinct in human terms, as 'the same grief flying' in a non-human sense, this leaves the question of 'answering skies'. Walford Davies (Davies, 2000) sees the phrase as ironic, like the 'unminding skies' of 'This side of the truth', the 'discovered skies' of 'How shall my animal' and 'The interpreted evening' of 'Vision and Prayer'; and it may be that the 'sound . . . from the green ground' and the 'answer' are the 'conversation' of bombers and anti-aircraft guns, a grim parody of prayer and divine response, making these prayers and their outcome 'turn on the quick and the dead' left after an air-raid.

The poem's calmness resists any urge to twist the familiar clichés with which it is replete, and it has a mesmeric quality; 189 of its 202 words are monosyllables, with 'the' occurring twenty-four times, 'his' seven times, 'who'/'whom' five times, and 'child', 'man', 'will', 'stairs', 'sleep' and 'prayers' four times. Korg (1965) argues that this is 'typical of the late style, in that the richness of repetition is matched by a paucity of imagery.' Yet for all that the minimalism and fastidious syntax seem to aim at clarity, the effect of the interwoven repetitions and torqued syntax is complex, even disorienting. The poem itself alerts us to this in stanza 2, as Goodby (2013) notes:

[I]t is not the meaning content of the prayers that 'turns' and converses / converts, but 'The sound' of them . . . in addition, the 'sounds' are only ever about to be said, they are never actually uttered. The poem . . . is one verbal event anticipating another – it is only ever a speculation, a potential suspended in its verbal web.

The form of this poem is one of Thomas's most admired: four five-line stanzas in hexameters, with crisscrossing end- and mid-line rhymes in successive lines; thus, *prayers-stairs* and *said-bed* in ll. 1–2, *love-move* and *room-whom* in ll. 3–4, with l. 5 rhyming with ll. 1–2. The crisscross-rhymes enact the theme of conversational interchange, the swapping of the man's and boy's prayers, except in the final line where *stairs* is an imperfect rhyme for *prayer-care*, although both *stairs* and *dead* rhyme back with stanzas 1–3.

2 **the man on the stairs** = cf. 'The colossal intimacies of silent / Once seen strangers or shades on a stair', 'Into her lying down head', and the ascending stair in Eliot's *Ash Wednesday* (1930), where each 'turn' is a stage in spiritual development. 8–9 almost exactly reverses ll. 1–2. 10–11 echoes ll. 3–4; Austin MS has 'For the sleep that will be found' and 'Who shall be calmed?' 14 **quick and the dead** = from Acts 10:42 and *The Book of Common Prayer*. 16–19 **high room . . . dark eyed wave** = cf. Keidrych Rhys's 'Garn Goch' (1939): 'Ideas of work in a broken mind / Of all a strange webbed future can find / In the pooled Van of a dark-eyed room.'

A Refusal to Mourn the Death, by Fire, of a Child in London

An early unfinished draft of this poem, never before published, written in pencil in Thomas's handwriting on the blank end papers of a copy of the anthology *New Road 1944* and dated 'Nov. '44', forms part of the Dylan Thomas MSS collection at the NLW. Titled 'A Refusal For An Elegy', it has many of the structural elements of the final version (stanza-form, rhyme-scheme, syntax), as well as much of its imagery, lexis and argument:

Never until the mankind-making
Bird beast and flower
Fathering & unsevered darkness
Tells with silence the last light breaking
And the still hour
Is come of the sea tumbling in harness

(Darkness, my accusing heart, for want
Of a syllable
Of elements Or an illumination
Of music blessing from the glad font
Of the miracle
Of the ~~last~~ skull ~~of the picture~~ under the dew of creation)

And I must enter again the round
Eye of the sea drop
And the syrup of the beating sun
Shall I let seed the wren's song of a sound
Or reap the white crop
Of a snow flake's field of the last one

Murmur & burning of the child's death.
I shall not murder
The mankind of her death with a single truth
Nor blaspheme down the stations of the breath
With any further
Mockery of Innocence and Youth

Thomas may have balked at a second stanza in which five lines start
with 'Of', and, in trying to recast it, decided to dispense with the
parenthetical structure and prolong the direct address of the opening
sentence. The more calculatedly majestic final version is the most
powerful of his Blitz elegies. Its title takes the form of a public
declaration in the opening 'hypotactic sentence', all of thirteen lines
long, in which the speaker tells us he will not mourn the child until
Doomsday or his own personal extinction (the same thing in Thomas's
universe of process). The second sentence gives the reason for this
deferment: to mourn now would be to murder her death, as a natural
('mankind') event we must all experience, with a 'grave truth' (com-
placent Christian promise of the afterlife, or elegiac platitude). The
third, which includes all but the last line of the last stanza, asserts –
seemingly as an alternative consolation – the kinship of the dead girl
with the 'first dead' (of London, and/or Adam and Eve), 'robed' in
the 'dark veins' of her 'mother' earth. The famous final line, a single
sentence with marked caesura, is an example of Thomas's trademark
magnificent closing cadences which proves, on examination, to offer

anything but closure. One meaning is that some form of eternal life begins (having suffered a death (and awoken from it) you shall not die again); but another is that after death there is nothing.

The movement of the poem is from the nominal 'refusal' of the title and opening two sentences, covertly offset by the tone of indignation and pity for the girl, towards an oblique act of commemoration in the final stanza, in which there is implied solace in her return to the organic cycle and in the fact that (contrary to Christian dogma) she will not have to suffer another death. Yet it is not simply an example of *occupatio*; the first sentence in particular, in its magnificent onrush, sweeps the reader over pockets of ambiguity without these initially being noticed. As Goodby (2013) observes, 'Never until' is a solecism (one may say 'never' or 'not until', but not 'never until'). This opens up an undecidable grammatical space in which the poem then unfolds, to be ambiguously framed by the final line, whose '*first* death' logically predicates a second, although we are reassured that there is 'no other'.

Moreover, as Carson (1996) claims, such ambiguities occur regularly, particularly in the opening sentence. Perhaps the key word is 'breaking', a participial adjective which modifies the direct object 'light', yet which, because it follows the noun, 'acts with a noun's force, as if "breaking" were an occurrence: a gerund co-serving as direct object.' This doubleness enacts the fact that 'breaking' can be taken to mean ending or beginning. Thomas, as Carson notes, 'so constructed the line as to preclude a definite answer – or, rather to include both answers.' The weak final syllable after three strong stresses inclines us hear an ending, and the 'breaking' / 'making' rhyme seems conclusive. Yet 'last light breaking' could just as easily mean the dawning of the last day, or even latest, or previous, day (other senses of 'last'), allowing hope as well as despair; 'it is both the climax and the anticlimax of the speaker's waiting'. This reinforces the ambiguity regarding the speaker's resolve not to mourn. 'Breaking', as Carson claims, 'is an apt word to signal the gateway to either immortality or oblivion, or both'.

The structure of 'A Refusal', then, is in some ways a more sophisticated version of that of 'And death', deploying and simultaneously disavowing a rhetoric of faith through the use of the double negative in order to avoid the draft version's 'single truth', and so creating a condition of undecidability, poised between cathartic mourning and paralysing melancholia. The attempt to embody the incommensurability of death and man's response to it, like other of Thomas's wartime poems, draws on Christian imagery and belief. In particular, the doctrines of atonement, the Last Judgement and eternal torment are central to its meaning; the 'other' death the child will not suffer is that threatened in Revelation ('the lake which burneth with fire and brimstone; which is the second death'). In line with the Unitarian tradition of his great-uncle Gwilym Marles, Thomas felt that the underwriting of atonement and resurrection by the doctrine of eternal punishment was morally repugnant, as suggested by his reported comment that '[t]he after life is one of the most terrible things you Christians have thought up. When I'm dead I want to be buried and feel the violets growing over me'. Less negatively, for Parkinson (1981), the speaker 'refuses mourning but identifies the child's death with Christ's and so elevates it'. One of the personal contexts may be, as James Keery (2006) has suggested, that Thomas was rejecting not only the conventional discourses for recuperating such deaths, but his own collusion with them in his wartime work of writing propagandistic film-scripts, perhaps even answering his disclaimer ('I know not . . . who was the first to die') in 'Ceremony After a Fire Raid'.

The poem's obvious magnificence contributed much to 'Thomas's apotheosis as "the arch-angel of a new Apocalypse"', as Keery puts it, and it has become something of a critical litmus test. To detractors, such as Henry Gibson (in Tedlock, 1960) and Terry Eagleton (2007), it epitomises what they regard as Thomas's faults: vague musicality, 'Celtic' verbosity ('absorbed in his own metaphorical pyrotechnics', in Eagleton's phrase), conceptual fudge. Others argue, to the contrary, that its impassioned simplicity is deceptive, the apparent vagueness a complex manipulation of readerly expectation and response which nevertheless grants the dead child a monumental dignity (like the non-personalised figures of Henry Moore's drawings of shelterers in the London Underground). They note that the poem yields allusions to the 'real world' of the Blitz Tube shelters and the Holocaust, if one is prepared to look.

In this sense, the first draft is revealingly transitional, since its date supports the hypothesis that the addition of 'Zion' and 'synagogue' reflected news of the Nazi death camps, not liberated by the Allies until 1945, when Thomas completed the poem. The case for the poem's success is strengthened by its rich intertextuality, albeit this raises further questions. Wilfred Owen's 'Dulce et decorum est', also a rebuke to official or approved responses to war deaths (the patriotic verse of Jessie Pope) is the most important predecessor and point of departure; others include Wordsworth's Lucy Poems and Browne's *Religio Medici*, 52: 'I can hardly thinke there was ever any scared into Heaven, they goe the fairest way to Heaven that would serve God without a Hell.'

1 **Never** = may allude to Winston Churchill's famously defiant usages of the word in his two most famous war speeches ('we shall never surrender' and 'never in the field of human conflict'). Although broadcast in 1940, these speeches were in the public mind ahead of the June 1945 General Election, as Churchill's virtues as war leader were weighed against his opposition to Beveridge's reforms; **mankind** = repeated in l. 15. 5 **still** = quiet (augmenting 'silence'); perpetual (apocalypse as a continuous condition). 8-9 **Zion . . . synagogue** = glancingly alludes to the Holocaust; the Red Army discovered Auschwitz in early 1945, but the liberation of Büchenwald by the US Army and Bergen-Belsen by the British Army in April 1945 had the biggest impact in Britain. Thomas's horrified awareness of this is likely to have played a role in the revision of the November 1944 draft. 13 **majesty and burning** = an example of the 'Blitz sublime', by which witnesses of the destruction felt simultaneously horrified and exalted; cf. also Dr Matthew Dante O'Connor's description of sheltering from a bombardment during WWI in chapter 1 of *Nightwood*:

> 'I was in the war [WWI] once myself', the doctor went on, 'in a little town where the bombs began tearing the heart out of you, so that you began to think of all the majesty in the world that you would not be able to think of in a minute, if the noise came down and struck in the right place . . .'

Eagleton, in line with his reading of the poem as narcissistically self-absorbed, denounces this line as 'meant to dignify its subject [but] simply succeed[ing] in making being burnt to death sound noble'. 15 **the mankind of her going** = war is a male occupation which has claimed a female child, in 'a poem of essentially female kindness

("London's daughter", "the dark veins of her mother")'; as Davies (1986) also notes, when Shakespeare uses 'mankind' in relation to a female it 'denotes unnatural cruelty'; **grave truth** = cf. *Romeo and Juliet*, 3:1, l. 98: 'Ask for me tomorrow and you shall find me a grave man'). Like some other commentators, Parkinson (1981) finds the pun too crude: 'the secondary context (death) is evident and the focusing of the pun is merely lurid'; it also has an 'almost sarcastic' edge, and 'ridicule has no place in this passionate elegy'. 19 **the first dead** = echoing 'the first death' of the final line. 21 **The dark veins of her mother** = mother earth (making 'veins' mineral); London (cf. also Richard Aldington's 'Life Quest': 'traffic-clots go curdling / Through the dark veins of the town . . . Breaking the rhythm of our blood / Until the soft swirl and lapse of Thames / Alone seem unreal'); cf. Browne, *Urne-Buriall*, III: 'the Earth, whereof all things are but a colonie; and which, if time permits, the mother Element will have in their primitive masse again.' 24 **After the first death, there is no other** = ostensibly, this is the reason given for not mourning; either *a* because no one can ordinarily die twice; *b* because, passing into the eternal processual cycle, one becomes part of the eternal life of the cosmos, however remote this is from a human concept of life; *c* because of Christian resurrection (the use of 'first death' presupposes that one is reborn after death and that there *could* therefore be another); *d* because the poet rejects the notion of the Last Judgement and the claim in Revelation 21:6–8 and elsewhere in Revelation that those damned at that judgement will suffer a 'second death' and eternal punishment (a similar notion, the weighing of the heart against the feather in Ancient Egyptian beliefs, features in Thomas's early poetry). However, while the line draws on something of the spirit of Revelation ('he that overcometh shall not be hurt of the second death'), its manifold intertextuality seems excessive if it is simply there to assert non-existence. Keery notes, against the charge that the line is vague, that it is in fact one of the most calculatedly allusive in all twentieth-century poetry: cf. among others to George Herbert, 'Mans medley' ('he . . . fears two deaths alone'); Browne, *Religio Medici*, 44 ('considering the thousand doors that lead to death [I] do thank my God that we can die but once'); Lionel Johnson, 'The Dark Angel' ('The second Death, that never dies'); Thomas Hardy, 'The To-Be-Forgotten' ('It is the second death') and 'In Tenebris I' ('Twice no-one dies');

Swinburne, 'The Triumph of Time' ('As the world's first dead . . . Made one with death'); J. F. Hendry 'The Toy Soldier' ('This was the first death'); and Thomas himself in 'I dreamed my genesis' ('sharp in my second death') and 'Ceremony After a Fire Raid' ('the first to die'). Ultimately, the line paradoxically holds all its elements in tension – its different meanings can all be accommodated in the poem – granting the eternity of death without resolving the issue of whether it is an eternal resurrection or eternal oblivion, and thereby embodying the enigma of death itself.

This side of the truth

This is a poem imbued with human tenderness, even as it denies its objective existence in the universe; 'the blinding country of youth' is 'blinding' to its inhabitants (children), but also dazzles and blinds external (adult) observers. Like 'A Refusal to Mourn', to which in some ways it is a companion piece, the poem therefore is not resigned, so much as poised on a knife-edge between consolation and near-despair.

29 **the wicked wish** = although all the poem's judgemental terms are shown to be relative, 'wish' seems to be more akin to 'life', or even 'the evolutionary process', with 'wicked' reflecting parental sadness that all living things, our offspring included, are born to die.

Sooner than you can water milk, or cry 'Amen'

Wynford Vaughan-Thomas told Paul Ferris in 1984 that Dylan Thomas 'gave me his splendidly bawdy pub poem on the night-life of New Quay' when they were drinking in Chelsea 'some time after September 1943'. Ferris surmises that it was written for Vaughan-Thomas 'by way of thanking him for an earlier gift of ten pounds', and notes that changes had been made by the time it was sent to Earp in May 1945. As in other convivial wartime verses, Thomas anticipates the kindlier, more fantastic vein, of 'Quite Early One Morning' and *UMW* in this portrait of Welsh sea-town life, down to the night-time antics of farmers and sailors with the town's good-time girls, the phrase 'bible-black' and the 'fish-heads' clutched by Lord Cut-Glass.

1 No comma after 'milk' in *TP71*. 2 **Cards** = Cardiganshire. 8 **atlantic thighs** = *TP71* has capital 'A' for 'Atlantic'. As the character of Ocky Milkman in *UMW* suggests, West Walian dairymen in London had a reputation for watering the milk they sold. 11 'from the mothy darkness of his black back house' in *TP71*. 12 'vinegar and paraffin' and no comma in *TP71*. 13 no comma, and 'and' for '&' in *TP71*. 14 *TP71* has 'Cross Inn and fouls' for 'Lion Inn to foul'. Both are New Quay pubs. 15 unpunctuated in *TP71*, and with uppercase 'Liz'; pun on 'bold'. 17–18 Additions to *TP71* version. 19–20 *TP71* has: 'Customers in the snugbar by the gobgreen logs / Tell other customers what they do with dogs'.

Unluckily for a death

'Poem (To Caitlin)' (1939), the earlier version of this poem, worried Thomas, perhaps because he came to feel the 'crudeness' he told Vernon Watkins was 'essential to the argument' was overdone. His 'completely rewritten' replacement for it, in the words of Maud (2003), nevertheless retains the original's argument and basic imagery.

6 **dedicate forever to my self** = the 'death biding two' will always lurk, waiting for the death of his love, because they are part of the psychic make-up of the couple (see l. 53). 27 **shoo the bird below me** = 'shoo' means 'scare away'; presumably, since he is rejecting the phoenix, this means that he will not acknowledge it by chasing it off. 28 **The death biding two** = the phoenix and the 'woman in shades'. 29 **tigron** = cross between a lion and a tiger, both kingly creatures, and thus taken as exemplar and leader of the 'striped and noon maned tribe' of l. 31. 32–3 **The she mule . . . broody in a milk of birds** = mules are a sterile cross of horse and donkey, the minotaur was the man-bull offspring of Zeus and Pasiphae, the platypus grotesquely combines avian and mammalian features, being 'duck-billed' and egg- laying ('broody'), but also suckling its young. 47 **Both shall fail if I bow not . . .**

immortality at my side = the first option would be an unreal sanctification of the 'ceremony of souls', capitulating to the 'woman in shades', the second a devaluing of the 'living flesh' in an attempt to gain eternal life. Typically, double negatives convey qualified positives, and the struggle to avoid the 'death'.

In my craft or sullen art

There is no surviving MS or mention of this poem in Thomas's correspondence, although it was must have been written pretty quickly in late summer 1945, when he was assembling *DE* and was perhaps thinking about the act of writing and its relationship to his reputation. He sent it to Dent's with 'Fern Hill' in a letter of 18 September 1945, observing: 'I have crossed out the poem on page 36 entirely, and am substituting another, and shorter, poem.'

In 'In my craft', Thomas probes the apparent opposition between notions of art as inspiration and the craft required to produce a lasting artwork. He seems, on first reading, to exalt the more plebeian 'craft' above a withdrawn, antisocial and potentially élitist 'art'. Davies (2000) argues that Thomas foregrounds 'craft' by attaching 'sullen' to 'art', inverting the image of 'bright metal on a sullen ground' of *1 Henry IV*, 1:2, l. 212. Yet, as Thomas noted, craft is a means to an end:

> You can tear a poem apart to see what makes it technically tick, and say . . . 'This is why the poem moves me so. . . .' But you're back where you began. You're back with the mystery of having been moved by words. The best craftsmanship always leaves holes and gaps in the works of the poem so that something that is not in the poem can creep, crawl, flash, or thunder in.

The opposition of 'craft' and 'art', then, is only apparently clear-cut.

Thomas's recent orientation towards the English pastoral-meditative tradition informs the poem's literary contexts, and its implicit claim on behalf of the solitude necessary for writing. 'Singing light' links him with others who wrote of burning the midnight oil, rejects thoughts of careerism, money and self-display, and affirms the traditional role of lyric – to extol love as a supreme value. Even as it paradoxically links solitude and solidarity, the poem's chief power, as a mantra-like 'charm', seems subliminal.

One way of tracing the poet's realisation that the lovers no longer acknowledge him, a falling short enacted in the second stanza ceding of a line to the first stanza, might involve noting how stanza 2 rings crafted and crafty changes on stanza 1 rather than simply repeating it, complex interlocking like the lovers, as rhymes ('art', 'arms', 'wages') and phrase-parts ('ivory' and 'towers') are shared but altered, exchanged but changed. The ending is crucial in this regard: it creates a circular effect, but the omission of 'sullen' does not quite close the gap between 'craft' and 'art'.

Goodby (2013) notes that 'labour', 'wages', 'trade' and 'pay' are economic terms ostensibly at odds with the poem's subject. They identify art's spiritualisation under the impact of commodification, forced to 'strut and trade', and hint at the dilemmas of the lyric poet under late capitalism. This informs the gulf between the poet's labours and the world of love, and the lovers' failure to pay tribute to a figure who was once central to courtship rituals and expressions of love. The wider context is also important; when 'griefs' returns in stanza 2 it applies to 'the ages' as well as lovers, hinting at 'arms' as weapons. In its own way, then, the poem was sensitive to Theodor Adorno's famous claim that it is barbaric to write lyric poetry after Auschwitz, and marks a shift from a late-romantic *mise-en-scène* – the poet rejected by an unfeeling world, but nevertheless welcomed by lovers – to a more extreme isolation, in which unpaid 'wages' are the only worthy form of reward. Anticipating their indifference, the poet writes for the lovers; they can give only themselves, and are only interested in giving themselves, to each other, and thus are alone capable of a pure, uncompromised relationship. Their love, like his art, has no exchange-value, and their ignorance of him is paradoxically why he can write only for them, this negative recognition modifying art's 'sullen'-ness.

1 **sullen** = deftly deflates the poem's quasi-Yeatsian tenor at its outset with very un-Yeatsian self-deprecation. 2 **exercised** = cf. *Cymbeline*, 4:2, l. 277 – 'No exorciser harm thee' – and the preceding lines, 'All lovers young, all lovers must / Consign to thee and come to dust.'

3 **moon rages** = the moon as a symbol of madness and poetic inspiration; then also (in the following line) of the madness of love 6 **labour** = the moon is associated with Diana, the goddess of childbirth and labour, the pangs of which resemble those of bringing a poem into existence. 10–11 **common wages** = develops 'labour', emphasising the 'craft' aspect of poetry. 15 **towering dead** = as well as Yeats at Thoor Ballylee, Thomas alludes to Shelley's solitary Platonist, and Milton in 'Il Penseroso': 'Let my Lamp at midnight hour / Be seen in some high lonely Tow'r'.

Fern Hill

One of the most famous of Thomas's poems was written about one rural dwelling in another, Blaen Cwm, where Thomas and his family spent the summer of 1945 with his parents (he described it in a letter to Oscar Williams of 30 July 1945 as 'a breeding-box in a cabbage valley [with] a parlour with a preserved sheepdog, where mothballs fly at night, not moths, where the Bible opens itself at Revelations . . . [in] a cottage row of the undeniably mad unpossessed peasantry of the inbred crooked country'). As a child, Thomas had spent many happy summer holidays at 'Fernhill', the farm owned by his Aunt Ann Jones (of 'After the Funeral' and 'The Peaches'). In writing it he took his formal and thematic cues from 'Poem in October', further developing its visionary landscape, syllabics and shapely stanzas to achieve a more complete realisation of the pastoral mode which dominates his later work. He described it in contradictory terms, as both a poem 'for evening and tears' and as 'that joyful poem' made of words which came 'at last, out of a never-to-be-buried childhood in heaven or Wales' (*CL*, 629, 652).

A complete success in its own terms, the poem's fame has prevented many from seeing past its nostalgic element, and even to dismissal of it as 'word-tumbling without gravity of point, or point of fun' for Geoffrey Grigson (in Tedlock, 1963), or 'emotionally dishonest' dilute Wordsworth (John Fuller, 1972). Many, however, have accepted its amplitude of feeling, while at the same time grasping its intense and complex bitter-sweetness. Tindall (1962), for example, sets out these ambiguities, noting how 'Fern Hill' is not about 'how it feels to be young . . . [but] how it feels to have been young', and how 'Thomas in time is hovering above a Thomas once below it'. Jack Jenkins (1966) explores the poem's 'green' theme; the colour of ferns – the very first plants – green is the alpha and omega of the poem, denoting growth and rot, while primeval ferns produced the coal burning in 'fire green as grass' at l. 22.

In the most exhaustive account to date, Alastair Fowler (Davies, 1972) takes 'Fern Hill' to be a childhood poem in the genre that looks back on childhood from sad maturity and values its innocence (Hood's 'I remember', Vaughan's 'The Retreat'; 'But I by backward steps would move, / And when this dust falls to the urn / In that state I came return.'). Similarly, Siobhán Parkinson (1981) notes Thomas's use of twisted idioms to give 'novelty and quaintness' and also a 'childlike quality' essential to the manipulation of perspectives on which the poem's irony is based, as well as the way we are simultaneously made aware of 'the child's vision of the farm and the adult's interpretation of it' (Parkinson, 1981). Fowler, however, goes on to unpick the intricate constructedness within 'Fern Hill's easy-going manner, detailing systematic phrasal manipulation, repetition ('easy', 'time', 'green', 'golden', 'stable', 'horses', 'simple'), colour- and sound-patterning, and the way this enacts larger, cosmic and symbolic symmetries (the four elements and the sun, moon and stars). This is 'Fern Hill' as creation poem, in which the alternation of day and night is central – the sun appears in every stanza – imbued with an implicit awareness of 'growing towards death' in what is, despite appearances, 'a tight, circular, almost sestina-like form'. That Thomas incorporates an aware-ness of the 'subjective selectivity of early fantasies', placing and ironising these, is endorsed by Davies (1986) who sees 'Fern Hill' as marking a shift from a materialist, process-oriented view of nature to a more 'conceptual' one ('human consciousness . . . is now more than merely "natural", having access to religious concepts and modes of feeling which are then applied *to* nature', but without this implying a 'specifi-cally Christian emphasis').

Stewart Crehan (1990) emphasises that the poem's child 'I' is happily isolated – there is no other human presence – but rebuts Russell Davies's jibe that it is therefore escapist, or 'as political as a mountain goat'. Adopting a Marxist-Freudian approach, he finds the radical optimism of 1945 in the poem's utopianism, 'anarchic paradise of play' and re-enactment of 'an unrepressed, unashamedly self-centred freedom'. For this reason, he claims, it is 'not essentially nostalgic', but allows for the realisation of the id (in which there is nothing that corresponds to the idea of linear time).

Against Crehan's at times rather stern advocacy, Alastair Heys (2004) asserts the poem's playfulness, Keatsian 'sensuous intelligence', 'material sublime', 'Romantic cult of childhood and the autumnal apple' and shamelessly oral and 'vulgarian pleasures', championing the pleasure principle. Although occasionally lapsing into stereotype ('sensual Celt in revolt'), Heys also reminds us that 'Fern Hill' is one of Thomas's first poems to display, rather than bury, its sources and intertexts: he discerns 'a quarrel between Milton, Wordsworth and . . . non-conformism on the one hand' and 'Shakespeare, Keats, Lawrence and the soul's sensual strut on the other.' This may be linked to Thomas's alteration of the farm's name to the more English- and suburban-seeming 'Fern Hill', 'analyzing the word to spell out a larger and wilder greenness' as Barbara Hardy (2000) puts it, and the tendency in his later poems to interweave English and Welsh landscapes and poetries. The most obvious English forbear is Wordsworth's 'Ode: Intimations of Immortality', but 'Fern Hill' also echoes Sidney, Shakespeare, the Bible, Donne, Herbert, Marvell, Clare, Whitman, Arnold, and Hopkins. Critics have rightly linked the poem to Thomas's re-reading of Lawrence's poems while he was at Blaen Cwm writing the poem; the letter to Oscar Williams, quotes 'Ballad of Another Ophelia' with its 'green glimmer of apples in the orchard'. But two other intertexts seem even more potent. The first is Thomas Traherne's *Centuries of Meditations*, in which childhood is described in similar terms. According to John Ormond, in David N. Thomas (2004), Thomas told him that this text was 'almost a keystone in [his] thinking':

The corn was orient and immortal wheat, which never should be reaped, nor was ever sown. I thought it had stood from everlasting to everlasting. The dust and stones of the street were as precious as gold: the gates were at first the end of the world. The green trees when I saw them first . . . transported and ravished me, their sweetness and unusual beauty made my heart to leap, and almost mad with ecstasy, they were such strange and wonderful things: The Men! O what venerable and reverend creatures did the aged seem!

Immortal Cherubims! And young men glittering and sparkling Angels, and maids strange seraphic pieces of life and beauty! Boys and girls tumbling in the street, and playing, were moving jewels. I knew not that they were born or should die; But all things abided as they were in their proper places. Eternity was manifest in the Light of the Day, and something infinite behind everything appeared which talked with my expectation and moved my desire . . . The skies were mine, and so were the sun and moon and stars, and all the World was mine; and I the only spectator and enjoyer of it. I knew no churlish proprieties, nor bounds, nor divisions: but all proprieties and divisions were mine: all treasures and the possessors of them. So that with much ado I was corrupted, and made to learn the dirty devices of this world. Which I now unlearn, and I become, as it were, a little child again that I may enter the Kingdom of God.

The second is Thomas Hardy's 'Regret Not Me':

Swift as the light . . .
Ecstatically I moved, and feared no night.

I did not know
That heydays fade and go,
But deemed that was would always be so.

I skipped at morn
Between the yellowing corn,
Thinking it good and glorious to be born.

I ran at eves
Among the piled up sheaves,
Dreaming 'I grieve not, therefore nothing grieves.'

These sources counterpoint Welsh idioms, religiosity and location; it is notable that Thomas, for example, uses *cynghanedd*-like sound-patterning in the opening lines of the first stanza (the reversed repetition of *ap/b* and *ou* sounds in 'apple bough . . . About . . . house . . . happy', repetition of *gr* in 'grass . . . green', repetition of long *i*, *t*, *m*(e) and *l* in 'Time let me hail and climb'. Like other Anglo-Welsh elements, this contributes to the sense of what James A. Davies (1997) calls a work 'at once within the text and in the margin – at the interstice – of mainstream English literature' (albeit his claim that it is a 'Unionist' poem may be felt to push this point too far). Like other key poems, 'Fern Hill' is also intertextual with Thomas himself, from the 'gold tithings' and 'cargoed apples' of 'I see the boys of summer' to 'the sea / Tumbling in harness' of 'A Refusal to Mourn'.

The poem has six stanzas of nine lines each, with only lines 6 and 52 breaking the syllabic count of 14, 14, 9, 6, 9, 14, 14 in the first seven lines of each stanza; the count for the two final lines, differently patterned, runs: 7, 9 (stanzas 1 and 2); 9, 6 (stanzas 3, 4 and 5); 7, 9 (stanza 6). As in 'Poem in October' there is assonantal end-rhyme (e.g. maiden-again-stable; barns-calves; rising-dying, etc.).

1 **apple-boughs** = as 'green' and 'golden', the colours of growth and maturity, like Hesperidean fruit (mixing pagan and Christian) and also sun-like. 2 **lilting** = 'the whole scene is . . . tilting, too, in the boy's excited vision' (Davies, 1986); **green** = a favourite Thomas word; echoing Marvell's 'green thought in a green shade' ('The Garden'), and common in Henry Vaughan. 3 **dingle** – cf. Matthew Arnold's 'Thyrsis': 'many a dingle on the loved hill-side . . . Hath since our day put by / The coronals of that forgotten time'. 7 **once below a time** = has the child both 'out of time to all appearances' and 'in time, subject of and to a time and future subject of another' (Tindall, 1962). The timeless stasis of the child's condition is central to the movement of the poem, which largely enacts it until stanza 4. 9 **windfall light** = 'windfall' is noun (light on the apples) and adjective qualifying light (referring to both the luck of having such a radiant memory of childhood *and* 'unmerited grace' (Fowler, 1972)). For Emery (1962), 'windfall' describes the light as 'largesse' and, simultaneously, as lost because fallen, blown down. The 'rivers' are those of apples / light under the orchard trees. 10 **green and carefree** = echoes 'young and easy', and anticipates 'heedless' and 'nothing I cared' in stanza 5; suggestion of 'naïve to be carefree', as in Hardy's 'Regret Not Me'. 14 **mercy of his means** = cf. Thomas's story 'The Visitors' (April 1934): 'Time was merciful enough to let the sun shine on his bed, and merciless enough to chime the sun away when night came'. 'Golden

mean', a common Traherne theme, is present in the line. 15 **I was huntsman and herdsman** = the boy's isolated self-sufficiency is less solipsism than the natural product of his raptness. 16 **sang to my horn** = 'the choice of instrument is deliberate, and reflects insight into the sexual character of fantasies of omnipotence . . . gently examin[ing] the basis of nostalgia in wish fulfilment' (Fowler, 1972); **foxes** = wild animals contrasted with domesticated ones ('calves', l. 15), hence 'huntsman and herdsman'. They recur in stanza 5 with 'pheasants', seemingly as the stuffed and tame one of the 'Fernhill' parlour in 'After the funeral' and 'The Peaches', perhaps symbolising the deleterious effects of time. 17–18 **the sabbath rang slowly / In the . . . holy streams** = Emery (1962) sees a contradiction: 'every day is a holiday and a holy day . . . [but also] sun's days, and they died with the light of the setting sun'. In 'The Crumbs of One Man's Year' (1946), Thomas refers to Josephus's Sabbatic River which flowed one day in seven: 'You could have thought the river was ringing – almost you could hear the green, rapid bells sing in it: it could have been . . . the river "in Judea that runs swiftly all the six days of the week, and stands still and rests all their Sabbath"' (*QEOM*, 44); cf. Traherne, *Centuries*, III:2: 'All Time was Eternity [in childhood], and a perpetual Sabbath. Is it not Strange that an Infant should be Heir of the World, and see those Mysteries which the Books of the Learned never unfold?' 19–21 **All the sun long** = 'as the word "day" is hidden but implicit . . . so the idea of time is implicit in childhood although the child is unaware of it' (Parkinson, 1981); **lovely . . . lovely** = term of approbation in South Walian English ('there's lovely'); deliberately lush, and a word 'chosen in despair of words . . . like "nice" in "A Prospect of the Sea" [it] proves the very word for childish joy' (Tindall, 1962). 20–2 the suggestion of the four elements (Davies, 1993) can be found in 'This side of the truth'. 22 **fire green as grass** = as bright and hot as grass is green: cf. 'bonfire green', in D. H. Lawrence, 'The Enkindled Spring'. 24–9 As in 'The hunchback in the park', Thomas alludes to the belief that very young children do not believe an object which can no longer be seen still exists (the phenomenon of 'object permanence'). 29–30 **it was all / Shining** = South Walian colloquial construction. 30 **Adam and maiden** = cf. Vaughan, 'Innocence', 'A little Adam in a Sphere / Of joys'. 31 **gathered** = cf. Genesis 1:9: 'let the waters under the heavens be gathered', with perhaps a hint of a poisoned eruption.

34 **the birth of the simple light** = cf. Wordsworth's Immortality Ode, 'The sunshine is a glorious birth'. 35 **spinning place** = Thomas associates spinning with creation (the spinning of the threads of Fate in Greek myth). 38 **new made clouds** = fresh, but perhaps anticipating the darkening of the child's sunlit world. 42 **sky blue trades** = cf. Wordsworth's 'Ode' on the child's 'work of his own hand' and 'the soul that rises with us, our life's star'. 44–5 **the children . . . Follow him** = as Betty and William Greenway note (Pursglove, Goodby and Wigginton 2000), the more sinister tale of the Pied Piper has replaced that of Little Boy Blue: 'it is almost as if, in the stories of childhood, is the prefiguring of our sad future, a subtext we can only read after it is too late.' 46 **lamb white days** = cf. Wordsworth's 'Ode': 'The young lambs bound / As to the tabour's sound'; also Henry Vaughan's 'Child-hood', 'Those white designs which children drive'. 49 **riding** = usually has a sexual connotation in Thomas; it perhaps means that in becoming an adult he falls into a 'sleep' concerning the un-selfconscious, vivid existence he enjoyed in childhood. 51 **childless** = because the child is now an adult. 52–4 These lines are inscribed on Thomas's commemorative plaque in Poet's Corner, Westminster Abbey. Crehan notes a return to the 'rocking movement' of the opening lines: 'Thomas makes the signifiers themselves mouth what the lips of infancy need and do . . . The pleasures of the breast are re-enacted'. They also remind us ('dying' often being sexual in Thomas) of the poem's blurring of childhood sexuality and adult desire, the revision of 'Fernhill' to 'Fern Hill' emphasising the allusion to the *mons veneris* (Goodby, 2013). 53 **held** = 'time . . . is not only a reaper: he is also a father . . . feared but also loved' (Fowler, 1972); **green and dying** – the child is no longer both green *and* golden, as previously; cf. 'The force', 'my green age'.

In Country Heaven [fragment]

Dylan Thomas: The Caedmon Collection (2002) includes a discussion ('In Country Heaven – The Evolution of a Poem') by Douglas Cleverdon and Humphrey Searle of the poem, and readings of its revisions and final (abandoned) version by Cleverdon, Searle, Hugh Griffiths and Basil Jones.

For Moynihan (1966), the poem shows that Thomas 'equates God, the human heart, and nature, and even more particularly the hill, and yet . . . retains the perception of God as an individual spirit. [It] shows the maker and first cause of Creation subsumed under a God of love and pity who cosmically prays and weeps for man', 'the symbol of heaven' being a '"canonized" nature', where all sleep sound because:

> [T]he fifth element is pity. This glimpse of paradise . . . was put aside in order to view eternity through human eyes, rather than the world through God's eyes. . . . [and] in the remembered tales [of the completed poems] Thomas sufficiently developed his mythopoeic vision of the regenerated world.

Hardy (2000) calls the 1951 fragment 'eloquent and polished' and notes the 'playful, very Joycean image of "All the Canterbury bells . . . Blithe in the tall telling"' in the 1947 fragment. But she also observes of the *In Country Heaven* project that it is 'a tragic reversal of Genesis and St. John, not "Let there be light" [but] "Let there be darkness"', a 'divine decreation' in which 'the god, author, and first cause weeps and in weeping reverses the creative fiat and makes the world turn dark. The darkness is seen by the dead in Country Heaven . . .'

In Country Sleep

Thomas wrote from Italy of 'working on a long poem' to his agent David Higham on 24 April 1947, of it 'coming on slowly' on 24 May, and of having up to one hundred lines by 20 June. He declared it almost finished on 11 July, and it was published in *Horizon* (UK) (where it contained '16 misprints, including Jew for dew' (*CL*, 745)) and *Atlantic* (USA) in December 1947.

Doubts have been expressed as to how complete Thomas felt this poem was; letters of 11 July 1947 to Tommy Earp and Margaret Taylor speak of a 'finished' poem, but on the 14th he told Bill and Helen McAlpine 'the first two parts of my poem are finished. I'm working on the third.' However, after a tentative stab at this, he decided against continuing. As it stands, 'In Country Sleep' is a successful free-standing work which moves to a logical conclusion.

In a radio broadcast of it on 25 September 1950, available on CD in *The Caedmon Collection*, Thomas said it was part of a work in progress provisionally called *In Country Heaven*.

Ostensibly, the poem addresses Thomas's daughter Aeronwy, and concerns his reading of bedside stories to her, placing it in the tradition of Coleridge's 'Frost at Midnight' and Yeats's 'A Prayer for my Daughter'. However, Thomas told Tindall (1962), that the poem 'was not addressed to a child at all but to his wife', and part II's 'haygold haired, my love asleep, and the rift blue / Eyed . . . so stilly / Lying' can suggest someone older. This suggestion is strengthened by Thomas's reading of 'riding thigh' for 'riding high' (at l. 101) in his recording of the poem. The sense of an exploration of complex, oedipally tinged paternal love and its entwinement with feelings of jealous desire towards a wife cannot be avoided, then, and may be reflected in the poem's evasive, convoluted syntax. In moving between two addressees, Thomas uses what Victor Golightly (2003) usefully calls 'proto-Magic Realism' to uncover the latent sexual content of the fairy-tales and dramatise his own situation. Even so, a purely Freudian interpretation of the Thief as rival for a daughter's love, or a sexual partner, is too limited to account for the poem's complex of interrelated symbolic values.

The chief question the poem raises is: if the Thief is to be acknowledged in a 'positive act of recognition', as claimed by Davies (1972, 2000), why fear him? For most critics the ambiguity of the role and nature of the Thief make him menacing; he clearly derives from 'the day of the Lord' that 'will come as a thief in the night' (2 Peter 3:10), and as Balakier (1996) notes he resembles the shape-shifting Satan of *Paradise Lost* (which would make father and daughter Adam and Eve). Part I ends on an ambiguous note of the naturalness of the Thief's 'falling', but with a hint of unnatural nuclear apocalypse; part II begins by bringing the speaker's anxiety out into the open. The speaker grasps that the girl has a 'faith' in the Thief coming to take her faith and needs this in order to confirm it. The core of her faith lies in the Thief's ability to make her grieve for him not coming.

'Designed', earlier in the poem, now acquires its full significance as 'has designs on'; but the speaker now sees that what he viewed as the Thief's predatory approach is desired by his daughter, and that this is part of a 'design' of her own, whereby her faith can only exist by being threatened, a process in which she has to collude. As often in Thomas, this is being conveyed by double negatives, as his efforts to gloss it reveal. In other words, while the Thief is not purely evil, he seems more than just the inevitability of ageing and death. For this reason the claim that he 'bears a strong resemblance to Blake's "spectre", a shadowy figure who is the enemy of "the Imagination which Liveth for Ever"' is suggestive (Balakier, 1996). The point is that, however defined, the speaker comes to be afraid that the girl will lose the faith-confirming fear that the Thief will not try to steal her faith. Or, as Maud (2003) puts it (calling it a 'triple negative'):

> She has this belief that each night [the Thief] will come to eliminate her fear that this is the night he will come only to leave her forsaken, feeling he will not come [in future]; the threat is that this belief will be stolen from her. Each night his presence negates her fear that he will not come.

In this sense, the poem is not so much about the seemingly threatened daughter/wife, or the Thief himself, but the process by which the speaker grasps the paradox of belief or faith. 'Faith' is less that in a 'God', more a general ontological condition.

Part I has nine seven-line stanzas with *abcbaac* rhyme; part II has eight six-line stanzas with an *abbcca* pattern. The fifth line of the stanzas in part I and the fourth line of those in part II are four syllables; the other lines alternate between twelve and thirteen.

16 **staved** = autograph alteration from 'stared' in Buffalo MS. 21 **tolled to sleep** = pun on 'told to sleep'. 38, 49, 93 **Thief** = for the ambiguous 'day of the Lord [that] will come as a thief in the night', cf. 2 Peter 3:10: 'For yourselves know perfectly that the day of the Lord so cometh as a thief in the night', 1 Thessalonians 5:2; 'Behold I [Christ] come as a thief! Blessed is he who watches and keeps his garments, lest he walk naked, and they see his shame.' Capitalised in first and third appearances in B431F25; second usage lower case, but with autograph correction. 51–4 **until the stern bell . . . the soul walks / The waters shorn.** = an apocalyptic trope similar to 'Never until . . . the still hour' of 'A Refusal to Mourn'. 59–63 **pounded islands . . . cyclone of silence** = perhaps also refers to Welsh legend

(Arthurian Afallon means 'island of apples'). 62 **yawning** = a reminder that the poem's *mise-en-scène* is a father reading a bedtime story to his daughter. 66 **And high, there . . .!** = cf. Hopkins, 'The Windhover': 'striding / High there'. 71 **pastoral** = of the poem's Cold War context, Richard Chamberlain (2003) notes how 'pastoral's power to integrate, without harmfully assimilating, disparate or opposing forces is felt in the way facts of nature are [here] pushed up against written text' and the 'mutually transforming, "pastoral" juxtaposition of joyful, redemptive art and the violence of war in the "dingle torn to singing"'. He adds, 'it introduces a challenge central to the pastoral logic of the late poems' by 'ghost[ing] the disturbing possibility that they celebrate the violence and ineluctable drive towards self-killing which have in effect already destroyed the beauty of the natural world'. 78 **Of blood! The bird loud vein!** = an Austin MS has 'Of the blood! The blood loud birds!' 93 lower case 'thief' given upper case 'T' in autograph in Buffalo MS (B431F25). 96 **designed** = Thomas now 'concentrates on words which suggest purpose and control: "designed", "truly", "ruly", "surely", "ship shape" etc' (Davies, 1993). 105 **lawless sun** = Austin MS has 'chained sun'. 111 **Your faith . . . the ruled sun** = Austin MS has variants 'steadfast' and 'constant' for 'ruled'. The contrast with the 'lawless' may involve not just the nuclear forces fuelling the 'sun', but 'the sun of scientific fact, against whose quantifications the imagination revolts' (Balakier, 1996). However, 'outcry' suggests Christ (as Son / 'sun' 'ruled' by God to die), and transposition of 'death' and 'faith' (Christ's death was faithless: 'And at the ninth hour Jesus cried with a loud voice, saying, Eloi, Eloi, lama sabachthani? which is, being interpreted, My God, My God, why has thou forsaken me?').

Over Sir John's hill

There is general critical agreement that this is one of the most satisfying of the of later poems, even if Geoffrey Johnson rather bizarrely claimed in 1954 that it was 'a loose association of impassioned words trusting to luck and chance alliteration for psychological linkage with the reader' (in Tedlock, 1960), and Hardy (1977) found its description too 'arbitrary' and lacking in 'feeling' before the 'calm melancholy' of its ending. The poem has a paradoxical premise which is often missed; in the originating action, the 'small birds' scattered by the hawk's presence fly *from* the safety of hedgerows and treetops and 'hare / *To* the hawk', who seemingly invites them to their deaths ('Come and be killed'). It is only when the speaker mentions 'guilt' that God appears; as Maud (1963) notes, this occurs late on, at l. 41, and it would be wrong to read religious belief into the religiose language. Davies (1986) and others argue that the poem exemplifies and critiques the human tendency to anthropomorphise the natural world, and the way this ends in metaphysics. That is, Thomas foregrounds the natural images as the vehicle by which this happens, and it is as illustrations of this process – rather than as 'word-painting' – that we should understand them. Man is separated from the natural world in trying to assert unity with it, just as much as in 'The force'.

3 **hoisted cloud, at drop of dusk** = those sentenced to death were 'dropped' through a trapdoor with the noose around their necks; or, in earlier centuries, simply pushed from a ladder or cart on which they had been 'hoisted'. 4 **rays** = continues the fire imagery, begun in l. 2, running throughout the poem: 'fiery', 'flash', 'fuse', 'flames', 'brand', etc. 21–2 **'dilly, dilly'** = 'Dilly', a reduplication from 'dally', means 'wait awhile' (Davies, 2001); but it also echoes 'Dylan' in the pronunciation (as 'Dillon') favoured by Thomas and his family and friends. 23–6 A Buffalo MS has:

I open the scriptural water at a passage
Of prophecies among the nutcracker sandcrabs prancing

And find in each wave-vext
Leaf, death's graveprint and text.

33 **leave shingle and elm** = B433F3 has 'leave greenwood & rest'.

Lament

A poem sent to Princess Caetani on 17 May 1951, and published in *Botteghe Oscure* without the current fourth stanza, the first three lines of which began what is now the fifth stanza. Stanza 4 had been restored, and revisions made, when it was republished, in its current form, in *Partisan Review* in 1952.

Goodby (2001) and Maud (2003) note the poem's roots in working-class, popular culture; its use of double entendres is even more marked in the MS material at Austin (e.g. 'through a slit in the moonshaft slag' and 'All night I could pick and choose'), which contains a wordlist that includes 'hustling', 'riggish', 'mischief', 'blackguard', 'rascal', 'scampish', 'hoodlum', 'lickerish', 'scapegrace' and 'doglocked'. However interpreted, claims that it expresses chagrin at Thomas's own sexual peccadilloes, or that it is a reprehensible revelling in promiscuity (Heaney 1992 and 1995), seem wide of the mark. Rather, 'Lament' is a playfully gross, Rabelaisian *performance*; glancing only obliquely at marital dilemmas, it rewrites the young-man-caught-by-marriage trope of 'Ballad of the Long-legged Bait' in the spirit of the verse-letters and radio features.

4 **gooseberry wood** = one working title in the Austin MS material was 'Lament or Gooseberry Wood'; cf. 'I was alone on the gooseberried earth' in the broadcast 'The Crumbs of One Man's Year' (*CB*, 154). 6 **big girls** = originally 'judies' in MS. 8 **wooed** = rhymes and puns back with 'wood', l. 4. 12 **coal black** = present in each stanza; **bush** = shrub; pubic hair. 22 **clover** = associated with sexual abandon, as in the bawdy folksong, 'Roll me over in the clover', very popular in Britain during and immediately after WWII. 43–8 **at last the soul ... woman's soul for a wife** = unabashedly phallic imagery; Thomas had used mouse and mouse-hole imagery in a consciously Freudian way in the 1930s to symbolise the 'stealthy scratchings of the unconscious' and sexual anxiety; cf. 'The Mouse and the Woman', 'How soon the servant sun'. With his ability to pursue sexual adventure gone, the speaker finds a spiritual side and uses it to find a wife, but can only describe this, incongruously, in terms of his previous thrusting, phallic career. 54 **a sunday wife** = the lower case makes an adjective of 'sunday'; i.e. his wife acts as though it is Sunday every day of the week. Cf. l. 16, 'When, like a running grave'. 57–60 the tone is tongue-in-cheek: 'He is not really a tragic figure, just pretending to be' (Maud 2003).

Do not go gentle into that good night

Thomas's much-loved father, D. J. Thomas, was chronically ill for many years; this poem was written a year before his death, in December 1952. In order to contain near-uncontrollable emotion, Thomas used the villanelle, a highly repetitive medieval form, in which five tercets are followed by a quatrain, with the first and last line of the first tercet repeated alternately as the last line of the subsequent tercets, and paired in a concluding couplet. Thomas's is the best-known example in English, and has affinities with Ernest Dowson's 'Villanelle of the Poet's Road' and 'To an Old Lady' by William Empson (cf. Thomas's truncated villanelle 'Request to Leda', an Empson tribute, of 1942). There are echoes of Yeats and his 'gaiety transfiguring all that dread' in 'rage', 'gay' and 'blaze'. The four central tercets follow part five of Yeats's 'Nineteen Hundred and Nineteen', which ironically mocks, in turn, the 'great', the 'wise', the 'good' and finally 'mockers' themselves. As Victor Golightly (2003) argues, Yeats's 'Come let us mock at the good / That fancied goodness might be gay', in particular, builds 'a strained background bitterness into Thomas's poem that catches the experience in grief where flows of emotion run inexplicably both ways.' *King Lear*, Blake and Byron add to the intertextual mix, and the threat of being stifled by the villanelle form is triumphantly faced down in a poem both powerfully public and movingly personal, as the ostensible plea to resist death is counterpointed by lulling rhythms as if to help the dying father on his way. MSS at Austin and Buffalo show it was composed in tandem with the rambunctious 'Lament', another deathbed lyric, and insights into both can be gained by reading them as a complementary pair; for all its dolorousness, 'Do not go gentle' has a grim humour.

1 **Do not go gentle** = the sense of gentle as 'A maggot, the larva of the flesh-fly or blue-bottle' (*OED*) may lurk here, as punningly used in *Anthony and Cleopatra*, V, ii. 58; **that** = Tindall (1962) notes '"That" was Thomas's favourite demonstrative', but it was also Yeats's; **good night** = a farewell, but a final one; cf. Yeats's 'From "Oedipus at Colonus"', 'a gay goodnight'. Golightly notes: 'Yeats's affected "that" turns an innocent farewell into a figure for blindness, for the dread of death, and death itself, "that good night"'. However, the

sense that 'night' is indeed 'good' and in the natural order of things is allowed by the splitting of 'goodnight', 2–3 **Old age should burn and rave at close of day; / Rage, rage against the dying of the light** = cf. Yeats's 'The Choice', applicable to both the painstaking work (and messy life) of Thomas, and the unfulfilled ambitions of his father, read in the light of the latter's blindness and proximity to death: 'The intellect of man is forced to choose / Perfection of the life, or of the work, / And if it take the second must refuse / A heavenly mansion raging in the dark.' 13 **grave men** = perhaps a pun on 'gravamen'; cf. 'A Refusal to Mourn'. 16 **on the sad height** = the predicament of Lear and Gloucester in *King Lear* and of Christ on Calvary (reversing the trope of the early poems, by which God the Father is seen as having betrayed the Son into crucifixion). 17 **Curse, bless, me now with your fierce tears** = Blake's *Tiriel* (1, ll. 12, 16–18) reworks *King Lear* (for 'bless' cf. also 'Poem on his birthday').

In the White Giant's Thigh

This is perhaps Thomas's most Hardyesque poem, lacking as it does the convoluted multiple negatives of 'In Country Sleep' or allegory and framed anthropomorphism of 'Over Sir John's hill'. Yet despite the brightly coloured, folk-tale tone, it weaves a particularly complex allusive weave, subtly grafting English pastoral scene and Welsh coastal landscape in order to problematise a sense of fixed location or identity, as well as confounding the notion of a purely 'English' or 'Anglo-Welsh' poetic canon. The bucolic relish of the poem ('wains', 'ox roasting sun') suggests a recollection of Breughel the Elder's paintings of peasant life. The notes towards the poem in Austin are extensive; they show Thomas considering the stanza form of Chaucer's *Troilus and Criseyde* as a model, contain the first use of the name 'Milk Wood', and contain numerous alternative lines, phrases and coinages. These are evidence of a highly fertile verbal imagination still working near its inventive peak; as well as such striking phrases as 'jussive bell', 'scrannel sun', 'kempt with brambles' or 'frogs jaw in the marish', there are longer passages such as this, presumably a draft for what became ll. 21–6: 'Stripling caliban straddle and fennish rooting sly / Cinder-eyed in the pitch, bullrush beds, the red groom / And roarer torched in the reek . . .'

16, 25 **milking, cows' tongues, buttermilk** = the Austin MS show that at one point Thomas considered developing this theme further, listing appropriate milkmaid names ('Meg, Mary, Nell, Peg of the Dairy') and coining 'Milk Wood' in the following passage:

And the weasels lean as reeves were the wayside wives
Of all the pilgrims of love on that April ground,
Or best bibbed and gowned in the Sundays of the dead
Proud walked Milk Wood that grew beneath the giant's hill
Now clasp me . . .

19 **clasp me to their grains** = 'grains' is a process word from the early poems; here, an expanded social context also suggests 'groins', 'groans' and 'grins'. 31 **furred small friars . . . in the thistle aisles** = imagery distantly related to the 'bare, ruin'd choirs' of Shakespeare's Sonnet 73, but with a sensual twist. Cf. *UMW*: 'Young girls lie bedded soft or glide in their dreams . . . bridesmaided by glow-worms down the aisles of the organplaying wood'. 35 **linked night** = For Kidder (1973) the primary sense is 'coupled'; 'the night is alive with sexual activity'. 50–3 **They . . . Teach** = syntax allows 'Who' to be the women ('they') and the narrator ('me') until the main verb is reached. 57 **long desirers** = cf. 'the long friends' in 'A Refusal to Mourn'. *ICS* and *CP52* had 'desires' for 'desirers', corrected by *CP88*. A worksheet at Austin has the phrase 'hay haired phantoms'.

Poem on his Birthday

In worksheets at Harvard this poem is titled 'Poem in October (1950)', and much of the writing seems to have been done in summer 1951. (Draft lines from stanza 4, heavily corrected, exist on the verso of a letter sent on 27 May 1951 to Edith Capon.) It first appeared, without the final three stanzas, in *World Review*, in October 1951; the full-length version was published in *Atlantic* in March 1952.

Like 'Over Sir John's hill', Thomas presents the view from his writing shed above the Laugharne estuary as a vision of nature 'red in tooth and claw', with humanity now even more driven by its death-instinct towards atomic self-destruction. However, there is less of a flourish in nature's acquiescence in the cycle of creation and destruction. The planet continues to have a 'beautiful' as well as a 'terrible' worth but Thomas's fears are made more explicit in a form of Atomic Age sublime, in which both unnervingly and apocalyptically fuse, a final form of the process poetic in which rhapsodic transfiguration and atomic extinction are almost inseparable.

The poem consists of twelve nine-line stanzas, alternately of six and nine syllables, with assonantal and full rhyme *ababcdcdac*.

1 **mustardseed sun** = Matthew 17:20: 'And Jesus said . . . If ye have faith as a grain of mustard seed, ye shall say unto this mountain, Remove hence to yonder place; and it shall remove; and nothing shall be impossible unto you'; in the parable told by the Son/sun, the mustard seed symbolises the different kinds of faith (in the natural world, God, heaven) of the poem. 4 **house on stilts** – in a draft, Thomas more prosaically describes the shed and the pictures of poets adorning its walls: 'In this estuary room / With Walt Whitman over my head.' 33 **turnturtle dust** = cf: 'How shall my animal', 'turn turtle'. 48 **fabulous** = Cf. 'impossible great God' of cancelled passage to stanza 3 of 'Into Her Lying Down Head'. Thomas's phrasing reflects a desire to accommodate belief and its lack; a Harvard worksheet has: 'O God who is nowhere, let me be / The least of your believers'. 53 **plenty as blackberries** = Falstaff, *1 Henry IV*, 2: v, ll. 243–4: 'If reasons were as plentiful as blackberries, I would give no man a reason under compulsion, I.' Cf. also Walt Whitman's 'Song of Myself': 'the running blackberry would adorn the parlours of heaven' (see Goodby, 2005). 62 **gulled and chanter** = other senses of 'gulled' (as 'duped') and 'chanter' (*OED*: 'one who sells horses fraudulently') suggest Thomas is qualifying the actuality of 'young Heaven' and belief in it. 69 **still quick stars** = paradoxically stationary and moving, dead and alive (the light of a star can be seen long after it has died).

Prologue to Collected Poems 1934–1952

Originally a verse-letter to John Malcolm Brinnin, written after Thomas's first US tour in 1950, which Brinnin was shown on a visit to Laugharne in July 1951 but never received. Thomas's letter of 3 March 1953 to Oscar Williams with the worksheets (now at Harvard) states that the 'first germ' was 'a piece of doggerel written to someone in the States on my return from there to Wales, but [it] soon grew involved and eventually serious' (*CL*, 975). But the worksheets have the title 'Letter On Returning to Wales from the United States of America, 1952', and record the poem's development after this later point, following Thomas's return from his second tour. It seems Ruth Witt-Diamant, his hostess in San Francisco, was now the intended recipient: one worksheet starts:

At home sweet Christ at last,
Wry, welsh, and far from Scotch,
My pecker at half mast,
This unamended potch
Of poppycock and love
I send, dear   Ruth

As *CP88* notes, 'after about twenty-three worksheets, the title "Prologue" begins to appear'. The further adaptation is explained by the fact that Thomas had just promised E. F. Bozman, his editor at Dent's, a prose preface to *CP52*, due to be published later in 1952. After telling David Higham on 28 June 1952 that he could not produce a 'prose-preface' he described the substitute poem to him, sending it off to Bozman two-and-a-half months later. As Thomas had hoped, the poem is an effective introduction to his work.

29 **these seathumbed leaves** = the pages of *CP52*. 33 **dogdayed** = the dog days, named after the dog star, Sirius, are the hottest of the year, stretching from early July to mid-August. 56 **deer** = as hunted by 'singsong owls'; cf. *King Lear*, II, 4, 135 ('mice and rats and such small deer'; quoted in the 'The Holy Six'). 65–6 **woe / In your beaks** = cf. 'the rook flew into the west with a woe in its beak', in

'The Enemies'. 79 **hollow farms** = farms in hollows between the hills. 84–5 **moonshine drinking / Noah of the bay** = primarily the sea ('bay') 'drinking' in moonlight and, via 'moonshine' as liquor. Seithenyn, the legendary Welsh ruler alluded to, neglected to close his sea defences after a night of carousing and his land (Cantre'r Gwaelod, now in Cardigan Bay) was flooded as a result. Legend has it that the 'drowned deep bells' of its churches can sometimes be heard tolling beneath the waves, an image found in Thomas poems such as 'I, in my intricate image' and 'It is the sinners' dust-tongued bell'.

An old man or a young man

From an untitled and undated fair copy in Thomas's hand at Austin; date assumed from handwriting to be in the early 1950s; first published by Walford Davies in the *Selected Poems* (2000).

Davies notes: 'some phrases on the reverse side, in the manner of Thomas's usual worksheets, show that the poem was in progress up to the point of this fair copy.' Echoing as it does such Yeats poems as 'The Three Bushes' and the Crazy Jane sequence, the pastiche is related to the Yeatsian tone of poems such as 'Do not go gentle'.

Verse and songs from Under Milk Wood

UMW derived from Thomas's earlier radio work, in particular 'Quite Early One Morning' (1945), which concluded with verses describing the inhabitants of the town. Though he had planned his 'play for voices' at least as early as 1939, and probably began work on it in 1947, Thomas never quite completed it. However, it had reached a coherent form when it was given a live performance in New York on 14 May 1953, with Thomas himself reading the parts of First Voice and the Reverend Eli Jenkins. He added substantially to it before his death later that year, and it was broadcast posthumously on 25 January 1954 in a recording which featured Richard Burton as the First Voice. It was part-published in *Botteghe Oscure* in October 1951, and fully published in book form in February 1954.

Excluded from *TP71* on the grounds that they were accessible in *UMW* (which Daniel Jones had recently edited) these lyrics are included in *CP14* as examples of the new, more public directions Thomas's work was taking just before his death. They are an essential part of *UMW*'s overall effect; some are songs, which were set to music by Daniel Jones, who surmised that the completion of *UMW* would have involved the addition of several more. Worksheets in Austin show that these would have been sung in a scene in The Sailor's Arms, with additional songs for Nogood Boyo, Mary Ann the Sailors, Evans the Death, Lord Cut-Glass and Gossamer Beynon.

i. Morning hymn of the Reverend Eli Jenkins / v. Evening hymn of the Reverend Eli Jenkins

1 **Gwalia** = an antiquarian name for Wales which suits the character of Eli Jenkins. 9–12 **Cader Idris . . . Plinlimmon** = Cader Idris (Powys: lit. 'the Chair of Idris [a giant]'); Moel y Wyddfa (Gwynedd; lit. 'Peak of Snowden', the highest mountain in Wales); Carnedd Llewelyn (in Gwynedd; lit. 'The Burial Mound of Ll[y]welyn); Plinlimmon (in Ceredigion; lit. 'Five Beacons'). 14 **Penmaen Mawr** = 'Great Stone Head'. 17–23 **Sawdde . . . River Dewi** = Daw is probably the Ddawn; as Davies/Maud (1995) note, it also functions in the alphabetic sequencing of the names in ll. 21–2, a device in traditional Welsh poetry. 'Dewi' ('David') is the patron saint of Wales, and a tributary of the River Taf, the estuary of which ran beside Thomas's work-shed in Laugharne. 25–8 conflates two stanzas published in the *Botteghe Oscure* version: the deleted lines, after this one, ran:

Our ruin in the spinet
Where owls do wink and squirrels climb
Is aged but half a minute

By Strumble or by Dinas Head.

ii. School children's song

Thomas included a copy of this song in a letter to Theodore Roethke of 19 June 1953. The children's song nicely counterpoints the adult world, reminding us the child-like nature of all the inhabitants of Llareggub. It is worth noting that *The Lore and Language of School-children* (1959), Iona and Peter Opie's classic study of school-children's street and playground songs and games, found Swansea to have the largest numbers of playground songs of any place in Britain. Also noteworthy is Thomas's visit to the Llangollen International Eisteddfod in July 1953 during work on *UMW*; the biggest success that year was of the Oberkirchen Girls' Choir, which he described in his radio feature on the event as singing 'like pigtailed angels'.

iii. Polly Garter's song

Also included in his letter to Theodore Roethke of 19 June 1953, where it has one minor difference from the published version ('was' for 'is' in the chorus).

Nursery and children's rhymes are a feature of *UMW* and, as Walford Davies and Ralph Maud (1995) note, 'it is . . . worth recalling that, in *Adventures in the Skin Trade*, another Polly pretends to lament Sam Bennet (a stand-in for the author) in the same terms: "His name was Sam and he had green eyes and brown hair. He was ever so short . . .". 'Little Willie Wee' inverts the name of Wee Willie Winkie in the eponymous nursery rhyme. Thus, as Laurence Lerner (Davies, 1972) puts it, it can be said that "Thomas's most brilliant invention was getting [Polly] to sing a nursery rhyme. This says to us what he nowhere says explicitly, that what she has lost is childhood.' The song's importance is evident from the fact that the dialogue in *UMW* ends with its final couplet – Polly is given the inhabitants' last word, and it is 'dead'.

8, 12 **little Willie Wee . . . Weazel** = compared with the other 'strong', 'big', 'thick' and 'tall' ex-lovers, it is hinted that Willie Wee's wee willie is small and/or only fit for micturation. This emblematic aspect of the name underlines the state of arrested yet flaunted sexuality which is one of the themes of *UMW*, and part of its subversion of puritan repression and hypocrisy.

vi. Mr Waldo's song

Called 'Mr Waldo's Pub Song' in an Austin typescript. I follow *CP88* with regard to punctuation and lineation. This is the only example of the evening exchange of songs in The Sailor's Arms, which, according to Daniel Jones, was to have closed *UMW*.

Elegy [unfinished]

Thomas put a good deal of work into his last, unfinished poem. A notebook at Austin contains eighteen pages of draft material, and there are also thirty-three separate numbered sheets, twenty of which contain material on both sides. Sheet number 31 includes a draft of a letter to E. F. Bozman dated 15 September 1953, indicating that Thomas was at work on the poem within a month of his departure on his final US reading tour. Sheet 2, bearing the title 'Elegy' (other working titles had been 'The Darkest Way', 'Too Proud to Die' and 'True Death') contains sixteen-and-a-half lines, rhymed in quatrains and written in six tercets, the latest stage the poem would reach before Thomas's death. Sheet 30 gave Thomas's plan for the poem (see *CP14*). The worksheets are shared with material for 'In the White Giant's Thigh'.

What survives suggests that Thomas intended that the poem would plead that D. J. Thomas should 'find no rest in the roots' and, born again, rejoin the 'roaring' life-cycle. There are references to the 'two darknesses' of blindness and death, and D. J. is imagined appealing to his mother. The numerous discarded phrases and lines give a moving sense of how the poem might have developed – 'The magnificence of suffering', 'Blue-veined / monkey hand', 'Live, damn you, again', 'Wounded and shy', 'Pain moved all over him, pawing as if blind', 'His body burnt until he died', 'All of a sudden, me holding his hand, / There was no man at all in the blind bed'.

Following Thomas's death, Vernon Watkins consulted the material at Austin and correctly identified the latest stage in the composition process. He 'completed' the poem by assembling lines and phrases from the MS material, and published the thirty-nine-line result in *Encounter* in February 1956. In June that year the poem was included in the tenth reprint of *CP52*, with a note by Watkins that quoted

Thomas's plan in full, and explained how his version had been written. He candidly admitted that the order of the lines used 'might well have been different' and that the poem 'might also have been made much longer'.

Acting on sound if rather severe scholarly instinct, in *CP88* Davies and Maud declared 'there is no justification for extending the poem as Vernon Watkins did, as all the extant worksheets lead up to the version printed here' (the sixteen-and-a-half latest version identified by Watkins, plus two crossed out but 'valuable lines' which it could reasonably be assumed would have been utilised 'if [Thomas] had had a chance to return to the poem'). They argue that they form a 'benediction from the poet to his recently dead father' and mark a 'new direction' not previously suggested by the plan or any of the worksheets.

Appendix 1

A note on the text of Collected Poems *(2014)*
and publication details for individual volumes

In determining the texts of individual poems for *CP14*, I had an eye
to the circumstances in which they were edited and proofed by Thomas
himself. We know that although he dealt pretty well with the proofs
for the *Collected Poems* (1952), he managed to miss several misprints,
and this has led me to check all the poems in it against the five individual volumes it incorporated. These present their own problems.
We know, for example, that *18 Poems* was well proofed, with no
typographical errors in the first edition. But a re-set 1942 edition by
the Fortune Press introduced many misprints; and this, not the 1934
edition, was used by Dent as their source text in 1952. Not all of its
errors were weeded out, and many survived until 1988. Some misprints
were notoriously long-lived. 'This bread I break' in *Twenty-five Poems*,
for example, has 'Once in this wind' for 'Once in this wine', and
though Thomas knew about it by 1937, he forgot to correct it in
1952. *TML* (1939), by contrast, has no textual errors; but there are
two points where stanza breaks coincide with the foot of a page, and
this led to the compositor of the 1952 *Collected* to eliminate them,
fusing stanzas which should have remained separate. The proof-sheets
of *DE* do not survive, but we know that Thomas missed three misprints, and that a line was lost from 'Ceremony After a Fire Raid'
which was not restored in 1952. Finally, Thomas made handwritten
changes to some poems in the copy of *In Country Sleep* owned by his
friend Ruthven Todd; following Davies and Maud, I have incorporated
these. The 1952 *Collected Poems* was quirky in other ways, too; it
placed fussy commas around parentheses, and dropped stanza six of

'When once the twilight locks'; the commas have now gone and the stanza is restored. The 1988 edition, otherwise exemplary, contained two misprints ('caldron' for 'cauldron' in 'Vision and Prayer', 'tonges' for 'tongues' in 'Shall gods be said'), both corrected in *CP14*.

The history of the publication of Thomas's volumes of poetry is a chequered one. His first book, *18 Poems*, appeared with Parton Books, but he moved to Dent for the publication of his second, *Twenty-five Poems*, in 1936, and stayed with them for the rest of his career. In the USA, his publishers were New Directions Press, who brought out *The World I Breathe* (1939), *New Poems* (1943), *Selected Writings* (1946) and *In Country Sleep* (1952) during his lifetime. The contents and ordering of the UK volumes contained in the centenary *Collected Poems* (*CP14*) in Appendix 6 does not contain publication details and these are given below.

A few further observations are in order. First, Thomas very rarely gave titles to his notebook poems, and the poems in *18 Poems*, *Twenty-five Poems* and *TML* are listed on the contents page in these volumes by their opening line, or a shorted version of it, and simply numbered in the text (in *18 Poems* and *TML*), or given no title at all (in *Twenty-five Poems*). Dispensing with titles was a modernist gesture which mingled both respect and challenge towards a reader: it signalled a refusal to predetermine responses, while enforcing an encounter unaided by clues as to subject or authorial intention. It was a common 1930s practice (Auden often does the same), and one particularly appropriate for Thomas, who opposed paraphrase on principle and saw his poems as autonomous verbal artefacts. However, the fashion changed at the end of the decade, and while the poems of *TML* are simply numbered, all of those in *DE* are prefaced by a title, albeit eleven are versions of the first line. By the time of Thomas's last collection, *In Country Sleep*, poem-titles are central to the reader's understanding of four of the six poems. All the poems in *CP52* appear in the text with a title, those from the first three collections being given the first-line titles of the contents pages of those volumes.

In compiling *CP52*, either Thomas or Dent eliminated certain inconsistencies in the use of capitals in titles; so, 'The Spire cranes' of *TML* became 'The spire cranes'. Some capitals were kept, however, where modern practice would be to eliminate them, and I have restored those removed by Davies and Maud in *CP88*. 'There was a Saviour' in *CP52* became 'There was a saviour' in *CP88*, for example. It may be that Thomas's revisions were inconsistent; not much seems to hang, at first glance, for example, on turning 'The Hunchback in the Park' (*CP52*) into 'The hunchback in the park' (*CP88*). However, it is impossible to be absolutely sure of this, and it seems to me that the last known preferences of a poet so keenly aware of the *gestalt* of a poem cannot easily be discounted. Given Thomas's trouble in juggling the upper- and lower-case forms of He/he when referring to the deity elsewhere, for example, disposing of the capitalised 'Saviour' is probably unwise. Much the same goes for other typographical conventions. Thus, 'To-day, this insect' (*Twenty-five Poems, CP52*) became 'Today, this insect' in *CP88*; yet, given that the poem plays with the etymology of 'insect', from the Latin *insectare*, meaning 'bisected', it seemed to me right that the bisected form of its first word should be restored. These and similar cases have persuaded me that it is safest to follow *CP52* in these minor matters.

18 Poems (1934)

On 22 April 1934, as author of 'The force that through the green fuse', Thomas was awarded the *Sunday Referee* prize of volume publication for the best poem to appear in its 'Poet's Corner' during 1933. The editor of 'Poet's Corner', Victor Neuberg, immediately invited him to assemble a collection. How seriously Thomas took this is evident from his many letters he wrote to Pamela Hansford Johnson on the subject of what to include in it. Above all, he wanted to match the benchmark established by 'The force that through the green fuse', and maximise the book's impact. He therefore chose thirteen of the thirty poems he had completed in the previous eight months, all from *N4*, and all in his recently perfected process style. But delay then set in as the *Referee* retreated from its promise to cover the £50 publication costs. As the delay lengthened through the summer and autumn Thomas added five more poems to the MS, but became increasingly frustrated, and tried to interest Cape and Faber in the collection. Before they could bite, however, David Archer of the Parton Bookshop stepped in, supplying £20 of the cost. *18P* was finally published under a joint Referee /Parton imprint on 18 December 1934.

Thomas was in London to see the book through the press and it was well proofed, with no typographical errors in the first edition, which I have taken as my copy-text (except to concur with a hyphenation introduced in *CP52*). On the flyleaf there is a note underscoring Thomas's desire that readers face his poems without preconception or the interposition of any biographical persona: 'This book . . . is unaccompanied by either portrait or preface, at the author's request.'

In 1942, Thomas sold the rights to *18P* to the Fortune Press. They re-set and reprinted it, with several misprints. Dent used this edition when setting up *CP52*, transcribing them. Thomas and the Dent editor caught most at proof stage, but two survived; I follow *CP88* in correcting both.

Twenty-five Poems (1936)

Thomas sent a batch of poems towards his second collection, including the first six 'Altarwise' sonnets, to Richard Church at Dent's, his new publisher, on 8 October 1935. Church liked the 'simple' poems among these (the lightly revised *N3* poems), but elsewhere detected the 'pernicious' influence of surrealism, and balked at publication. Thomas denied all knowledge of surrealism with inventive brazenness and tongue firmly lodged in cheek, refusing to sacrifice the denser, more recent work his editor objected to, and Church eventually gave way: 'I have decided to put myself aside and let you and the public face each other. I am accordingly taking steps to have the book set up in type.' On 17 March 1936 Thomas sent him an expanded MS titled *Twenty-three Poems*, now containing 'Altarwise' I-VIII; on 22 June he sent 'Then was my neophyte' and the revised 'And death shall have no dominion', plus 'the last two sections, IX & X, of my long poem', making a total of twenty-five poems. An advance proof of *Twenty-three Poems* shows that several misprints were corrected and lines changed at proof stage by Thomas; in the proofs for *25P*, however, the celebrated 'wind' for 'wine' misprint in 'This bread I break' escaped him, as did a line lost from 'Out of the sighs', together with a few lesser errors. *25P* was published on 10 September 1936.

The Map of Love (1939)

On 20 December 1938 Thomas informed Vernon Watkins: 'I went to see Dent's . . . about a new book. I'm making it an odd book: 15 poems & 5 stories: all to be called In the Direction Of The Beginning. It may look a mess, but I hope not.' This was to become *TML*. Dent hoped to make a splash with Thomas's third collection, placing material from Edith Sitwell's laudatory review of *25P* on the front cover; they also commissioned Augustus John to paint a portrait of Thomas, and included a monochrome reproduction of it as a frontispiece. The volume was divided into two sections headed 'VERSE' and 'PROSE', and contained seven, not five, stories: 'The Visitor', 'The Enemies', 'The Tree', 'The Map of Love', 'The Mouse and the Woman', 'The Dress' and 'The Orchards'. Page proofs at Harvard, corrected in Thomas's autograph, show that he made four typographical corrections and no other changes. The collection was published on 24 August 1939.

Deaths and Entrances (1946)

A Buffalo MS shows that a volume to be called *DE* was being planned by Thomas as early as July 1941, confirming Gwen Watkins's account in *Portrait of a Friend* (see note to 'Deaths and Entrances', above). This volume was put on hold at the outbreak of the war, and poems for it further slowed by Thomas's poetic silence in 1942–4. In October 1944, now writing again, he submitted a book-length MS to Dent's. He added new poems after that date, and again after proofs were sent to him on 30 May 1945. Returning these on 18 September 1945, he enclosed 'Fern Hill', 'In my craft or sullen art' and a revised 'Unluckily for a death'. *DE* was published on 7 February 1946. No proof-sheets have survived, but the edition makes a good copy-text, apart from a few minor misprints, in 'The Conversation of Prayers', 'Vision and Prayer' (one, 'caldron' for 'cauldron', was missed in *CP88*) and 'Ceremony After a Fire Raid' (in which l. 19, 'Give', was lost; *CP88* restored this from the text of the poem's journal publication, and I follow suit).

In Country Sleep (1952)

A letter of 14 December 1951 to his agent shows Thomas read the proofs for this US-only published chapbook without copies of the poems as they were to appear in the UK edition of *CP52*, having returned his sole copy of the *CP52* proofs to Dent's in November. Under the circumstances, there are surprisingly few variants between the editions. Thomas made some corrections in his friend Ruthven Todd's copy of *ICS*, and following *CP88* I have incorporated these as reflecting Thomas's final wishes. However, for reasons they do not give, Davies and Maud state that they 'do not accept that the order of the six poems in that volume [*ICS*] is preferable [to that of *CP52*], and . . . [restore] the basically chronological order of the poems' – that is, place 'In Country Sleep' before the other five poems. It is worth noting the point made by Daniel Jones in *TP71* that what is most striking about the *In Country Heaven* project is Thomas's indifference during his lifetime to the ordering of the poems which were to have made it up – the sequencing in the 1950 broadcast and in *CP52* is different again (and in *CP52* the sequence is interrupted by two poems which do not belong to it), while to different correspondents he suggested both that 'In the White Giant's Thigh' was the opening piece, and that he had not made his mind up about where it would go. Like others, Jones observes that the idea of writing a long work 'suggested itself gradually and was often abandoned' and surmises that Thomas may have wondered whether he possessed the ability to create a large, overarching poetic structure.

Collected Poems 1934–1952 (1952)

For his *Collected Poems*, Thomas opted to simply collect his five collections to date. The exception was 'Paper and Sticks' from *DE*, which, at a late stage, he asked to be dropped declaring that he had 'the horrors' of it. 'Do not go gentle', from later in the volume, was therefore moved forward to take its place just after 'Into her lying down head' in the *DE* section. Thomas also included 'Once below a time', which had not made it into *DE* in 1946, placing it after 'Ceremony After a Fire Raid'. However, he seems to have been too preoccupied with writing a preface to proof-read very thoroughly. The preface eventually took the form of short, almost casual 'Note' (see Appendix 5 in *CP14*), followed by a very elaborate poem, titled (by Dent, not Thomas himself) 'Author's Prologue'. Thomas's haphazard proof-editing was not helped by Dent's use of the error-riddled Fortune Press 1942 edition of *18P*.

After Thomas's death, Vernon Watkins assembled 'Elegy', Thomas's poem for his father, from his notes. This was included in *CP52* from 1956 onwards with a note explaining its provenance, but dropped in *CP88*; in my edition I follow *CP88*.

Dylan Thomas's Notebooks (1967)/Poet in the Making (1968)/ The Notebook Poems (1989)

In 1967 Ralph Maud published a US edition of the four then-known surviving poetry notebooks from the period 1930–4 held in the Special Collections section of the Margaret Lockwood Library Special Poetry Collection at the State University of New York at Buffalo. (The first notebook [B432F]) runs 27 April 1930–9 December 1930; the second notebook [B432F6] runs December 1930–1 July 1932; the third notebook [B432F5] runs 1 February 1933–16 August 1933; the fourth notebook [B432F4] runs 17 August 1933–30 April 1934.) They were republished in a UK edition as *Poet in the Making*. This volume contains a substantial Introduction on Thomas's youthful poetic evolution, and notes which are exhaustive and scholarly; an appendix contains eleven examples of juvenilia and eight of adolescent poetry, conjectured to be from a notebook, now lost, of July 1932–February 1933. In 1989, a version of this book, *NP* was issued to complement the new *CP88*, with an updated Introduction and stream-lined notes for a non-scholarly readership. It also contained three of the previously included juvenilia, all eight of the missing notebook pieces, and fifteen poems which were either juvenilia, poems taken from the *Swansea Grammar School Magazine*, poems deleted from the first notebook, or poems from the short story 'The Fight'. In the notes I have specified origins for these early poems where necessary; almost all, however, are from the notebooks.

The Poems (1971)

After his death in 1953, poems not included in *CP52* gradually emerged in Thomas's letters (1957 and 1965), both uncollected journal poems and under other circumstances (i.e. of 'Jack of Christ' in the *Western Mail* in 1960). With Maud's *The Making of a Poet* (1967), it was evident that thirty-seven of Thomas's published poems were revised versions of notebook poems, and this altered the understanding of his development. Together with the errors in the 1952 edition, these additions to the corpus prompted a new edition, published jointly by Dent and New Directions, and edited by Daniel Jones .

To the ninety-one poems of the post-1956 *CP52*, Jones added fifty-six from the notebooks, the 1933 verse letter to Pamela Hansford Johnson, the revised version of 'That the sum sanity', 'O Chatterton', 'I, the first named', 'The Molls', 'Paper and Sticks' (included in *DE*, but dropped in *CP52*), 'The Countryman's Return', Request to Leda', 'Last night I dived my beggar arm', 'Your breath was shed', and the verse-letter 'New Quay'. He added all poems except the early version of 'Especially when the October wind' from the BL MS 48217, dated to Autumn 1932 (seven poems), and two from the other poems collateral with the notebooks (but not 'That sanity be kept', although it was a published poem). Jones also included a thirty-eight line version of 'In Country Heaven' and Vernon Watkins's version of 'Elegy in an appendix titled 'Unfinished Poems'. In another appendix, titled 'Early Poems', he gave thirty-six poems 'written before the poet's sixteenth birthday'. This made a total of 201 poems.

Jones included an introduction explaining his aims – greater representativeness than *CP52* in poem selection, and a chronological arrangement in order to 'reveal the relationship between poems written at the same time', 'the development of the poet in technique and imagery', and the poems' historical contexts. His reasons for excluding the verses from *UMW* (it was 'easily accessible' and 'should be heard or read in the context for which it was intended') are less compelling, and may be connected to the fact that he had recently edited an edition of the play. The edition also contained a 'Note on Verse-Patterns', and poem notes. These mainly confine themselves to publication details, but occasionally offer commentary, and Jones' friendship with Thomas means that both the 'Note' and notes contain many shrewd insights. The edition lacks such important items as the film-script *Our Country*, but it established the principle of a fuller, warts-and-all selection. Its editorial apparatus is limited, however – just twenty-eight pages of notes, largely publication details – and despite Jones's consultation of archive material, many errors from *CP52* remained. In addition, the production values of the volume were poor.

Collected Poems 1934–1953 (1988)

Reacting strongly against Daniel Jones's 1971 edition, Walford Davies and Ralph Maud adopted a radically conservative approach to the task of editing Thomas, returning to the published-collections-only format of *CP52* (to the extent of inserting separating pages bearing the names of Thomas's five collections between the different sections). They took the five volumes as their copy-text rather than *CP52* itself, adding 'Once below a time' to the *DE* section, restoring 'Paper and Sticks' to it, and returning 'Do not go gentle' to its place in the *ICS* section. Vernon Watkins's version of 'Elegy' was dropped; a final section included the latest stage of its composition in MS, plus the two lines which seemed its likeliest continuation. Maud and Davies also added a sixteen-line version of 'In Country Heaven' which they conjectured to be the latest version of the poem, consigning the thirty-eight line version to a final note, and dating it to March–April 1947, just before Thomas's visit to Italy. One misprint was introduced ('tonges' for *CP52* 'tongues' in 'Shall gods be said').

Lacking any introduction, *CP88* follows the poems with a 'General Preface to the Notes' and 'Textual Preface to the Notes'. The first of these explains why Jones's approach was reversed, and justifies the provision of individual poem notes. Though a great improvement on Jones, these are, however, patchy, and often over-reliant on biography. In the 'Textual Preface' Davies and Maud chart Thomas's attentiveness as a proof-reader for his own collections and give tables of the punctuation and other minor changes between the proofs, collections and *CP52*.

Note on editions of the Collected Poems
1952, 1971 and 1988

Every editor of Thomas is faced with the problem of what to do with the poems in the four notebooks of April 1930–April 1934. At the most basic level, this is an insoluble problem; Thomas did not destroy most of his adolescent verse, and this overbalances the surviving poetic corpus from a publisher's (and from most readers') point of view. If included in a *Collected Poems*, largely mediocre items would take up three-fifths of the space, irritating all but the hardiest of scholars and making it commercially unviable. In addition, the dating of the material Thomas mined from the notebooks makes the dating and placing of these poems problematic. On the other hand, placing the notebook poems (or a selection of them) in an appendix would fly in the face of the fact that published and unpublished poems mingle inextricably in the last two notebooks; it is therefore neither possible nor desirable to draw a line between them. Davies and Maud's apportioning of Thomas's poetry of this period to either *CP88* or *NP* reasserts a strict division between the poems in the notebooks, sealing off the canonical items from the process by which Thomas found his poetic voice, and suppresses the variety of his subsequent work. *CP14* therefore returned to Jones's pragmatic solution of including a chronologically arranged selection of un-published as well as published notebook poems and juvenilia to show Thomas's poetic development during his formative years.

In an article published in *P.N. Review* of 2004, Davies and Maud justified their decisions on three grounds: Jones's over-subjective criteria for placing reworked notebook poems; the innate 'triviality' of the additional poems he had included; and Thomas's authority for the *CP52*. They argued that their separate presentation of *NP* and *CP52* 'respect[ed] the integrity of two discrete bodies of poetry, each with its own rationale', and provided 'the most satisfactory way of having all the Thomas poems one is likely to feel the need of'. However Thomas's personal authority could hardly be credibly invoked thirty-six years after his death in an era of different editorial protocols. A key to the ordering of poems in individual volumes is easily supplied (as, say, Anthony Thwaite does in the Philip Larkin *Collected*). Secondly, 'trivial' is itself a 'subjective' judgement. Thirdly, undoing Jones's chronological arrangement in *CP88* made it very difficult for readers to grasp Thomas's development and the interplay of poems. Finally, the claim for two 'discrete bodies of poetry' ignores their common origin, as already noted. Thus, 'Before I knocked' (dated 6 September 1933 in *N4*), included in *18P*, is followed in *N4* by the unpublished 'We see rise the secret wind' (8 September), 'Not forever shall the lord of the red hail' and 'Before we mothernaked fall' (both 16 September). Each tackles closely related questions of faith, origin and process, and shares a 'rationale' that cuts across the distinctions between published and unpublished. The three later poems are of high quality; not only do they not warrant separation from 'Before I knocked', they demand to be presented with it.

Davies and Maud were right, of course, to query Jones's too-impressionistic criteria for placing reworked notebook poems in his chronological schema. It was also true that his scholarly apparatus was substandard. But this did not justify throwing the baby out with the bathwater. The final claim in the *P.N. Review* article – that a two-volume solution provided 'all the Thomas poems one is likely to feel the need of' – rather highhandedly forestalls a reader's right to decide the matter. A reader owning both *CP88* and *The Notebook Poems*, and who wanted 'all of' Thomas's poems would still need seven more books, a very rare pamphlet and two hard-to-find journals. Such assumptions, with other shortcomings detailed above, give the 1988 *Collected Poems*, despite its invaluable scholarship, a somewhat airless, mausoleum-like feel.

Appendix 2

The fifth notebook (N5)

In late October 2014, I was contacted by Sotheby's about the forth-coming sale of a hitherto unknown poetry notebook in Dylan Thomas's hand dating from summer 1934 to August 1935 – the successor to the four surviving existing notebooks held at SUNY Buffalo, which concluded in April 1934. They wanted me to agree to speak to the press when they made the discovery public by publishing their catalogue online the following week, on Monday 2 November. Agog at the discovery, and assured of its authenticity by a photocopied sample, I was happy to agree. Seeing the notebook was quite another matter, however; a timetable crowded by Dylan Thomas himself (a festival in Sheffield, a Dylan Thomas panel at a Conference in Pitts-burgh) intervened. Briefly, it even seemed that BBC 2's *Newsnight* might feature the notebook on 10 November, when I arrived back from the US, but a juicier story intervened. On 12 November, however, Sotheby's asked if I would appear on BBC 1's *Breakfast* to discuss the notebook the following morning, and I made my way to Salford, where Gabriel Heaton, Sotheby's in-house manuscripts expert, and his colleague Toby Skegg, generously permitted me to make its brief acquaintance before we went on air.

The sale was to be on behalf of relatives of Louie King (1904–84), a former maid at the home of Yvonne MacNamara, Dylan Thomas's mother-in-law, in Blashford, Hampshire. A note in Louie King's hand, found with the notebook, read: 'The Book of Poetry by Dylan Thomas was with a lot of papers given to me to burn in the kitchen boiler. I saved it and forgot all about it until I read of his death.' Notebook, note, and two newspaper clippings had been placed in a paper Tesco bag and kept in a drawer for decades, unappreciated until the centenary year.

The auction day duly arrived, and on 2 December 2014 the notebook was sold, amid great excitement, to Swansea University, for £85,000 (£104,500 after fees and tax).

N5, like *N1–N4*, is a lined school exercise book. Its covers have been lost, and its forty-nine surviving pages contain nineteen poems and parts of poems, numbered and usually dated. Three are the component sections of 'I, in my intricate image, and two are groups of two and three sonnets respectively from 'Altarwise by owl-light'. There are revisions to fourteen of the items, while others contain variant readings to the published text. Most of the poems exist in no other surviving manuscript form. They are as follows:

1. 'All all and all'
2. 'My world is pyramid'
3. 'Do you not father me'
4. 'Especially when the October wind'
5. 'I dreamed my genesis'
6. 'I fellowed sleep'
7. 'When, like a running grave'
8. 'Now'
9. 'I low soon the servant sun'
10. 'A grief ago'
11. 'I, in my intricate image' (part I)
12. 'They see the country pinnacle' ('I, in my intricate image', part II)
13. 'Hold hard these ancient minutes'
14. 'They suffer the undead water' ('I, in my intricate image', part III)
15. 'Incarnate devil in a talking snake'
16. 'The seed-at-zero'
17. 'Altarwise by owl-light', I and II
18. 'Foster the light'
19. ' Altarwise by owl-light', III, IV and V.

The poems have been entered in chronological order, as composed, and many have been ascribed a location as well as a date for their copying-out. Based on this, and knowledge of Thomas's whereabouts, it is possible to link the poems to the following locations: Swansea (poems 1–7), London (poems 8–12), Disley, (poems 13–14) and Glen Lough (poems 15–19).[1] The revisions of several poems not among this final group are also dated and located in Glen Lough. What *N5* shows, then, is that Thomas's first, rather self-dissipating bout of life in London, from December 1934 to spring 1935, did not, as is so often assumed, prevent him from writing and/or copying up several important poems. He then returned to Swansea to recuperate (a brief interlude glanced at in 'Hold hard, these ancient minutes'), before going to stay with the Taylors, and then on holiday with Geoffrey Grigson. These retreats were intended to isolate him from the temptations of the capital's fleshpots, so that he could concentrate on a follow-up collection to *18P*. In this, as *N5* now proves, he succeeded admirably. The *N5* poems reveal a steady evolution from the less to the more complex, and a steadily increasing amount of revision, culminating in that of 'I, in my intricate image' and 'Altarwise'.

N5 is unlike the other four notebooks in that it contains no poem which had not been already published by 1936, and therefore nothing which Thomas could rewrite. By the time he and Caitlin arrived at Mrs Macnamara's house for the first of their sojourns there, in October 1937–April 1938 (there were others, in November 1938–March 1939 and January–March 1940), its poems were already in the public realm. Why, then, did he keep *N5*, take it to Blashford, and then leave it there? The answer is probably that Thomas – who often took his notebooks with him on his travels, and could be careless with them – simply left it behind, probably on the first or second visit. He would have made no attempt to reclaim it because he had no further use for it.[2] Things changed in 1941, when he learned that his manuscripts had a monetary value and sold the four surviving notebooks; but by then it was too late.

---

[1] Thomas was a guest of Margaret and A. J. P. Taylor at their cottage in Disley, Cheshire, in April–May 1935, and went on holiday to Glen Lough, near Ardara in County Donegal, Ireland, with Geoffrey Grigson, in July–August 1935.

[2] In 1941, for example, Thomas left the first four poetry notebooks, and the 'Red Notebook' containing his early short stories, at John Davenport's house in Gloucestershire, and had to write to Davenport asking him to look for them.

This scenario was insufficiently sensational for some, and more than one newspaper article suggested that Mrs Macnamara had deliberately destroyed her turbulent son in-law's work ('Saved: the revelatory notebook Thomas's fiery mother-in-law sent off to be burned'). They cited as evidence a letter in which he slated her and Blashford:

> This flat English country levels the intelligence, planes down the imagination, narrows the a's, my ears belch up old wax and mis-remembered passages of misunderstood music. I sit and hate my mother-in-law, glowering at her from corners and grumbling about her in the sad, sticky, quiet of the lavatory' (*CL*, 403).

But this is standard grumbling for humorous effect. Thomas may not have been an easy son-in-law, but the likeliest reason for Yvonne Macnamara's incendiary order was that, having been left in her house, whether by accident or design, the notebook was simply clutter. There is no trace, in Thomas's letters of the time or anywhere else, of concern about its fate, as we would expect if it had meant anything to him.

To the student of Thomas, however, *N5* is immensely significant. If the order of the poems in it corresponds to the order of their composition and completion (and the datings make this almost certain), then it is necessary to revise the order suggested by all previous scholars and editors. Although the publishers of *CP14* did not allow me to correct the order in the 2016 paperback edition, the list given above allows a reconstruction of it. It shows, to take my own case, that while I managed to locate all of its poems within the right time-frame (albeit, while managing to interpolate 'Should lanterns shine' and 'Grief thief of time' among them), and placed poems 1, 2, 4, 8 and 9 in correct sequence, the majority of my attempts were out. I place 'Foster the light' too early, 'Do you not father me' too late, put 'A grief ago' before 'I, in my intricate image', not after it, and so on.

Still more important is the evidence of compositional labour *N5* contains. Thirteen of its sixteen poems were altered after being fair-copied, some substantially; this is a greater proportion than in any of the earlier notebooks. I take this to reflect the rate at which Thomas was developing in 1934–5, and the fact that, as the complexity and daring of the poems increased with his working-out of the potential of the new style, they demanded increased revision. In short, if *N4* is the record of Thomas's perfection of the process poetic, *N5* is the record of his attempt to see how far it could be pushed – that is, of his most experimental phase as a poet. While no poem in it is wholly rewritten, several underwent major revision, and almost all bear some signs of a final sharpening and enrichment.

Appendix 3

Errata for Collected Poems
(2014 and 2015 hardback editions)

p. 6,	'How shall the animal', l. 15: no comma after 'Speak'.
p. 8,	'To-day, this hour I breathe', l. 23: 'his' should be 'in'.
p. 9,	'Rain cuts the places we tread', l. 22: delete 'into'.
p. 15,	'Before the gas fades', l. 39: 'Nor' should be 'Not'.
p. 18,	'Out of a war of wits', l. 25: delete 'good'.
p. 19,	'Their faces shone', l. 6, delete comma; l. 11, first 'cheap' should be 'summer'.
p. 23,	'And death shall have no dominion', l. ?: insert 'they' after 'naked'.
p. 26,	'Within his head revolved a little world', l. 56: 'at' should be 'as'; l. 83: 'weight' should be 'weights'.
p. 32,	'"Find meat on bones"', l. 6: should be 'winding-sheets' (hyphenated).
p. 34,	'Ears in the turrets hear', l. 25: 'Hands' should be 'Ships'.
p. 41,	'Before we mothernaked fall', ll. 5, 6 and 12: delete commas; l. 16: 'is' should be 'are'.
p. 48,	'See, says the lime', l. 31: comma after 'gut' should be semi-colon.
p. 51,	'This bread I break', l. 6: the first 'the' should be 'this'.
p. 56,	'Where once the waters of your face', l. 14: change 'love beds' to 'lovebeds'.

p. 58,   'In the beginning', l. 14: 'light' should be 'alight'.

p. 61,   'I dreamed my genesis', end l. 4: change comma to
                    full stop; l. 10: insert comma after 'I' (also
                    corrects Davies and Maud, 1988).

p. 68,   'Especially when the October wind', l. 24: 'make'
                    should be 'tell'.

p. 75,   'Hold hard, these ancient minutes', l. 16: first 'the'
                    should be 'and'.

p. 78,   'Do you not father me', l. 8: 'Adorn' should be
                    'Adore'.

pp. 87–8,   'The seed-at-zero', l. 2: change first 'The' to 'That';
                    l. 9: change first 'The' to 'That'; l. 36: change
                    'village' to 'planet'.

p. 94,   'I make this in a warring absence', l. 11: no comma
                    after 'Or'; l. 36: 'jawbone' not 'jaw bone'.

p. 98,   'The spire cranes', l. 7: delete 'the' before 'silver'.

p. 105,   'The tombstone told', l. 10: should read: 'More the
                    thick stone cannot tell'.

p. 114,   'Once below a time', l. 10: insert 'a' after 'with'.

p. 121,   'Into her lying down head', l. 23: delete 'newborn'.

p. 140,   'Among those Killed', l. 4: delete 'had'.

p. 141,   'Lie still, sleep becalmed', l. 5: no hyphen in
                    'mile-off'.

p. 165,   'Holy Spring', l. 24: add full stop at end of line.

pp. 167–70,   'A Winter's Tale', l. 7: delete second 'the' (before
                    'hay'); l. 38: 'into' should be 'in'; l. 60: delete
                    third the' (before 'water'); l. 70: 'breasts' should
                    be 'breast'; l. 98: add hyphen to 'she' ('she-').

p. 174,   'This side of the truth', l. 28: insert full stop after
                    'years'.

p. 175,   'Unluckily for a death', l. 7: insert comma after
                    'occurred'; l. 9: insert comma after 'forehead'.

p. 177,   'In my craft or sullen art', l. 5: insert comma after
                    'arms'; l. 18: insert comma after 'ages'.

p. 182,   'In country sleep', l. 49: delete 'that'; l. 53: delete
                    second 'of'.

pp. 185–6, 'Over Sir John's hill', l. 35: remove comma after 'I';
l. 41 should be justified to left-hand margin;
l. 48: 'tilted' should be 'tilting'; l. 52: insert comma
after 'elms'; l. 60: insert 'souls of the' after second
'the'.

p. 191, 'Lament', l. 23: 'coal' should be 'coal-'.

pp. 199–200, 'Poem on his Birthday', l. 55: 'might he' should be
'he might'; l. 96: no comma after 'then'; l. 98,
no comma after 'said'.

Bibliography

Writings by Dylan Thomas

Poetry

18 Poems (London: Parton Press, 1934).
Twenty-five Poems (London: Dent, 1936).
The Map of Love (London: Dent, 1939).
The World I Breathe (Norfolk, CT: New Directions, 1939).
New Poems (Norfolk, CT: New Directions, 1943).
Deaths and Entrances (London: Dent, 1946).
Twenty-Six Poems (London: Dent, 1950).
In Country Sleep (New York, NY: New Directions, 1952).
Collected Poems 1934–1952 (London: Dent, 1952).
The Notebooks of Dylan Thomas, ed. and intro. Ralph Maud (New York, NY: New Directions, 1967) (repr. as *Poet in the Making*, London: Dent, 1968).
The Notebook Poems 1930–1934, ed. Ralph Maud (London: Dent, 1990).
The Poems, ed. Daniel Jones (London: Dent, 1971).
Collected Poems 1934–1953, eds Walford Davies and Ralph Maud (London: Dent, 1989).
Letter to Loren, ed. Jeff Towns (Swansea: Salubrious Press, 1993).
Collected Poems, a new centenary edition, ed. John Goodby (London: Weidenfeld & Nicolson, 2014).

Prose

Portrait of the Artist as a Young Dog (London: Dent, 1940).

Quite Early One Morning, ed. Aneurin Talfan Davies (London: Dent, 1954).
Adventures in the Skin Trade and Other Stories (repr. in *Collected Stories*, 1983).
A Prospect of the Sea and Other Stories and Prose Writings, ed. Daniel Jones (London: Dent, 1955).
A Child's Christmas in Wales (Norfolk, CT: New Directions, 1955).
Dylan Thomas: Early Prose Writings, ed. Walford Davies (London: Dent, 1971).
The Death of the King's Canary, with John Davenport, intro. Constantine Fitzgibbon (London: Hutchinson, 1976).
Collected Stories, ed. Walford Davies and intro. Leslie Norris (London: Dent, 1983).

Dramatic, film and radio writings

The Doctor and the Devils (London: Dent, 1953).
Under Milk Wood, eds Ralph Maud and Walford Davies (London: Dent, 1995).
Dylan Thomas: The Broadcasts, ed. Ralph Maud (London: Dent, 1991).
Dylan Thomas: The Complete Screen Plays, ed. John Ackerman (New York, NY: Applause Books, 1995).

Miscellanies

Selected Writings by Dylan Thomas (New York, NY: New Directions, 1946).
Miscellany One: Poems, Stories, Broadcasts (London: Dent (Aldine Paperback), 1963, rep. 1965, 1969, 1974, etc.).
Miscellany Two: A Visit to Grandpa's and Other Stories and Poems (London: Dent (Aldine Paperback), 1966, repr. 1971, etc.).
Miscellany Three: Poems and Stories (London: Dent (Aldine Paperback), 1978).
The Omnibus Dylan Thomas (London: Phoenix Press (Orion plc), 1995).

Correspondence and critical writing

See also *Quite Early One Morning* and *Dylan Thomas: The Broadcasts* (above).
A Pearl of Great Price: The Love Letters of Dylan Thomas to Pearl Kazin, ed. and introd. by Jeff Towns (Cardigan: Parthian Books, 2014).

Letters to Vernon Watkins, ed. and intro. Vernon Watkins (London: Dent, 1957).
'Poetic Manifesto', *Texas Quarterly*, 4 (Winter 1961), 45–53.
'Replies to an enquiry', *New Verse*, 11 (October 1934), 8–9.
The Collected Letters, ed. Paul Ferris, 2nd edn (London: Dent, 2000).

Critical works on the poetry of Dylan Thomas

Book-length studies

Ackerman, John, *A Dylan Thomas Companion: Life, Poetry and Prose* (London: Macmillan, 1991).
— *Welsh Dylan: Dylan Thomas' Life, Writing and his Work* (London: John Jones, 1979).
Barfoot, Rhian, *Liberating Dylan Thomas: Rescuing a Poet from Psycho-sexual Servitude* (Cardiff: University of Wales Press, 2014).
Davies, Aneurin Talfan, *Dylan: Druid of the Broken Body* (London: Dent, 1964; repr. Swansea: Christopher Davies, 1977).
Davies, James A., *A Companion to Dylan Thomas* (Greensborough: University of Kentucky Press, 1997).
Davies, Walford, *Dylan Thomas* (Cardiff: University of Wales Press, 1990) (repr. 1972).
— *Dylan Thomas* (Milton Keynes: Open University Press, 1986).
Fraser, G. S., *Dylan Thomas* (London: Longmans, 1957).
Goodby, John, *The Poetry of Dylan Thomas: Under the Spelling Wall* (Liverpool: Liverpool University Press, 2014).
Hardy, Barbara, *Dylan Thomas: An Original Language* (Athens and London: University of Georgia Press, 2000).
— *The Advantage of Lyric: Essays on Feeling in Poetry* (Bloomington and London: Indiana University Press, 1977).
Holbrook, David, *The Code of Night* (London: Athlone, 1972).
— *Llareggub Revisited: Dylan Thomas and the State of Modern Poetry* (London: Bowes and Bowes, 1962) (repr. as *Dylan Thomas and Poetic Dissociation* (Carbondale, IL: Southern Illinois University Press, 1964)).
Jones, T. H., *Dylan Thomas* (Edinburgh and London: Oliver and Boyd, 1963).
Kershner, R. B. Jr, *Dylan Thomas: The Poet and His Critics* (Chicago, IL: American Library Association, 1976).

Kidder, Rushworth M., *Dylan Thomas: The Country of the Spirit* (Princeton, NJ: Princeton University Press, 1973).

Kleinman, Hyman H., *The Religious Sonnets of Dylan Thomas: A Study in Imagery and Meaning* (Berkeley, CA: University of California Press, 1963).

Korg, Jacob, *Dylan Thomas* (New York, NY: Twayne, 1965) (repr. Hippocrene Books, 1972).

Maud, Ralph, *Entrances to Dylan Thomas' Poetry* (Pittsburgh, PA: University of Pittsburgh Press, 1963).

Moynihan, William T., *The Craft and Art of Dylan Thomas* (Oxford: Oxford University Press, 1966).

Olson, Elder, *The Poetry of Dylan Thomas* (Chicago, IL: University of Chicago Press, 1954).

Pratt, Annis, *Dylan Thomas' Early Prose: A Study in Creative Mythology* (Pittsburgh, PA: University of Pittsburgh Press, 1970).

Stanford, Derek, *Dylan Thomas: A Literary Study* (London: Neville Spearman, 1954).

Treece, Henry, *Dylan Thomas: 'Dog Among the Fairies'* (London: Lindsay Drummond, 1949).

Wardi, Eynel, *Once Below a Time: Dylan Thomas, Julia Kristeva, and Other Speaking Subjects* (New York, NY: SUNY Press, 2000).

Wigginton, Chris, *Modernism from the Margins: The 1930s Poetry of Louis MacNeice and Dylan Thomas* (Cardiff: University of Wales Press, 2007).

PhD theses

Hornick, Lita, '"The intricate image": a study of Dylan Thomas' (Columbia University, 1958).

Golightly, Victor, '"Two on a Tower": The influence of W. B. Yeats on Vernon Watkins and Dylan Thomas' (University of Wales Swansea, 2003).

Parkinson, Siobhán, 'Obscurity in the *Collected Poems* of Dylan Thomas' (University College Dublin, 1981).

Essay collections

Bold, Alan, ed., *Dylan Thomas: Craft or Sullen Art* (London and New York, NY: Vision Press, 1990).

Brinnin, J. M., ed., *A Casebook on Dylan Thomas* (New York, NY: T. Y. Crowell, 1961).

Cox, C. B., ed., *Dylan Thomas: A Collection of Critical Essays* (London: Prentice-Hall, 1962) (repr. Englewood Cliffs, NJ: Prentice-Hall, 1966).

Davies, Walford, ed., *Dylan Thomas: New Critical Essays* (London: Dent, 1972).

Ellis, Hannah, ed., *Dylan Thomas: A Centenary Celebration* (London: Bloomsbury Press, 2014).

Goodby, John and Chris Wigginton, eds, *Dylan Thomas: New Casebook* (Basingstoke: Palgrave, 2001).

Tedlock, E. W., ed., *Dylan Thomas: The Legend and the Poet* (London: Heinemann/Mercury Books, 1963).

Special journal issues

Glyn Pursglove, John Goodby and Chris Wigginton, eds, *The Swansea Review: Under the Spelling Wall*, 20 (2000).

Les Années 30. Dylan Thomas (Université de Nantes), 12 (Juin 1990).

Poetry Wales: Dylan Thomas Special Issue, 9/2 (Autumn 1973).

Adam International Review, Dylan Thomas memorial number, 238 (1953).

Book chapters, journal essays and reviews

Aivaz, David, 'The Poetry of Dylan Thomas', *The Hudson Review*, viii/3 (autumn 1950) (repr. Tedlock, 1963), 382–404.

Balakicv, James J., 'The ambiguous reversal of Dylan Thomas's "In Country sleep"', *Papers on Language and Literature*, 32/1 (1996), 21–44.

Bayley, John, 'Dylan Thomas', in *The Romantic Survival* (London: Constable, 1957).

— 'Chains and the Poet', in Walford Davies, ed. (1971).

Beardsley, Monroe and Hynes, Sam, 'Misunderstanding Poetry: Notes on Some Readings of Dylan Thomas', *College English*, XXI (March 1960), 315–22.

Berryman, John, review of *The Loud Hill of Wales*, *Kenyon Review*, 2/4 (Autumn 1940), 481–5.

Bigliazzi, Silvia, 'Fable versus Fact: Hamlet's Ghost in Dylan Thomas's Early Poetry', *Textus*, V (1992), 51–64.

Caines, Michael, 'Buying Dylan Thomas a pint', *Times Literary Supplement* 5829/30 (Christmas Double Issue) (19 and 26 December 2014), 7–8.

Carson, Ricks, 'Dylan Thomas's "A Refusal to Mourn the Death, by Fire, of a Child in London"', *The Explicator*, 54/4 (Summer 1996), 240–2.

Conran, Tony, '"After the funeral": The praise-poetry of Dylan Thomas', in *The Cost of Strangeness: Essays on the English Poets of Wales* (Llandysul: Gomer Press, 1982).

— '"I saw time murder me": Dylan Thomas and the tragic soliloquy', in *Frontiers in Anglo-Welsh Poetry* (Cardiff: University of Wales Press, 1997).

Crehan, Stewart, 'The lips of time', in ed. Alan Bold, *Dylan Thomas: Craft or Sullen Art* (New York, NY and London: Vision Press, 1990) (repr. in Goodby and Wigginton, 2001).

Davies, James A., '"A Mental Militarist": Dylan Thomas and the Great War', *Welsh Writing in English*, 2 (1996), 6–81.

— 'Dylan Thomas and Paternal Influence', *Welsh Writing in English*, 1 (1995).

Davies, Walford and Maud, Ralph, 'Concerns about The Revised New Directions Dylan Thomas', *P.N. Review*, 31/2 (November–December 2004), 67–70.

Empson, William, 'Review of the *Collected Poems* of Dylan Thomas', *New Statesman and Nation* (15 May 1954), 643–6.

Garlick, Raymond, 'Shapes of Thought', *Poetry Wales: A Dylan Thomas number*, 9/2 (Autumn 1973), 40–8.

Goodby, John, '"The Rimbaud of Cwmdonkin Drive": Dylan Thomas as surrealist', in eds Elza Adamowicz and Eric Robertson, *Dada and Beyond: (Vol. 2) Dada and its Legacies* (Amsterdam and New York: Rodopi Press, 2012).

— 'Bulbous Taliesin': Dylan Thomas and Louis MacNeice, in eds Fran Brearton and Edna Longley, *'Incorrigibly plural': Louis MacNeice and his Legacy* (Manchester: Carcanet Press, 2012).

— 'Djuna Barnes' as a source for Dylan Thomas, *Notes & Queries*, 58/1 (March 2011), 127–30.

— 'Dylan Thomas's sources in Whitman and the use of "sidle" as noun', *Notes& Queries*, 52/1 (March 2005), 105–7.

Graves, Robert, 'These Be Your Gods, O Israel!', sixth Clark Lecture on Professional Standards in English Poetry, delivered at Trinity College, Cambridge, Michaelmas Term, 1954; pub. *Essays in Criticism*, 5 (1955), 129–50; repr. in Brinnin (1961).

Hawkins, Desmond, 'Poetry', review of *18 Poems*, *Time and Tide*, XVI (9 February 1935), 204, 206.

Heaney, Seamus, 'Dylan the Durable? On Dylan Thomas', *The Redress of Poetry* (London: Faber, 1995) (orig. published as *Dylan the Durable? On Dylan Thomas* (Bennington, VT: Chapbooks in Literature series, no publisher, 1992).

Heys, Alistair, 'Dialectic and Armistice: Dylan Thomas's Reception of Keats', *Keats-Shelley Review*, 18 (2004), 217–38.

Holroyd, Stuart, 'Dylan Thomas and the Religion of the Instinctive Life', in Tedlock, 1960.

Hopwood, Mererid, *Singing in Chains: Listening to Welsh Verse* (Gomer Press, 2004).

Horan, Robert, 'In Defense of Dylan Thomas', *The Kenyon Review*, vii/3 (Spring 1945), 304–10.

Huddlestone, Linden, 'An Approach to Dylan Thomas', *Penguin New Writing*, XXXV (1948), 123–60.

Keery, James, 'The burning baby and the bathwater', *P.N. Review* 151, 29/5 (May–June 2003), 49–54; *P.N. Review* 152, 29/6 (July–August 2003), 57–62; *P.N. Review* 154, 3/2 (November–December 2003), 26–32; *P.N. Review* 156, 30/4 (March–April 2004), 40–2; *P.N. Review* 159, 31/1 (September–October 2004), 45–9; *P.N. Review* 164, 31/6 (July–August 2005), 57–61; *P.N. Review* 170, 32/6 (July–August 2006), 59–65; *P.N. Review* 171, 33/1 (September–October 2006), 56–62.

Korg, Jacob, 'Imagery and universe in Dylan Thomas's "18 Poems"', *Accent*, xvii/1 (Winter 1957), 3–15.

Loesch, Katharine T., 'Welsh Poetic Stanza Form and Dylan Thomas's "I dreamed my genesis"', *Transactions of the Honourable Society of Cymmrodorion* (1982), 29–52.

Mathias, Roland, 'Lord Cutglass, twenty years after', in ed. Danny Abse, *Poetry Dimension 2* (London: Sphere Books, 1974), pp. 61–89.

Maud, Ralph, 'Dylan Thomas astro-navigated', review of *The Poetry of Dylan Thomas* by Elder Olson, *Essays in Criticism*, 5 (1955), 164–8.

McKay, Don, 'What Shall We Do With A Drunken Poet?: Dylan Thomas' poetic language', *Queen's Quarterly*, 93/4 (1986), 794–807.

— 'Crafty Dylan and the Altarwise sonnets: "I build a flying tower and I pull it down"', *University of Toronto Quarterly*, 55 (1985/6), 357–94.

McNees, Eleanor J., *Eucharistic Poetry: The Search for Presence in the Writings of John Donne, Gerard Manley Hopkins, Dylan Thomas, and Geoffrey Hill* (Lewisburg, TN: Bucknell University Press, 1992), pp. 110–46.

Miller, J. Hillis, 'Dylan Thomas', in *Poets of Reality: Six Twentieth Century Writers* (Cambridge, MA: Harvard University Press, 1966), pp. 190–216.

Mills, Ralph J., 'Dylan Thomas: The Endless Monologue', *Accent*, XX (Spring 1960), 114–36.

Montague, Gene, 'Dylan Thomas and *Nightwood*', *Sewanee Review*, 76 (Summer 1968), 420–34.

Morgan, George, 'Dylan Thomas's "In the Direction of the Beginning": towards or beyond meaning?', *Cycnos*, 20/2 (2003), 1–17 (see 'Selected online resources').

— 'Dylan Thomas and the ghost of Shakespeare', *Cycnos*, 5 (1989), 113–21.

Moylan, Chris, 'Thomas's "O make me a mask"', *The Explicator*, 54/1 (1995), 39–43.

Mundye, Charles, 'Lynette Roberts and Dylan Thomas: Background to a Friendship', *PN Review*, 41:2 (November/December 2014), 18–23.

Neill, Michael, 'Dylan Thomas's "Tailor Age"', *Notes & Queries*, 17/2 (February 1970), 59–63.

Nowottny, Winifred, *The Language Poets Use* (London: Athlone Press, 1962 (repr. 1975)).

Perry, Seamus, 'Everything is Good News', review of centenary edition of the *Collected Poems, A Dylan Thomas Treasury* and reissues of *Under Milk Wood* and *Collected Stories, Times Literary Supplement*, 36/22 (20 November, 2014), pp. 5–8.

Riley, Peter, 'Thomas and apocalypse', *Poetry Wales*, 44/3 (Winter 2008–9), 12–16.

Scarfe, Francis, 'Dylan Thomas: a pioneer', in Francis Scarfe, *Auden and After: The Liberation of Poetry 1930–41* (London: Routledge, 1942 (repr. 1945)).

Roberts, Harri Garrod, '"Beating on the Jailing Slab of the Womb": The Alleged Immaturity of Dylan Thomas', *Embodying Identity: Representations of the Body in Welsh Literature* (Cardiff: University of Wales Press, 2009).

Silkin, Jon, 'Dylan Thomas', *The Life of Metrical and Free Verse in Twentieth-Century Poetry* (Basingstoke: Macmillan, 1997).

Simpson, Louis, 'The Color of Saying', in Louis Simpson, *A Revolution in Taste* (New York, NY: Macmillan, 1978).

Stearns, Marshall 'Unsex the Skeleton: Notes on the Poetry of Dylan Thomas', *The Sewanee Review*, LII:3 (1944), 424–40.

Sweeney, John L., introduction to *Dylan Thomas: Selected Writings* (New York: New Directions Press, 1946), ix–xxiii.

Thomas, M. Wynn, '"Marlais": Dylan Thomas and the "tin bethels"', in *In the Shadow of the Pulpit: Literature and Nonconformist Wales* (Cardiff: University of Wales Press, 2010).

— '"He belongs to the English": Welsh Dylan and Welsh-language Culture' (in Pursglove, Goodby and Wigginton, 2000).

— 'Portraits of the Artist as a Young Welshman', in M. Wynn Thomas, *Corresponding Cultures: The Two Literatures of Wales* (Cardiff: University of Wales Press, 1999).

Thurley, Geoffrey, 'Dylan Thomas: Merlin as sponger', in Geoffrey Thurley, *The Ironic Harvest: English Poetry in the Twentieth Century* (London: Edward Arnold, 1974).

Watkins, Vernon, *Vernon Watkins on Dylan Thomas and other poets and poetry*, eds Gwen Watkins and Jeff Towns (Swansea: Parthian Books, 2013).

Weick, George P., 'Dylan Thomas's "When, like a running grave"', *The Explicator*, 62/3 (Spring 2004), Washington, 172–6.

Young, Alan, 'Image as structure: Dylan Thomas and poetic meaning', *Critical Quarterly*, 17 (1975), 333–45.

Guides and bibliographies

Emery, Clark, *The World of Dylan Thomas* (Miami, FL: University of Miami Press, 1962).

Gaston, George M. A., *Dylan Thomas: A Reference Guide* (Boston, MA: G. K. Hall & Co., 1987).

Maud, Ralph (with Albert Glover), *Dylan Thomas in Print: A Bibliographical History*, (Pittsburgh, PA: University of Pittsburgh Press, 1970).

— *Where Have the Old Words Got Me?* (Cardiff: University of Wales Press, 2003).

Rolph, J. Alexander, *Dylan Thomas: A Bibliography* (London: Dent, 1956).

Tindall, William York, *A Reader's Guide to Dylan Thomas* (New York, NY: Farrar,

Strauss and Giroux, 1962) (repr. 1996, Syracuse University Press).

Biography

Brinnin, John Malcolm, *Dylan Thomas in America* (Boston, MA: Little, Brown and Co., 1955).

Davies, James A., *Dylan Thomas's Swansea, Gower and Laugharne* (Cardiff: University of Wales Press, 2000).

Ferris, Paul, *Dylan Thomas* (Harmondsworth: Penguin, 1978).

Fitzgibbon, Constantine, *The Life of Dylan Thomas* (London: Dent, 1965) (repr. Plantin Paperbacks, 1987).

Grigson, Geoffrey, 'Recollections of Dylan Thomas', in Tedlock, ed., 1960.

Hardwick, Elizabeth, 'America and Dylan Thomas', in Brinnin, ed., 1961.

Hawkins, Desmond, *When I Was: A Memoir of the Years between the Wars* (London: Macmillan, 1989).

Heppenstall, Rayner, *Four Absentees* (London: Barrie and Rockliff, 1960).
Holt, Heather, *Dylan Thomas: The Actor* (Llandebie: Dinefwr Press, 2003).
Janes, Hilly, *The Three Lives of Dylan Thomas* (London: Robson Press, 2014).
Jones, Daniel, *My Friend Dylan Thomas* (London: Dent, 1977).
Lycett, Andrew, *Dylan Thomas: A New Life* (London: Weidenfeld & Nicholson, 2003).
Sinclair, Andrew, *Dylan Thomas: No Man More Magical* (New York, NY: Holt, Rinehart and Winston, 1975).
Thomas, Aeronwy, *My Father's Places: A portrait of childhood by Dylan Thomas's daughter* (London: Constable, 2009).
Thomas, Caitlin, *Double Drink Story: My Life With Dylan Thomas* (London: Virago, 1998).
— *Caitlin: A Warring Absence* (London: Secker & Warburg, 1986).
— *Leftover Life to Kill* (London: Putnam, 1957).
Thomas, David N., *Dylan Thomas: A Farm, Two Mansions and a Bungalow* (Bridgend: Seren Books, 2000).
— ed., *Dylan Remembered: Interviews by Colin Edwards, Vol. 1 1914–1934* (Bridgend: Seren Books, 2003).
— ed., *Dylan Remembered: Interviews by Colin Edwards, Vol. 2 1935–1953* (Bridgend: Seren Books, 2004).
Watkins, Gwen, *Dylan Thomas: Portrait of a Friend* (Talybont: Y Lolfa, 2005).

Selected online resources

Hannah Ellis: Dylan Thomas site: *http://www.discoverdylanthomas.com*
Ruthven Todd's letter to Louis MacNeice concerning Thomas's death: *http://www.dylanthomas.com/index.cfm?articleid=45898*
Home page for the Boathouse, Laugharne, Dylan Thomas's last residence: *http://www.dylanthomasboathouse.com/*
Home page of the Dylan Thomas Society of Great Britain: *http://www.thedylanthomassocietyofgb.co.uk/*
Dylan Thomas blog run by Andrew Dally: *www.dylanthomasnews.com* and twitter feed @dylanthomasnews
Essays by Victor Golightly, Richard Chamberlain, Nathalie Wourm, Harri Roberts, John Goodby and Chris Wigginton: *http://www.dylanthomasboathouse.com/education/essays-academic-papers/*
John Goodby, 'Dylan Thomas', *Oxford Bibliographies Online*: *http://www.oxfordbibliographies.com/view/document/obo-9780199846719/obo-9780199846719-0057.xml?rskey=o0p49f&result=41&q=*
George Morgan, essay on 'In the Direction of the Beginning': *http://revel.unice.fr/cycnos/index.html?id=84*

Index